God, Evil, and

To Jessica and Sean, book lovers

# God, Evil, and Design

*An Introduction to the Philosophical Issues*

David O'Connor

**Blackwell**
Publishing

BLACKWELL PUBLISHING
350 Main Street, Malden, MA 02148-5020, USA
9600 Garsington Road, Oxford OX4 2DQ, UK
550 Swanston Street, Carlton, Victoria 3053, Australia

First published 2008 by Blackwell Publishing Ltd

1    2008

*Library of Congress Cataloging-in-Publication Data*

O'Connor, David.
    God, evil, and design : an introduction to the philosophical issues / David O'Connor.
        p. cm.
    Includes bibliographical references and index.
    ISBN 978–1–4051–5770–4 (hardcover : alk. paper) – ISBN 978–1–4051–5771–1 (pbk. : alk. paper)   1. Theodicy.   2. Good and evil.   I. Title.

    BT160.036 2008
    214—dc22

                                                                                2007046400

A catalogue record for this title is available from the British Library.

Set in 11/13pt Dante
by Graphicraft Limited, Hong Kong
Printed and bound in Singapore
by Markono Print Media Pte Ltd

The publisher's policy is to use permanent paper from mills that operate a sustainable forestry policy, and which has been manufactured from pulp processed using acid-free and elementary chlorine-free practices. Furthermore, the publisher ensures that the text paper and cover board used have met acceptable environmental accreditation standards.

For further information on
Blackwell Publishing, visit our website at
www.blackwellpublishing.com

# Contents

# Preface

1   In the poem "The Stolen Child," W. B. Yeats (1865–1939) reminds us that we live in "a world more full of weeping than [we] can understand." It is a memorable line and, for many people, a true description. Terrible things often happen, causing immense, undeserved suffering. Diseases and natural disasters waste vast numbers of lives. Many times, neither the victims nor anybody else can discover a point or a purpose in such terrible occurrences. In many cases, the victims seem to be just unlucky.

In the view of the monotheistic religions, the universe is a divine creation. Those religions are Judaism, Christianity, and Islam. According to this view, the creator is a supernatural person, essentially omniscient, omnipotent, and perfectly good.

Do the two things square with one another? Or does the fact of "nature, red in tooth and claw" "shriek" against the theist's "creed"? The words are those of Alfred Lord Tennyson (1809–92), from the poem "In Memoriam."

Some religious believers go beyond asserting compatibility. Some believers maintain that, even though terrible things happen in it, the world still provides good evidence of its divine origin.

I take up two questions here. First, does the idea of a perfect creator square with the fact that there is a vast amount of seemingly pointless suffering and death? And second, with that fact taken into account, does the world testify to a divine source?

2   In investigating these two questions, I hope to introduce readers to fundamental issues in the philosophy of religion. That raises two related worries. Can a worthwhile investigation be a good introduction? Can an introduction remain introductory while pursuing a genuine investigation? Don't the two things pull against each other? To some extent, perhaps they do. However, we must keep in mind a fundamental fact about the

discipline of philosophy itself. It is that, in its very nature, philosophy is investigative. So it may be that proper philosophical introductions will always be investigations.

My hope is that beginning philosophers will see the competing ideas in this book as live options. An idea is a live option for us when we take it seriously as something that might be true. So, when competing ideas are taken seriously in this way, it is a small, as well as a natural, step to try to sort out and adjudicate those rival claims on the truth. And to take that step is to engage philosophically with the ideas themselves, which is to be underway in investigating them.

Not all readers of this book will start out more-or-less unfamiliar with the issues discussed. What about them? For one thing, they may notice my omission of much of the detailed analysis and development of ideas conducted in the secondary literature. Despite that, as well as other accommodations I make to keep the main story-lines in clear focus, I hope readers already familiar with the issues examined find the discussions here to be worthwhile.

An investigation that is also both an introduction and relatively short will only go so far. Accordingly, when we are finished, it will be clear both that a lot remains unsaid on the issues discussed and that nothing has been said on some neighboring ones. But I hope that enough will have been said to provide a good introduction to the contemporary debates on the issues discussed, to make some contribution to those debates, and to lead to further inquiry.

3   The aim of investigation is discovery. In our investigations here, I think that, up to a point, we do discover which ideas are the better supported by the evidence considered. And verdicts are issued accordingly.

4   Verdicts often provoke disagreements. So, perhaps you will disagree with mine or with how I arrive at them. Whether you do or not, I hope that, in one respect, disagreeing with me is easy.

If I am easy to disagree with, whether in the end or along the way, then the odds are good that I have been clear. If you are unsure what I am saying, then you are not in a good position to agree or disagree with me. Furthermore, if you disagree with some, or even with all, of this book, then perhaps you are engaging in your own philosophical reflection. And I would be pleased if some things in this book had some of the responsibility for that.

The same benefits will be found in agreeing with me, and I hope that happens some of the time as well.

In another respect, though, I hope disagreeing with me is not easy. For I hope I am more right than wrong in this book. Furthermore, if and where I am right about things, I hope it is for persuasive reasons. However, whether my reasons are persuasive or unpersuasive, let me be the first to stress that, having written this book as an introduction, I make no claim to say the last word on any topic discussed in it.

5   I have incurred various debts in writing this book, and, while I cannot repay my creditors, I would like to acknowledge them. I am grateful to my children, Sarah, Jeremy, and Adrian, for their continuing interest in this book and for their encouragement along the way. I am grateful to Anna Muster for the same. I am grateful to the chair of the philosophy department at Seton Hall University, Vicente Medina, and to the then dean of the university's College of Arts and Sciences, Molly Easo Smith, for a reduced teaching load in the spring of 2006. The reduction helped me to make a good start on this book. In the fall of that year, I taught a course on the topics of the book. By that time, I had more or less a first draft in hand, and I am grateful to students in that course for their help, as I tried out ideas and illustrations of ideas. I hope their philosophical education didn't suffer too much in the process. Two anonymous readers for the publisher made useful criticisms and suggestions, and the book is the better for them. I thank them for their help. Blackwell's Gillian Somerscales did a first-rate job of copy-editing, and I thank her for many improvements. Finally, I am grateful to Jeff Dean of Blackwell for his interest in this book from start to finish, and for good advice at several stages in its development.

# Part I

# Introduction

# Part 1

## Introduction

# 1

# What We Are Going to Investigate, and How

## I Two Investigations

*A fact, a belief, and the friction between them*

This is a world in which terrible things happen for no apparent good reason. Think of the tsunami that struck Indonesia and several other countries at Christmas 2004, killing over 230,000 people, injuring many more, and leaving almost 2,000,000 homeless. Since then, we saw Hurricane Katrina cause great destruction along the Gulf Coast of the United States, a major earthquake in Pakistan and another in Indonesia, and, in the summer of 2006, a second tsunami on the Indonesian island of Java. As reported in the *New York Times* on February 2, 2006 and on June 21, 2006, the Pakistani earthquake in October 2005 killed more than 73,000 people, caused serious injury to about the same number, and left between 2,500,000 and 3,000,000 people homeless. In addition to the human toll in these disasters, vast numbers of animals were killed or injured.

Along with large-scale disasters that dominate the news for a while, there are many small-scale tragedies. We all know of situations like the following: a seven year-old little girl dying of the tumor that has caused her and her family so much suffering and fear in the two years since it was diagnosed; a young woman whose breast cancer will leave her children motherless in a year, or two at the most, and who is anguished at the prospect; a man whose rich life is fading away through Alzheimer's disease; a young deer, badly burned in a forest fire caused by lightning, lying in agony for days before dying.

A common thread in the foregoing list of calamities is that there is no human responsibility for them. In the unintentionally ironic term used in insurance policies, they are 'acts of God.' But many horrors do trace to human responsibility, and there too the scale can be unimaginably vast or specific to one individual person. Think of the Holocaust and the murders of over 6,000,000 people in the Nazi death camps, or the brutal torture of an abducted child.

The facts listed above, and many more like them, are well known to us all. For context and perspective now, let us put them alongside another fact, also well known to us.

It is the fact that many people, including many thoughtful and sophisticated people, believe the world was made by God. That is a core teaching of the monotheistic religions – Judaism, Christianity, and Islam. In those religions, God is understood to be a perfectly good, all-knowing and all-powerful, supernatural being. As creator of the world, God is believed to watch over it with loving concern for all creatures and especially for us humans.

At face value, there is friction between the facts of destruction and suffering, on the one hand, and the belief in a good creator God, on the other. How could a world with so much pain and misery, so much devastation and waste of life, be made by God? Aware of those facts, how could any thoughtful or sensitive person hold the belief?

## A natural friction

The friction is natural. Why? Principally because God is understood to be a perfectly good person, with limitless knowledge and power, and we expect the goodness of a good person to show itself in tangible ways. For instance, all other things being equal, we expect a good person to prevent terrible things that are within the person's power to prevent. The expectation is both natural and reasonable. After all, if a good person, who has the power to do so, does not prevent such things, in what does his or her goodness consist?

Suppose you see a young child trip and fall, bumping his head and lying face down in a shallow stream. Suppose there is nobody else about and that you are a healthy adult, not occupied at the time in any overwhelmingly important task. You see the child. All of us who know you believe you are a good and decent person. Wouldn't we expect you to help? And later, when we hear the child was left to drown, what are we to think of your goodness?

True, there may have been a good reason for your inaction, and because of our prior belief in your decency, we keep an open mind for the present. The point here is not that, at this stage, we judge you a certain way. It is that your behavior on this occasion seems to conflict with our justified expectation, based on thinking of you as a good person. The point is that we have good grounds for a serious question.

To drive home the point about our legitimate expectations, change the example in one respect. Suppose that all of us who know you believe you are a miserable, selfish wretch. We believe you are prone to cruelty and to enjoying the misfortunes of others, especially the weak and vulnerable. How surprised would we be now to hear that the child was left to die?

Why are the expectations in the two cases different? The reason is our different beliefs about the kind of person you are. We are surprised and puzzled in the first case, but not in the second, or at least much less so in the second.

Now switch back to the original example, and change it one more time. We believe you are a good and decent person, although we are still puzzled and troubled that you did not help that little boy who was left to drown. Then, several more times, we hear of your inaction on occasions when help or kindness from you would have cost you very little, but would have meant a great deal to another. How long is it reasonable to continue believing in your goodness?

## Bill Gates and God

The world could be better in many ways. Obviously we believe it would be better with cancer curable, or smallpox and AIDS eradicated, and so on. After all, that is why people work hard for those results, why governments fund their efforts, and why the rest of us hope for their success. But progress is slow, and many terrible things seem completely beyond our power.

Now suppose that five years ago, Bill Gates, Warren Buffett, George Soros, the Saudi royal family, and a large number of other billionaires and governments pledged huge sums of money for a great philanthropic project. Suppose Bill Clinton joined them to co-ordinate efforts to raise billions more, and to arrange for hundreds of thousands of volunteers. The initial aim of the project is to make significant progress against poverty and disease over a five-year period.

Someone special would be needed to direct this ambitious venture. Suppose the person hired for the job is the best possible candidate, being omnipotent, omniscient, and perfectly good. For the sake of argument, let's suspend disbelief and suppose that. This person is put in complete charge of the project, with no strings attached, for the initial period of five years.

Suppose those five years have passed, and that it is now the present day and time to take stock. Ask yourself – as you compare things now to five years ago, as you think about diseases, starvation, droughts, ongoing genocides, and so on – would you be surprised to find things as they are, that is, seemingly no better than before? Would you be inclined to judge that the project had met expectations? Would you think the project director should be rehired, perhaps paid a bonus?

### A question

Let us go back now to the idea of God. It is the idea of a personal being who is perfect in goodness, knowledge, and power. If you were to pause and think about the idea of such a being, what expectations would you legitimately have about a world that was brought about by that supernatural person?

As our supposition about the imaginary Gates philanthropy seems to show, our reasonable expectation would be simple and straightforward. All other things being equal, we would expect omnipotence, omniscience, and perfect goodness to make a discernible difference for the better.

Now place alongside that expectation what you know about the world in actuality. There are many good things, of course, but nonetheless the world is obviously imperfect in many ways. Perhaps there are good reasons for things to be this way. The point right now is not to reach a verdict. It is to see an obvious and legitimate question clearly.

That question is this: How well do the idea of God and the fact that there is a vast amount of seemingly pointless suffering, death, and destruction in the world fit together? Do they square with one another? Or do the enormous quantities and varieties of such seemingly pointless and terrible things justify a reasonable person in thinking there is no God?

### Who is asking the question, and why?

On May 29, 2006, the *New York Times* reported that Pope Benedict XVI had visited the site of the Nazi extermination camp at Auschwitz in Poland the previous day. As reported in the paper, the pope said this: "Why, Lord, did you remain silent? How could you tolerate this?"

For a reflective believer, surely, these are urgent questions. They arise at the intersection of faith and reason. But the friction is equally apparent to reflective unbelievers, and the question arising from it is important for them too. For the core theistic idea is remarkable, and, if true, could perhaps be the most important truth of all.

It is the idea that everything that there is, the entire universe, exists at all only because of the choice of a unique supernatural being. That the universe exists on purpose is an idea worth examining seriously. Accordingly, our question about how well the core theistic idea fits with the existence of enormous destruction and suffering is a question of interest to all reflective persons, not just believers.

Certain variations on that philosophical question arise for believers alone. The variations I have in mind are questions intended to be resolved within faith, perhaps in scripture, or in conversation with a minister or rabbi, or in prayer. The goal of those questions is peace of mind. Perhaps the pope's questions were so intended.

But the underlying point is the same, whether it comes up as a philosophical question in a fair-minded effort to discover the truth, regardless of whether the things discovered support the theistic idea or undercut it, or as a religious question aimed at clarifying or solidifying faith. It is that, at face value, there is a clear friction between the idea of a perfect creator, on the one hand, and a supposedly created world that is obviously imperfect in many ways, on the other.

Our examination here is of philosophical questions only. Purely religious questions will receive no further discussion.

### A second question

To this point, our question is whether the idea of God squares with the fact that many terrible things happen for no apparent good reason, or whether that fact is good reason to think there is no God. But even if, at face value, the fact of seemingly pointless suffering, waste of life, and so on counts against the existence of God, do not other things support it? For instance, there are pleasure and happiness as well as pain and misery. There is great natural beauty. The universe is vastly complex, yet orderly and regular, and basic conditions at its origin almost fourteen billion years ago were right for the eventual emergence of life. Are these not things that count in support of the idea that God is the original source or cause of the world?

Let us grant, for the sake of argument, that they are. That raises a second question. It is whether, all things considered, the good as well as the bad, it is reasonable to conclude that God is the original source or cause of the universe.

The keys to this second question are the words 'all things considered' and 'conclude.'

### All things considered, and believing and concluding

What things are being considered in the second question? There is the fact that, even though the world is massively complex, it is orderly and regular. In addition, there are its conduciveness to life, the development of morality, the existence of great natural beauty, and so on. In the view of many believers, these things testify to the world's divine origin.

But there are bad things in the world as well as good: pain as well as pleasure, death as well as life, destruction and ugliness as well as growth and beauty.

Our second question, then, is whether, all those things considered, good things and bad, it is reasonable to conclude there is a God? Is the idea of God a good explanation of the existence of a world containing all the things mentioned, good and bad?

The second key to our second question is the word 'conclude.' All things considered, is it reasonable to conclude that God exists? This is not the same as asking whether, all things considered, it is reasonable to *believe* that God exists. It is narrower in scope than that.

Believing and concluding are not the same. Concluding or inferring something involves deliberately moving from evidence to judgment. While it is true that we acquire some of our beliefs that way, we do not acquire them all, or perhaps even most of them, like that. For example, think of a child acquiring many of his beliefs just by the experience of living and interacting with others, or by being told, and not by figuring things out for himself. The process is more absorption than inference.

The difference holds up in the other direction too. We may conclude something without believing it.

Our second question, then, is not about religious belief as such, at least not directly. Neither is it directly about the justifiability of such belief. Instead, it is about the justifiability of concluding or inferring that God exists.

## Two investigations

We are going to pursue two investigations. First, does the idea of God square with the occurrence of vast amounts of seemingly pointless suffering and waste of life? Second, when the occurrence of such terrible things is taken in conjunction with the fact that vast amounts of good things happen too, would it be reasonable to conclude that the best explanation of the existence of the world is a perfect, supernatural creator? All things considered, would that be a reasonable conclusion?

## Another difference between the two questions

Because the two questions cover some of the same ground, it is important to be clear about their essential differences. In addition to the difference already noted, that between the justifiability of believing something and of concluding something, respectively, here is another: In our first question, the idea of God is part of the investigation from the start, but in the second investigation it is not.

Our first question is directed to discovering how well the idea of God squares with certain known facts about the world. In this investigation, then, both of those things, the idea of God and the facts of suffering and waste of life, are part of our evidence from the start.

But in our second investigation, if the idea of God comes in at all, it can only be as a conclusion, at the end of the inquiry about the nature and origin of the universe. In that investigation, the idea of God is deliberately excluded from the evidence.

There is good reason for the exclusion. It is to avoid committing the fallacy that logicians call 'begging the question': that is, the kind of fallacious reasoning which presupposes its conclusion from the start. We cannot genuinely arrive at a conclusion if we have been assuming it all along.

When we exclude the idea of God from the evidence in our second investigation, we do not thereby deny the idea. If we did that, we would be guilty of the same fallacy in the other direction. Instead, the point is that, in our second inquiry, we will be strictly neutral on the idea of a creator God, unless and until there is impartial evidence to justify introducing the idea.

## The stakes in our questions

Our first question is directed to discovering how well the idea of God squares with certain known facts about the world. If it does not square well with those facts, then, in proportion to the lack of fit between the two things, those facts will be reason to think there is no God.

Our second question is whether, all things considered, it would be plausible or reasonable to conclude that God is the original source or cause of the universe. For the sake of argument, suppose the answer is no. This would mean that, on the evidence considered, we would not be justified in arriving at the idea of God.

But, in itself, this failure would not be sufficient reason to think there is no God. In itself, failure to prove something, that is, to establish it as a conclusion on the strength of evidence and argument, does not mean that the thing in question is false or ought not to be believed.

To illustrate the point, take Al Capone. The authorities tried to prove he was a racketeer, a bootlegger, a murderer, and head of the mob in Chicago. But they failed. He was convicted on tax fraud, and on none of those other charges. Now, does this mean that he was not a racketeer, bootlegger, murderer, or head of the Chicago mob, or that we should not believe he was those things? Of course not. The point stands up to generalization. It is that, sometimes, we can be well justified in believing something we cannot prove.

The upshot is that the stakes are higher for theistic belief in posing the first question than in posing the second. Failure to square the facts of evil with the idea of God provides reason to think there is no God, while, in itself, failure to prove the existence of God does not.

The rest of this book runs on the two tracks of the different, but related, questions just set forth. Because the inclusion and exclusion, respectively, of the idea of God in our two investigations is a crucial difference between them, understanding that difference is crucial to the overall enterprise in this book. For that reason, I am going to stay with it a while longer.

## Two tales of headhunting

Here, from the world of business, is an illustration of the difference. Suppose you work for an executive search firm as the director of a regional office.

Just to be clear, executive search firms specialize in screening and hiring high-level personnel, for instance, presidents, vice-presidents, chief operations officers, and so on, on behalf of various kinds of public and private institutions. You may have heard such firms or their employees referred to as 'headhunters.' Anyway, now that we have you working in such a firm, I want to describe two scenarios, each involving an executive search that you undertake on behalf of a large institution.

*First search*

Suppose your firm is hired by a teaching hospital in a major city. A search is already underway for a new head of emergency medicine. You and your firm are being brought in now, after the search has been going on for almost two months. At this point in the search process, a clear front-runner has emerged among the candidates who have been screened and interviewed. The chair of the hospital's board of directors has explained to you that the board is close to offering the job to this candidate. However, before doing so, they want further advice about how well the candidate fits the profile of the kind of head of emergency medicine that the board has in mind. The chair of the hospital's board tells you that she wants you to see if there is a good match, a good fit, between the candidate and the institution, and to advise the board accordingly.

You are quite clear that you are not being hired to recommend other candidates, or to address aspects of this candidate's credentials other than his fit with the job description and the institution. You understand what you are being hired to do, and what you are not hired to do, and you accept the commission.

After meeting the board's candidate, perhaps you will think you could have found them a better candidate. But if so, you will keep that opinion to yourself, for you know it does not mean that the candidate in place cannot be a good fit with the institution. Being a good fit does not require being the best fit.

*Second search*

Suppose your firm is hired by a teaching hospital in a major city. The hospital's board of directors wants to hire a new head of the emergency medicine department. The board wants the search to be national and international, and your firm is hired to run the search from start to finish. You will assist the board in drafting the advertisement for the position, you will then advertise the position, solicit recommendations and applications from your contacts in the field, screen the applications, conduct preliminary interviews of promising candidates, run credential checks as well as other kinds of background checks on the finalists, and then present a shortlist of candidates to the board for consideration. You will participate in the board's interviews of those finalists, and afterwards give advice on each of them. Then the board will make its selection of the candidate who, in its judgment, best meets the advertised description of the job.

*Comparison*

As a business person, it is important for you to be quite clear about the differences between the two commissions. Otherwise, you may not explain the task in hand well to your staff or do a good job. That task is more limited in the first search than in the second. In the first search, you start from a position where there is already a candidate in view, and your job is to judge the quality of the fit between candidate and institution. But in the second search, you start with a blank slate, commissioned to come up with the candidate who best fits the institution.

I'm sure you see quite clearly what I have in mind in contrasting the two searches, and how the contrast applies to our two lines of inquiry in this book. Nonetheless, let me briefly state it anyway.

In the one investigation, we are attempting to discover how well the idea of an all-perfect creator squares with the world, as we find it to be in experience. In particular, how well does it square with the enormous amounts of suffering, death, and destruction that seem to have no point or purpose whatsoever? But in the other investigation, starting from a description of the world neutral in respect of religion, and taking into account the mix of good and bad in the world, we are attempting to come up with the best explanation of the fact that such a world came to exist at all.

## II   The Veil of Ignorance

Our second investigation calls for us to exclude the idea of God from the evidence. But isn't that unrealistic? After all, won't any person engaged in that inquiry be familiar with the idea that the world was initially brought about by God? And that being so, how can we realistically expect to exclude the idea from the evidence? Isn't it naïve to think that could be done?

The objection seems to go further. In addition to being the case that most people are familiar with the idea of a creator God, isn't it also likely that very few are neutral regarding it? Isn't it probable that, like you and me, most adults already have some opinion on the matter, either belief or disbelief? And even if they don't come down firmly on one side or the other, isn't it likely that they have at least some tendency to believe or disbelieve it? And won't that opinion, or that tendency, undercut impartiality in trying to understand and explain the origin of the universe? Again, isn't an expectation to the contrary just naïve?

Similarly, in our first inquiry, won't religious believers be inclined to think that the existence of God does somehow square with the occurrence of terrible things? So won't they automatically think that belief in God is not undermined by those things? And won't unbelievers automatically incline to the opposite view? Again, how can we expect impartiality?

These are good questions. They bring up difficulties we must face.

The worry about impartiality does not apply uniquely to philosophical questions about religious topics. It applies also to other controversial issues in philosophy, for instance, the moral permissibility or impermissibility of abortion, the fairness or unfairness of affirmative-action policies, the metaphysical idea that the mind is nothing above and beyond the functioning brain, and so on. So the question is really about the possibility of genuine philosophical reflection on issues about which some people have strongly held views.

I am not mentioning these other areas, where the same worry quickly comes up, in order to dilute the problem in our investigations here. To the contrary, I think that the reluctance to suspend pre-existing opinions may be stronger and more common in philosophical discussion of religious topics than it is in discussion of other subjects.

Nonetheless, I think genuine philosophical investigation of the various issues mentioned is indeed possible. I hope so, for it is perhaps our most strongly held opinions that should least escape serious scrutiny. And I do not only mean scrutiny by people who do not themselves hold the views in question. I especially mean serious scrutiny by the holders of those views themselves. After all, if I am going to hold an opinion strongly, as opposed to tentatively or provisionally, then I want to be as sure as I can that I have good grounds for my view. And if I don't, I certainly want to know that too.

### Impartiality and Rawls's veil of ignorance

But my optimism is not a solution of the problem, nor a tactic to deal with it. For tactics, I propose to borrow an idea from John Rawls (1921–2002), one of the most influential thinkers of modern times. Rawls was a political theorist, whose principal objective was to develop a theory of social justice.

In his theory, the primary emphasis is on the kinds of social institutions and governmental policies that would have to be in place to ensure fairness for all citizens equally. But in modern mass societies, the United States for example, there are large and deep differences among citizens, differences of social class, race, education, income, access to health care, and so on. What is equal justice for all in a society like that?

The question of Rawls's that I want to pick up here is a procedural one, not the foregoing substantive question about the nature of justice. The procedural question comes to this. How can we examine the issue, or try to solve the problem, without bias stemming from our own self-interest? After all, we come to the question of equal justice and its achievement with a vested interest in our own social and economic status, our own prospects for success and a good life, in a society where vital resources are relatively scarce.

The brilliance of Rawls's idea is to use self-interest to get to a fair-minded discussion of the demands of justice and, from that, perhaps to justice itself. He proposes a thought experiment in which, through an imagined negotiation with other citizens, we are to work out the blueprint for the society in which we will live out our lives. Each of us comes to the negotiation with the goal of working out the best possible arrangements and circumstances for ourselves and our families. That is, self-interest rules.

But certain restrictions apply. The principal restriction is that, in this imagined negotiation, we do not know who we are. This extraordinary thought is the key to Rawls's proposed solution to the problem of bias.

Suppose we do not know our own actual life-circumstances. That is the procedural idea I propose to borrow from Rawls's thought experiment. It is the idea that the discussions take place behind a veil of ignorance, a kind of selective suspension of memory. The details of how to bring about the kind of selective ignorance that the thought experiment calls for don't matter. What does matter is that anything that might reflect bias is beyond our awareness.

### The veil of ignorance and our investigations here

Let us adapt Rawls's procedure to our own investigations, with a view to coping with our problem of bias. Let us agree to pretend along the lines that Rawls suggests. In reality, we have nothing to lose. For, just as the participants in Rawls's thought experiment are, all the while, people with specific life-situations, so we too, all the while, are believers or unbelievers. By agreeing to pretend for the sake of argument, we agree to see how the issues would look from neutral ground. It's hard to see the harm in that.

### First investigation

Does the idea of God square with the fact that terrible things happen for no apparent good reason? To investigate this question, we will imagine we do not know whether we believe or disbelieve in God. While imagining or pretending this, we will retain all of our knowledge about religion, as well as everything else we know. We just won't know, temporarily, our own individual religious preference.

So, not knowing whether we are believers or unbelievers, we cannot be guided in our investigation by whatever personal stake that we might, in reality, have in the answer to the question. But we retain all of our normal desire for understanding and knowledge. So we have a strong desire to investigate the question and to learn the answer, whatever it is, as best we can. We also retain our ability to reason and to think critically as well as imaginatively.[1]

### Second investigation

To investigate our second question, we will imagine, as before, that we do not know if we are believers or not. But now, in addition, we will make believe we know nothing at all about religion, not even that there is such a thing. We will pretend to know nothing about philosophy either. We will imagine we know nothing about anything that might be called

---

[1]  William L. Rowe, an influential philosopher whose work on the problem of God and evil we will discuss in detail later on, proposes a context of ignorance similar to that in our first investigation. See William L. Rowe, "The Evidential Argument from Evil: A Second Look," in Daniel Howard-Snyder, ed., *The Evidential Argument from Evil* (Bloomington: Indiana University Press, 1996), 265.

supernatural. We will attach no meaning to the word 'God,' no more than we do now to the collection of letters 'Hsz.'

On the positive side, we will be as rational, lucid, and curious as ever. From our experience of making decisions in daily life we will continue to be good judges of adequate and inadequate evidence, of reasonable as opposed to unreasonable interpretations, of bias and impartiality, of justified and unjustified conclusions. True, these things are studied by philosophers and there are philosophical theories about them. But, behind the veil of ignorance, we will not know this. Back there, our knowledge of good reasoning will be practical, not theoretical.

We will be free to pursue any line of investigation we wish, in any direction we choose. We will start with no religious or theological concepts, nothing supernaturalist, and nothing philosophical or metaphysical, but we will be free to come up with such ideas, to invent them in effect, if that is where our inquiry leads. Apart from these gaps in our knowledge, we will be our normal selves. Insofar as some people you know are concerned, you may wonder how to tell the difference from their normal state, but I leave that issue for you.

When an actor gets in character in a play or film, her outlook is that of the fictional person the writer created. If she cannot suspend her own personality or beliefs for the life of the performance, then she is hardly an actor at all, let alone a poor one. We likewise, by suspending our religious belief or unbelief, as the case may be, and by remaining in character for the life of each investigation, enable ourselves to explore ideas here minus the filter of our own pre-set beliefs. In addition, we put aside any form of group-think to which we may be susceptible in real life. We get to try various controversial ideas on for size.

Trying ideas on for size is not fundamentally different from trying on shoes for size. It only works if we first take off our own. And there is no obligation to buy, so we can always leave with our own shoes in the end. Likewise, when we try on ideas.

The benefit of the tactic is this. Our ability to engage in fair-minded, impartial inquiry determines our ability to discover the truth. Our willingness to engage in such inquiry reflects our desire to know the truth.

### A near-precedent to reassure believers

There are precedents or near-precedents, even in the history of theistic philosophy, for this veil-of-ignorance approach to trying to understand the origin of the universe. The most famous is the effort by Thomas Aquinas (*c.*1225–74) to explain various fundamental facts about the natural world.

Experience shows the world to be an orderly, cause-and-effect universe (nowadays we might qualify this by adding, at least above the quantum level, the level of sub-atomic particles). These facts of order, regularity, and causation are presupposed in all scientific inquiry. Consequently, it may be that we cannot expect science itself to provide an ultimate explanation of them. If so, what does explain them?

Aquinas pursued that question. Starting just from the recognition of such fundamental facts about the universe as that it is orderly and regular, that its order is cause-and-effect order, and so on, Aquinas tried to account for the coming into existence of such a universe in the first place. The point I'm emphasizing is that Aquinas's only tool was the application of intelligence and reason to those basic facts of nature. True, he did not set the stage for his inquiry with a gimmick like the veil of ignorance, but the effect is the same as if he had.

Committed theist that he was, Aquinas believed that a satisfactory explanation could be found only in the idea of a certain kind of supernatural being. But the point to note right now is not Aquinas's view of the answer to the question, but the procedural idea embedded in his approach to finding an answer, and especially in his approach to persuading others that he had found the right answer.

His procedure reflected the idea that if supernaturalist ideas came into the investigation it would be to answer questions that otherwise would be unanswerable. But no such idea would be an assumption or a piece of evidence in the inquiry to begin with. So, if such ideas did come into play, they would do so only on the strength of the evidence and in proportion to the evidence; and therefore, such ideas would come in only in the conclusion.

Accordingly, on this characterization of his inquiry, I think Aquinas would have had no objection to stepping behind our veil of ignorance.

## Suggested Reading

Aquinas, Thomas (2003) "The Five Ways," in Louis P. Pojman, ed., *Philosophy of Religion: An Anthology*. Belmont: Wadsworth. Most philosophy-of-religion anthologies contain these arguments of Aquinas's.

Gaskin, J. C. A. (1988) *Hume's Philosophy of Religion*. Atlantic Highlands: Humanities Press. Chapter 3 addresses the difference between our two investigations.

Hume, David (1998) *Dialogues Concerning Natural Religion*, ed. J. C. A. Gaskin. Oxford: Oxford University Press. Of the twelve parts comprising the work, Parts I and XI, in particular, are relevant. The second of our two investigations is sketched out in Part I, while in Part XI the distinction between our two investigations is described. Several editions of the *Dialogues* are available. Any will do.

Peterson, Michael L. (1998) *God and Evil: An Introduction to the Issues*. Boulder, CO: Westview Press. A good introduction to the main issues and debates, with a point of view a bit different from mine in this book.

# 2

# Terminology

Starting out, we need to be clear about the meanings of key terms. The principal ones are in the title of this book. They are 'God,' 'evil,' and 'design.'

## I God

### Many concepts of God

I'm sure you have heard people say that, even though there is a variety of different religions, believers all worship the same God in the end. This is typically said with good intentions and in a spirit of solidarity, but it is false nonetheless. Not all religious people, not even most religious people, worship the same God. For, among the various understandings of divinity, some of the major ones are incompatible with one another.

Buddhism is one of the world's main religions, as it has been since well before the start of Christianity. There are different forms of Buddhism, but in none of them is there a concept of God such as the one reflected in the main theistic religions. Furthermore, that theistic concept of deity as a unique, perfect, infinite, supernatural person is rejected as incoherent and undesirable. In some forms of Buddhism a variety of Gods is acknowledged, while in others, Theravada Buddhism for instance, there are no deities at all. Either way, Buddhists are unbelievers, atheists, insofar as the God of Jews, Christians, and Muslims is concerned. And the same applies in reverse: Jews, Christians, and Muslims are unbelievers in the various deities proposed in the polytheistic versions of Buddhism.

Viewed historically, polytheisms, religions centered on the concept of multiple Gods, are not solely or predominantly religions of Asia or the Far East. In ancient times, polytheistic religions were commonplace in Europe too. Think of the Gods of ancient Greece and Rome respectively, with whose names and stories most of us are reasonably well acquainted. For other examples from ancient times, think of the various pagan religions of northern Europe, for instance the polytheisms of Ireland and Scandinavia.

Another ancient polytheistic religion, albeit one still strong today, is Hinduism. Like Buddhism, it is one of the principal religions of Asia. However, unlike those forms of Buddhism that acknowledge deities, Hinduism has monotheistic leanings. For its many Gods and Goddesses are seen within that faith as ultimately offshoots of one great God.

The point in this very brief survey is to emphasize that today, as throughout human history, the word 'God' means different and even conflicting things in different cultures.

Nonetheless, with Buddhism as an exception, the same basic claim seems to be implicit in all of the major religions. It is that theirs alone is the true concept of divinity, and that rival concepts are false. Sometimes the claim is explicit. For an obvious example, think of the first of the Ten Commandments in the Christian Old Testament: "I am the Lord, thy God . . . Thou shalt not have other gods besides me . . ." But the claim to ownership of the one true concept of divinity cannot be true in all, or even most, cases. So, in starting out on our investigations here, it is important to be clear and specific in the meaning that we are attaching to the word 'God,' and to recognize that the questions we are investigating pertain to a particular cultural concept of divinity.

### The God of Jews, Christians, and Muslims

From this point on, I will use the word 'God' to mean the God of the three main theistic religions. It is the concept of an eternal, supernatural person, perfect in all respects. The medieval philosopher St Anselm (*c.*1033–1109), famously described the God of theism as the being, greater than which none could be conceived.

To give a bit more specificity to the concept, as well as to prepare the ground for our investigations, let us look briefly at four qualities essential in the theistic concept of God. They are omnipotence, perfect goodness, omniscience, and being a person.

#### Omnipotence

To say that God is omnipotent means that God is able to do all things that are possible in themselves, and that are consistent with all of the essential divine attributes. As this qualified phrasing suggests, some restrictions apply.

First, there is the restriction to things that are possible in their own right. A shape that is square all over and round all over at the same time is impossible. So God cannot make a round square, or a vacuum that is not empty, and so on. But these inabilities do not stem from any lack or deficiency in God's power, or, for that matter, in ours either. For round squares are just verbal combinations. The very idea of such a thing is intrinsically incoherent and self-canceling. No such thing could ever exist, no matter what. This means that, regardless of what kind of power upgrade it might be possible to get, rounding squares that stay square all the while remains a thing that could not be done.

The other restriction mentioned in the concept of divine omnipotence concerns things that are incompatible with some other essential characteristic of God. To talk about this we will need to get a little bit ahead of ourselves, for we will need to bring in a divine attribute not yet explained. But, as this problem is an unavoidable part of describing a package deal piece by piece, we won't worry about it.

God is omnipotent, but God could not steal that CD for personal gain. Not just would not, but could not. By contrast, you or I probably would not steal it for personal gain either, but not because we could not, for in the right circumstances we could. So why could God the omnipotent not culpably steal it? The reason is that it would be incompatible with another of God's intrinsic qualities, namely, perfect or infinite goodness. In effect, then, God's power is the power to do anything that is possible, while always acting in character.

Now you and I, most of the time anyway, act in character too. So, acting in character is not unique to God. But the point is that God is said to be infinitely good, whereas you and I are at best only good up to a point. And behavior that is consistent with perfect goodness is going to have more restrictions for that reason than behavior consistent with being pretty good.

There is a bit of oddity and paradox here. For it means that we can do things that omnipotent God cannot: for instance, steal that CD for personal gain, lie about something, be unsympathetic to a friend in need, be selfish or cruel, and so on.

### Perfect goodness

Part of what it means to say that God is perfectly or infinitely good is that God has absolute moral goodness. Essentially, that means God cannot do anything that is overall bad. On the contrary, a morally perfect being will always and only do what is overall good. Clearly, knowledge of overall goodness and badness is involved here, and shortly we will come to the concept of knowledge.

The phrasing I am using here, "overall" good or bad, suggests restrictions and qualifications. For one thing, there may be no upper limit to the number of good actions that an omnipotent, perfectly good being could perform. Or there may be no greatest amount of overall good that could be done. If so, then no matter how good a thing a perfectly good being does, something even better is always possible.

Furthermore, certain good things may be impossible without something bad in them, some amount of pain or frustration, for instance. So, while a morally perfect being will not cause, or permit, pain or frustration for their own sakes, perhaps in bringing about an overall good situation it proves necessary sometimes to permit pain or frustration to occur. For instance, perhaps perfect justice sometimes requires punishment, and consequently the pain of punishment received, as well as, at the other end of things, the pain or unhappiness we feel in punishing a person or animal we love.

The upshot is that a perfectly good being will only do, or permit, things that are good overall. But a thing that is overall good may not be good in all respects. For perhaps some things that are good overall can only be achieved at the cost of some pain. And pain in its own right is never a good thing.

### Omniscience

Omniscience means that God knows everything that is knowable. Note that, here too, certain restrictions may apply. For instance, perhaps the future is unknowable. The future does not exist now, for it has not yet happened. And, being non-existent, perhaps it is impossible to know ahead of time. If so, then not knowing the future would not negate the concept of omniscience, any more than the impossibility of making a circular square defeats the idea of divine omnipotence.

### Being a person

The theistic God is understood to be a person, although not of flesh and blood like you and me, but a wholly spiritual or non-physical person.

By emphasizing that the concept of being a person is intrinsic to the concept of God, the theistic religions are trying to make it plain that God is not to be understood as an abstraction, or as just a force or a power. Instead, the God of the theistic religions is understood to have intentions and beliefs, to perform actions, and so on.

The idea of an omnipotent force may, perhaps, be coherent and intelligible. If so, then we could not deduce from the attribution to God of omnipotence alone that God is a person. But the same does not seem to be true of either omniscience or perfect goodness. With respect to those qualities, there is good reason to think that only a person could possess them.

### Omniscience and being a person

Non-human animals may plausibly be said to know things. But there is much that they do not, and could not, know. For instance, they do not know that they know things. And, given the nature of their brains, they could not. They are not built for such self-reflectiveness. So horses and cats and chimpanzees may be ruled out as candidates for omniscience. Even though they occupy places on the knowledge scale that peaks in omniscience, they could never make it all the way to the top, or even much further up, without ceasing to be the very sorts of animals that they are.

The best case of knowers that we know of is ourselves. In our case, in addition to the kinds of things that non-human animals can know – let's call that sensory or perceptual knowledge – we have reflective and abstract knowledge. For instance, we know that we have knowledge in the first place. And we know things that are not present in our perceptual field.

Our best understanding of such knowledge is that only persons possess it. So, if we attribute limitless knowledge to God, we seem to be required to attribute personhood to God too. Otherwise, we will not be able to include reflective or abstract knowledge in what God knows.

### Perfect goodness and being a person

A parallel line of reasoning would seem to take us from the attribution to God of perfect goodness to the attribution to God of personhood. For, while animals can be good or bad in various ways, as mothers providing for their young, say, or as hunters, or as herders of sheep, or as guards and so on, their goodness or badness do not seem to include moral goodness or badness. For instance, we do not have any knowledge of an animal injuring another animal for the sake of the pain to be caused. Typically, animals injure other animals in the process of killing them for food, or in defending their territory. With the possible exception of certain primates, our best understanding of animal brains seems to rule out the possibility that animals could have the concept of causing pain to others, or of choosing to cause pain to others.

True, there may be continuity between morality in humans, on the one hand, and animal experience and behavior, on the other. That would be so, for instance, if morality were ultimately rooted in feeling. But morality also requires reflection. It requires not just doing good things and avoiding bad things, danger or pain for instance, but also understanding what is good or bad in a particular situation, and either choosing or avoiding it for that reason. And, understanding that, it requires being able to project that understanding on to other situations as well, even though they may not have yet occurred, and to judge them good or bad too. We humans seem to be the only animals capable of this. Thus it would seem that attributing moral goodness to God also commits us to attributing personhood to God.

As these considerations about divine knowledge and goodness show, it is by analogy to ourselves that personhood is attributed to God.

*A glitch in attributing personhood to God, and a stipulation*
But attributing personhood to God is not plain sailing by any means. For one thing, in the two previous examples, I fudged something in a way favorable to theism.

It is not true that our experience of abstract knowledge, or of moral goodness, requires us to call the possessors of such qualities persons, pure and simple. Instead, what follows from our experience is to call the possessors of those things human persons. That is, our only knowledge of persons is restricted to animals of a certain kind, physical beings of a particular species, *Homo sapiens*.

That poses a problem, then, insofar as the theistic notion of God as an essentially or intrinsically spiritual or non-physical person is concerned. For we have no experience at all of non-physical persons. We have no experience of thinking, or feeling, or evaluating, or intending, occurring in any organism that does not have a functioning brain or central nervous system. Moreover, our best knowledge is pretty convincing on the point that this is no coincidence. Furthermore, we have good reason to think that the mental and linguistic natures of humans and other advanced primates are those of essentially social beings.

Nonetheless, for the sake of argument, let us stipulate acceptance of the idea of God both as a one-of-a-kind individual and as intrinsically a wholly spiritual person. This includes stipulating that God is omnipotent, omniscient, and perfectly good, as those qualities have been sketched out here. This stipulation enables us to proceed with our two investigations. But strains in the analogy by which God is understood to be a person, and a good person in particular, will develop later on in our investigations.

## II  Evil

### *Moral evils*

There is a lot of cruelty in the world, cruelty to persons and cruelty to animals. There is a lot of deception, too: for instance, cheating and exploitation. There is a lot of mockery and humiliation, viciousness and sadism. There is a lot of violence in the world, much of it perpetrated by human beings. There is torture and murder. Any newspaper or news broadcast will give plenty of examples of all of the above and more.

Some are scarcely imaginable. Think, for instance, of a mother repeatedly pressing the hands and face of her screaming, terrified, two-year-old on to the hotplate of the stove. An entirely different dimension of scarcely imaginable horrors caused by human beings is the Holocaust, the murders of over 6,000,000 people in death camps during World War II – to say nothing of the suffering caused to those who happened to survive those camps. And we have not yet mentioned the Soviet camps, the gulags, or the death toll in the Cultural Revolution of Chairman Mao, or the murders of millions of Cambodians by the forces of Pol Pot, or, reaching back further into history, the massacres in North Africa by the Christian crusaders of the late Middle Ages, or the slaughter in Constantinople in the Fourth Crusade. And history tells us of many others.

The two-year-old horribly tortured by his mother for crying at night. The victims of the Holocaust. Do we count these as two terrible things? Or as some six million and one? The latter, surely. For each victim suffered his or her own individual torment, and each of those deaths was the unjustified death of an individual person. And the same goes for the victims of the Stalinist purges, the Christian crusades, and so on.

We need a word to cover all the many varieties of wickedness together, a group name by which to know them. In the philosophical literature on this topic, the term 'moral evil' is often used as the group name for the kinds of things I have just been describing. Let us follow the common philosophical practice, and employ the term for the same purpose here.

Moral evils, then, are the harmful and hurtful things for which persons are morally responsible and culpable. Moral evils include both wicked doings and also wicked omissions, which are things that should have been done but are culpably not done. Moral evils are not just unfortunate happenings, like lightning striking a tree, causing a fire that burns a forest, destroys a home, and kills a family. They are by definition not accidents. The concept is pretty much the same as what people who favor religious language call sins.

Certain restrictions apply. For instance, a child might be said to be willfully responsible for causing pain and suffering, but, depending on the age or development of the child, the child might not be responsible in the moral sense of responsibility. Likewise, a mentally retarded adult might not be morally responsible, even though he or she is the cause of the pain or harm. Furthermore, not all cases where normal adults are blamed for an action or an omission are moral evils. A student turning in his term paper late, without a good reason or excuse, is held responsible and likely penalized. But, as described, his action is hardly a moral evil.

Noting that certain restrictions and qualifications apply, the term 'moral evil' does a good job of displaying its meaning in the very name itself. The same, however, cannot be so readily said of its companion term, 'natural evil.'

### Evil happenings

I began the previous chapter with a reminder of the recent Indonesian tsunamis, the Pakistani earthquake, the Gulf Coast hurricane. We usually refer to such things as 'natural disasters.' The term is appropriate, for they are obviously disastrous occurrences for their victims, and their causes are purely natural forces, without any contribution from us.

These are happenings, not doings. There is no plan or intention or omission behind them. They just happen as a consequence of certain other non-intended things happening before them, and so on back in a sequence of effects brought on by causes, which are themselves effects.

Unfortunately, distinguishing between doings and happenings does not give us the precise distinction between moral evils and the other main kind. Consider the terror of a deer fleeing from a predator, and then its agony upon being caught, mauled, and bitten into. The hunting, catching, mauling, and biting are all doings. But obviously they are not culpable. The lion couldn't help it, just as, perhaps, the mentally retarded adult couldn't help injuring a child. These kinds of things, while doings, are more like happenings, for present purposes. So let us add them to those things I have been citing as examples of evil happenings.

Together, they are examples of pain and suffering and death that result from the unscripted operations of nature itself, without being responsibly intended by any human person. The next question is: What term best fits these things?

### Natural evils

The term 'natural disaster' works fine for earthquakes, hurricanes, mud slides, tidal waves, and the like, when there is a heavy toll of victims. But it seems forced and out of place, if applied to the child dying of lymphoma, or to the Alzheimer's patient. It seems too big a term for single cases, even though there is no denying that each individual case is a disaster for the victim and the victim's family. Likewise, there is no denying that each of them is the result of natural causes alone.

The truth of the matter is that there is no particularly good term for the range of things being gathered together now, that is, pain and suffering and waste of life that result just from forces in nature itself. Among philosophers who work on the topic, the term 'natural evil' is often used to refer to these sorts of things.

The word 'natural' is apt, for it picks up the point that such things result solely from occurrences in the natural world itself. The word 'evil' is intended to pick up the felt badness of the sorts of things in question, that is, the pain and loss and suffering that result for the victims.

But the term is not a really good fit. Mainly, this is so because, in everyday speech, we usually employ the word 'evil' when there is a person at fault. In everyday contexts, we typically use the word 'evil' for things like child abuse, or genocide, or torture, or for the perpetrators of such things. For instance, the terms 'evil doer' and 'evil deed' reflect the common kinds of everyday uses of the word 'evil.'

But here, in regard to many kinds of cancer, or Alzheimer's, or sudden infant death syndrome, or earthquakes, there is, by definition, no doer. The insurance-policy term 'acts of God' is not meant literally. So, by simple logic, there is no deed either. These are examples of things that happen, not of things that are done. And, for the reason given earlier, it includes such things as killings by animals in the wild.

So, when used of diseases and earthquakes and so on, the word 'evil' is being stretched beyond its normal range, leaving us with a widely used term, 'natural evil,' that is neither ideal nor self-explanatory. But no other term comes to mind as any better. So, both for that reason and because, in philosophical circles, the term is already commonly used for the sorts of things under consideration, let us put aside our misgivings and join the majority by using it too.

Natural evils, then, are instances of pain and suffering, of harmful or destructive occurrences, for which no human being is morally respons- ible. Natural disasters, diseases not due to human beings, killings by animals in the wild, and so on, are the most obvious examples.

## III   The Problem of God and Evil

Suppose for a moment that, throughout the whole of human history, the idea of God had never occurred to anybody. Suppose it is just the same in that regard as the idea of Hsz. Suppose also that the world otherwise is just as we now find it to be, insofar as both moral and natural evils are concerned. In this imagined world, there are theft, cruelty, torture, murder, and so on, to the very same extent that there are these things in the actual world. Likewise, there are the very same earthquakes and floods and diseases that exist in the actual world.

In this imagined world, then, with all of the evils and horrors of the actual world in it, there would be one problem fewer to deal with than in the actual world. For, in the imagined world, there would be no problem of trying to make sense of all of these terrible things in terms of a supposedly perfect creator. In this imagined world, wonder- ing whether a particular evil occurrence was justified or not would be restricted entirely to pain and suffering and so on caused by human beings. In this imagined world, natural disasters, diseases, killings by animals in the wild, and so on, would be neither justified nor unjustified. They would simply be things that happen. In this respect, this imagined world would be like the actual world of the atheist.

The missing problem would be philosophical in nature. There would be no philosophical problem of evil, even though all the very same evils would exist as in the actual world, and so would all the same problems of coping with such things as diseases, crimes, natural disasters, and so on.

This would be so because the philosophical problem of evil is not the philosophical problem of evil as such. Rather, it is the philosophical problem of God and evil. There is no philosophical problem about the latter without the concept of the former.

## IV Design

When something is designed, it is planned to be a certain way. It is organized and implemented according to a certain intention. By definition, a design represents purpose and premeditation. There is no such thing as accidental design. Accidents come about by chance, but things that happen by design are planned. And things that are planned are things that trace back to minds of a certain sort as their ultimate source. We ourselves are the best and obvious example of this, but animals of other species have intentions and act on purpose too, and, in the case of certain higher primates, seem to make plans. But leaving aside the zoological details, the fundamental point that is relevant here is that intention and design come from minds of a certain sort, and that without such minds nothing could occur by design or on purpose.

It is important to distinguish between the concept of design and the concept of order. It is important because they are neighboring concepts, with close connections. If they were different like black and white, we would not need to remind ourselves to be careful not to confuse them with one another. The core of the difference between them is reflected in the contrast between the two following points. Accidental order is possible, in fact it is common, but accidental design is impossible, and so is nowhere to be found.

You look at the clouds in the sky or the sand dunes on the beach and you see order. But the order you see is what wind or the ebb and flow of the tides bring about. There is order, but that order is not the same as a design or a plan. We might say the sand dunes look as if they were designed, but we know they were not. By contrast, when you look at your cellphone or your watch, you see order that is due to intention and design. Cellphones and watches do not just come about. They exist on purpose.

Order of the one kind, the kind you see in the sand dunes, is natural order. It is order found in nature itself, occurring by the forces and processes of nature, with no help from us. Order of the other sort is brought about by humans. It is the product of design.

Our second investigation asks if there is evidence to warrant concluding that the universe itself came to exist by design; whether in that respect it resembles the cellphone more than the sand dune.

# V   Faith and Reason

## *Four views of the relationship between faith and reason*

Both questions under investigation here involve the relationship between faith and reason. There are four main interpretations of that relationship in the theistic tradition. Of those, two are receptive to one or both of our investigations and have a stake in the outcome, while two are unreceptive and acknowledge no stake in either of them. I will now sketch out the four interpretations.

### Instinct

One of them is the idea that religious belief is instinctual. It is the idea that we cannot but believe in God. This is a claim not just about religious belief, but about human nature too. Viewed as a claim about human nature, it seems to be false.

Among several reasons, here are two. First, it is a fact that many people are unbelievers. Second, believers sometimes abandon their faith. But it is hard to see how either could be so, if faith were a matter of instinct.

For those reasons, I will give no further consideration to this idea.

### Faith only

Another interpretation is the fideistic, or 'faith only,' interpretation of religious belief. It is unreceptive in principle to any counter-evidence to the idea of God. As such, it gives itself veto power over anything that might count against its core beliefs. It is, then, not open to discussions in which those beliefs might be at risk. As such, it has no stake in either of our investigations. Later, we will have cause to think that prominent defenses of theism have a pronounced fideistic leaning.

In contrast with the first two, both remaining interpretations of the relationship between faith and reason do have a stake in what we discuss here.

*Religious experience*

The first of the remaining pair shuns any effort to prove that God exists, or to provide philosophical arguments as support for belief in God. It sees faith as adequately sustained and supported either by individual experience or by the experience of living in a particular kind of community. As such, religious belief is said to be properly basic. On this view, religious belief is seen not to need grounding in a set of beliefs more basic than itself.

Nonetheless, this view accepts a need to defend religious belief against potentially damaging counter-evidence. In particular, it sees the need for a defense against the counter-evidence of vast amounts of terrible evils that seem pointless.

The American philosopher William Hasker calls this view 'experientialism.'[1] Among contemporary philosophers, the most prominent experientialist is the influential American philosopher Alvin Plantinga (b. 1931). We will come back to him in chapter 4.

*A role for supporting evidence*

The fourth interpretation of the connection between faith and reason agrees that, typically, faith arises in a person's experience of living in a certain kind of community. But it maintains also that a proper understanding of the physical universe, as well as of the nature of human life, both corroborates belief in God and provides a sufficient basis for a reasonable person to conclude that God is the original source of the universe. In this way, it reflects a more ambitious understanding of the relationship between reason and faith than the experientialist view espoused by Plantinga and others. This view is broadly characteristic of the Roman Catholic intellectual tradition.

In addition, like the experientialist view, it accepts the need for a defense of theistic belief against the counter-evidence of vast amounts of terrible evils. I will follow precedent and refer to this view as 'evidentialism.' The name is appropriate, in that this view is interested in accumulating evidence to support religious belief, as well as in countering evidence brought against it.

---

[1]   William Hasker, "Evidentialism," in Robert Audi, gen. ed., *The Cambridge Dictionary of Philosophy* (New York: Cambridge University Press, 1995), 253.

## VI   Our Two Investigations

Does the existence of vast amounts of evil square with the idea of God as omnipotent, omniscient, perfectly good creator, or does it undercut that idea, either by showing it to be outright false or, short of that, improbable? That is one question.

From a description of the world that includes reference to its lawlike orderliness, its enormous complexity, its suitability for the evolution of life, its containing beings who feel pleasure and pain, including vast amounts of seemingly pointless pain, would a reasonable and truth-seeking person conclude that the world traces to a perfect creator? That is a second question.

In the first investigation, both the idea of God and the facts of evil are present in our inquiry from the start, as we attempt to discover whether, and how well, they fit together. Both are essential parts of the question itself.

In our second investigation, by contrast, the idea of God plays no part in the question. If the idea comes up at all in that investigation, it can only be in the answer, on its merits as a solution to the problem under examination.

### Suggested Reading

Peterson, Michael L.; Hasker, William; Reichenbach, Bruce; and Basinger, David (1998) *Reason and Religious Belief.* New York: Oxford University Press. Chapters 3 and 4 are relevant here.

Rowe, William L. (2007) *Philosophy of Religion.* Belmont: Wadsworth. Chapters 1 and 6 provide a good account of things discussed in this chapter.

# Part II

# The Logic of God and Evil

# 3

# Is the Existence of God Impossible?

Does the idea of God as perfect creator square with the fact that terrible things happen, or does that fact provide good reason to judge there is no God?

*Two senses of squaring and not squaring,
and our first investigation*

Things may not square with one another in either of the following ways.

One way is when something counts against the probability that something else is true, or against the reasonableness of believing it to be true. In this sense, when one thing gives us reason to think that another is either false or unreasonable, there are degrees of not squaring. In this first sense, one thing may count heavily against another, or it may count against it only a little, or something in between.

Another way is when one thing rules out even the possibility of another. In this second sense, the two things are logically inconsistent with each other, and there are no degrees of that. In this sense of not squaring, two things are absolutely mutually exclusive.

In this chapter and the next, we will investigate whether the existence of evil in the world is logically inconsistent with the existence of God. If it is, then the fact that evil exists means, not just that there is no God, but that there could not possibly be a God.

A decision on the issue turns upon the precise meanings of certain concepts, more than on facts in the world. Accordingly, we will need those precise meanings clearly before us. The concepts in question are logical possibility and impossibility, logical necessity, and contradiction.

# I    Logical Possibility and Impossibility

## *Possibilities and impossibilities*

"Anything is possible." How often have you heard people say that? Perhaps you have said it or thought it yourself. Usually people say it to hedge their bet, or to remind someone of the difference between reality and fantasy. Typically, when we qualify something by saying "anything is possible," we mean that we want to focus on realistic options, as opposed to wild conjectures far beyond the range of things that we need to worry about in a particular situation.

So, is anything possible? No. Lots of things are not possible at all, for instance, something's being a circle and not a circle at exactly the same time, or something's being a shapeless circle, or a five-sided triangle. What about traveling faster than the speed of light, or surviving a 10,000-foot fall, or a brain transplant? Are they possible?

Now here the answer is not so simple. For there are different meanings of the terms 'possible' and 'impossible,' and we need to be clear about which meaning is in play in a particular question. In the questions about going faster than light and about surviving that fall, it is physical possibility/impossibility that is meant. But in our investigation into the possibility or impossibility of God's existence, we are using the terms in their strictly logical sense. Then there is the meaning when we say something is medically possible or impossible – a brain transplant, for instance. In addition, we talk about something's being politically possible or impossible, psychologically possible or impossible, financially possible or impossible, possible or impossible as a practical matter, and so on. There are many contexts where things are said to be possible or impossible, and there will often be overlaps among them. Let us bring the strictly logical sense into focus by way of contrast with two other meanings.

## *Practical possibility/impossibility*

It was impossible for me to meet you for lunch yesterday. The plumber was due to come between ten and four, and I had to be home to let him in, and you know how difficult it is to get an appointment with a plumber. Here, 'impossible' means inconvenient. For of course I could have met you for lunch, of course it was possible, in a different sense of the term. After all, I hadn't been taken hostage, or fallen into a coma, or otherwise become incapable of moving.

Some things are more inconvenient than others, and sometimes we exaggerate the inconvenience of doing something. The word 'impossible,' used to express impracticality and inconvenience, is always an exaggeration, relative to strictly literal impossibility, which is logical impossibility. Similarly, we sometimes exaggerate the difficulty of doing something, which takes us to, or at least close to, physical impossibility.

### Physical possibility/impossibility

"Given Agassi's position and world-class quickness, Federer had to send that ball down a two-inch pipe of space in order to pass him, which he did, moving backwards, with no setup time and none of his weight behind the shot. It was impossible."

Thus, the *New York Times*.[1] Was it impossible? Well, it happened. Thousands saw it in person at the final of the 2005 US Open tennis tournament, and millions more, myself among them, saw it on television. Here, the word 'impossible' means exceedingly difficult, perhaps unprecedented, awe-inspiring.

And then there is Tom Cruise. At face value, *Mission: Impossible* suggests something that, quite simply, cannot conceivably be done. An impossible mission, understood literally, is a far more daunting prospect than even a suicide mission. A suicide mission offers the hope of success at least, even if the cost is going to be steep. But a mission that is impossible suggests that the best thing would be to stay home.

As it turns out in the movies, though, the success rate for supposedly impossible missions is remarkably high. The reason of course, as everyone in the cinema knows, is that for Tom Cruise the impossible is not, strictly speaking, impossible at all. Instead, it is something very improbable or difficult, at least for the rest of us – fending off a helicopter while clinging to a train speeding through the chunnel, say, or surviving a fall from an airplane in flight.

Compared to the tennis and falling-from-an-airplane examples, the strict meaning of physical impossibility is violating a law of nature. To travel faster than the speed of light is perhaps the best or purest

---

[1] *New York Times Sports Magazine*, Sept. 2006, 48.

example of this strict sense of physical impossibility, at least above the level of sub-atomic particles.

This raises the question whether the strictest sense of physical imposs-ibility is the strictest sense of impossibility, period. For instance, can we meaningfully speculate about something above the level of sub-atomic particles traveling faster than light, or does the speculation simply cancel itself out?

In a science-fiction context, or in contemplating discoveries that physi-cists may make centuries from now, or as an example of a miracle, per-haps we can speculate about it. Even David Hume (1711–76), perhaps the best-known skeptic about miracles, accepts that a miracle is theoretically possible.

At any rate, the point is that, if we can coherently speculate about the possibility of traveling faster than light, then there is exaggeration even in the idea that a violation of a law of nature is absolutely impossible. And if that is so, then there is always exaggeration in the term 'physical impossibility.'

By contrast, when something is logically impossible, it is literally impossible, impossible without exaggeration, so not just at present but at all times. Not even a miracle could violate it.

## Logical impossibility

He survived a 10,000-foot fall from an airplane. Just from hearing or reading that sentence, you do not know with absolute certainty that it is false. For instance, you do not know that a miracle didn't happen and he survived.

He survived that 10,000-foot fall, but was dead before he hit the ground. X is a circle and X is not a circle at the very same time. Just hearing or reading those sentences, you know with absolute certainty that, if meant literally, they have to be false. Charitably, you might suppose there was a typo in them, or that, for some other reason, what the sentences literally say is not what is meant. For there is no exaggera-tion in the judgment that those sentences have to be false, that they are necessarily false. Saying such things are impossible would be the strict and literal truth of the matter.

Consequently, we do not have to check all the places where this alleged X might be found, as there are no places for things that are all over simultaneously circular and non-circular. Nor do we have to see the faller afterwards, or see the film of the fall, and especially the landing, to know for sure about his simultaneous survival and death. The impossibilities here are not physical, or practical: they are logical.

In logical impossibility, there is no space whatever into which an exception, no matter how remote or fantastic, could creep, not even a miracle. (True, some theistic philosophers and theologians have maintained that God can do what is logically impossible. But saying this does nothing to get around the fact that the very idea of doing a logically impossible thing is incoherent, so we will ignore it.)

When something is logically impossible, the very concept of it is self-defeating or self-canceling. That, essentially, is what logical impossibility is. It is an absolute concept. Its meaning is not relative to context. There are no degrees of it.

We can say or write examples of logical impossibilities, but we could never find an example in reality. For, by definition, things that are logically impossible could not occur even in a dream, or fantasy, or exaggeration, or miracle. We can imagine seeing a picture of the person who survived the 10,000-foot fall and marveling at his luck, or whatever did the trick. But we cannot imagine seeing a circle that at the very same time is not a circle at all, or a circle that is a square. We can, of course, imagine a circle and a square overlapping, or a circle transforming in a flash into a square. But neither is imagining a circle that is also not a circle at all but a square.

## Logical possibility

If logical impossibility is the kind of impossibility that comes from the very idea or concept of something, when the idea is necessarily self-defeating or self-canceling, what is logical possibility? Well, the short answer is that it is anything which is not impossible in that way, no matter how wildly far-fetched or improbable. Anything not ruled out by the very intrinsic nature of itself is a logical possibility.

It is the most permissive kind of possibility. For instance, not only is it logically possible for you to survive the 10,000-foot fall, it is logically possible for you to survive such a fall each hour, on the hour, for the next twenty years.

The two concepts, logical possibility at one end, logical impossibility at the other, are each maximally extreme. Something can be logically possible, although physically impossible. Think of surviving that fall every hour for the next twenty years. But, at the other end of the spectrum, something that is logically impossible is impossible in all the other ways that things can be impossible too, that is, physically, medically, psychologically, and so on.

## Contradiction and logical necessity

A statement or idea that self-cancels in the way that "X is a circle and at the same time X is not a circle" does is a self-contradictory statement or idea. Likewise, two statements that cannot possibly both be true at the same time, no matter what, and that cannot possibly both be false at the same time either, contradict each other. Taken either way, their combination necessarily self-destructs. For instance, the statement "X is a circle" and the statement "X is not a circle" cannot possibly be true simultaneously, or false simultaneously either.

This use of the word 'contradiction' is more restrictive than its everyday use. In effect, we are restricting the term to the meaning it has for logicians, which is to refer to necessarily self-canceling statements and to combinations of statements that would necessarily self-cancel. Such statements and combinations are necessarily false.

By contrast, the everyday use of the word 'contradiction' is more liberal and tolerant than this. For sometimes in everyday life we say two people contradict each other when all we mean is that they disagree.

Not every false statement or belief is a contradiction. But every contradiction is false. Furthermore, as we saw in the examples above, a contradiction is necessarily false. The following contrast will bring out the meaning of this key word, 'necessarily,' that I have been using.

"John Kerry is the president of the United States." This statement is false. But it didn't have to be false. And for you to know it is false, you have to know certain facts about the world, over and above knowing the meanings of the words in the sentence itself. You have to know something about the result of the 2004 presidential election in the United States. If, this minute, you just woke up from a coma that started on October 31, 2004, you would not know, merely from reading that sentence, that it is false. For the sentence is not forced to be false by the literal meanings of the words that comprise it. What makes it false is the non-linguistic fact of the electoral vote for George Bush in November 2004.

Some false statements are false because they misrepresent facts in the world. They are false for reasons beyond their own internal make-up, and they would be true if the external facts were different. Most false statement are like that. They are not contradictions. But other false statements are beyond reprieve, for instance, "He survived the 10,000-foot fall that killed him." Taken literally, they could never be true, no matter what facts in the world change. They are false because, in their very meaning, they self-cancel. They are strict contradictions. They don't just happen to be false, they are necessarily false.

The argument we are going to consider claims there is a strict contradiction between the two following statements: "God, understood to be an omnipotent and perfectly good being, exists" and "Evil exists." The claim is that, because the second statement is true, the first is necessarily false.

## Explicit and implicit contradictions

Sometimes a contradiction is explicit. A case in point is our earlier example, "X is a circle and X is not a circle." In real life, however, it is very rare to find an explicit self-contradictory statement, apart from typos and statements used to illustrate the error. And the reason is the obvious one, namely, the obviousness of the error.

Typically, then, contradictions are implicit. They occur between statements or beliefs that, when interpreted, show themselves incapable of forming a conjunction that could ever possibly be true.

Consider these two statements: "X is a circle" and "X is not a curved shape." Could both statements be true at the same time of the same X? No. Why not? After all, they do not explicitly affirm and deny the same thing at the same time, namely, being a circle. The second statement does not even mention circularity.

But just a very small bit of analysis and interpretation reveals that being a circle necessarily means having a curved shape. Having a curved shape is part of the essential meaning of being a circle. So, with the add-on of that implication, namely, the necessarily true point that a circle has a curved shape, we find that the statement "X is a circle" does contradict the statement "X is not a curved shape." Implicitly, although not explicitly, they contradict one another. That is, the conjunction of the three statements "X is a circle," "Being a circle, X necessarily has a curved shape," and "X is not a curved shape" amounts to an explicit contradiction.

In real life, implicit contradictions will typically require more analysis and interpretation than that example. Nonetheless, the example suffices to illustrate the point at issue. It is that seeing an implicit contradiction between two statements, or within a two-part statement, requires some additional interpretation. Just looking at the two statements themselves is not usually enough to see the contradiction. Consequently, pointing to the statements themselves is not usually enough to explain it.

Furthermore, the example shows the principle involved in proving an implicit contradiction between two statements. It is that the additional interpretation must include a third statement which is necessarily true and which, when added to the original two, results in a three-part conjunction that contains an explicit contradiction. In the example above, the third statement is "Being a circle, X necessarily has a curved shape," while the original two are "X is a circle" and "X is not a curved shape." Conjoining the three of them generates an explicit contradiction.

Now let us apply this principle to the claim that there is an implicit contradiction between the two statements "God, understood to be an omnipotent and perfectly good being, exists" and "Evil exists." To prove this claim, a third statement must be found which is necessarily true, that is, which could not even possibly be false, and which, when conjoined with the original two, results in an explicit contradiction. Short of this, an implicit contradiction will not be proved.

As we take up the claim to prove a contradiction between God and evil, the questions to keep in mind are these: What is the pivotal third statement, the one that is necessarily true? And do the three statements together generate an explicit contradiction? As these questions suggest, the burden of proof in proving this claimed contradiction is heavy.

## II   J. L. Mackie's Argument

Approximately fifty years ago, the Australian philosopher J. L. Mackie (1917–81) argued for the following position:

> I think . . . that a . . . telling criticism can be made by way of the traditional problem of evil. Here it can be shown . . . that religious beliefs . . . are positively irrational, that the several parts of the essential theological doctrine are inconsistent with one another . . . so that the [believer] can maintain his position as a whole only by . . . [being] prepared to believe . . . what can be disproved from other beliefs that he also holds.[2]

---

[2]   J. L. Mackie, "Evil and Omnipotence," in M. M. Adams and R. M. Adams, eds, *The Problem of Evil* (Oxford: Oxford University Press, 1990), 25.

I will examine Mackie's argument for a contradiction between God and evil in two installments, one here in this chapter, the other in the next. My division of labor reflects a division in Mackie's presentation of his case. He develops his argument, first, by presenting what he calls the "simplest form" of it, then, second, by responding to various attempts to show there is no contradiction between God and evil. I will concentrate on the first stage now, postponing the second until the next chapter.

Mackie begins with the following synopsis of his attempted proof:

> In its simplest form the problem is this: God is omnipotent; God is wholly good; and yet evil exists. There seems to be some contradiction between these three propositions, so that if any two of them were true the third would be false . . . However the contradiction does not arise immediately.[3]

His task is to bring this alleged implicit contradiction out into the open.

The core of the enterprise is his analysis of the essential meaning of each of the two concepts, goodness and omnipotence. Mackie sets forth his understanding of their respective essential meanings as follows:

> good is opposed to evil, in such a way that a good thing always eliminates evil as far as it can,

and

> there are no limits to what an omnipotent thing can do.[4]

## Essential meaning

Since Mackie's argument turns on his understanding of the essential meaning of each of those two terms, we need to be clear what the essential meaning of a term (or concept, or idea) is.

It is what the term or concept has to mean, what it necessarily means. The contrast is with the conventional, or merely agreed-upon, thus changeable, meaning of a term or concept. The conventional meaning of a concept can change with context or circumstance. But its essential meaning cannot change. It is always the same, regardless of context.

---

[3]    Mackie, "Evil and Omnipotence," 25–6.
[4]    Mackie, "Evil and Omnipotence," 26.

For instance, it is part of the essential meaning of the geometrical concept 'circle' to be a closed plane curve, every point of which is the same distance from a fixed point within the curve. Anything not having those properties is not, and could not possibly be, a circle, in the geometrical sense, at all.

By contrast, the confectionery concept of a biscuit, for example, is different in different places. If you go shopping for biscuits in Ireland you will get one sort of thing, whereas in America you will get something quite different. And an Irish child may be disappointed in America, when the promised biscuits are produced.

Before the suffragette movements in Great Britain and the United States, being a voter meant being a man, as does being a priest in the Roman Catholic branch of Christianity. But in the Episcopalian branch, the word 'priest' can mean either a man or a woman. Even in their respective confectionery, electoral, and clerical contexts, then, the words 'biscuit,' 'voter,' and 'priest' can mean different things. But in the context of geometry, the meaning of the word 'circle' is fixed. That is not the only meaning of the word 'circle,' of course, nor its only context. After all, there is the Circle Line in the London Underground and the famous group of philosophers and scientists in the 1920s and 1930s known as the Vienna Circle.

In a line quoted just above, we saw Mackie emphasize that, in its essential nature, omnipotence means unlimited power. In a moment, we will see him qualify this, but in a way that will not affect any crucial point in his argument. In another line quoted just above, we saw him emphasize that, in its essential nature, the goodness of a good person means eliminating evil as much as possible.

### Mackie's proposed 'third' statement and his conclusions

Putting those two things together, Mackie concludes: "From these it follows that a good omnipotent thing eliminates evil completely."[5] This is the sought-after third statement, the one that will bring success to his argument if it meets the two criteria mentioned earlier. They are: (1) in its own right, the statement must be necessarily true, and (2) when the statement is conjoined with the original two statements, the result is an explicit contradiction.

[5]   Mackie, "Evil and Omnipotence," 26.

Now, it is a plain fact that evil exists in the world. So Mackie further concludes, "the propositions that a good omnipotent thing exists, and that evil exists, are incompatible."[6]

By the word 'incompatible' in the second conclusion Mackie means contradictory, so that the simultaneous existence of both God and evil is logically impossible. Either alone would be possible, but not the conjunction of both together, just as either one alone of "X is a circle" and "X is not a curved shape" is possible, but the pair together is not. So, as the existence of evil is a plain and obvious fact, Mackie's conclusion is that the existence of God is logically impossible.

## Measuring success

A circle is a figure that does not have a curved shape. A reliable car is one that breaks down a lot. These two statements seem to be implicit contradictions, that is, statements forced to be false by the essential meanings of their key terms.

It seems obvious, and so it seems easy to prove, that a car that breaks down a lot could not possibly be a reliable car. Suppose we are talking about that, wondering if it is really true. And suppose I say I'm going to prove that a reliable car could not possibly be one that breaks down a lot, because there is an implicit contradiction between reliability and breaking down a lot. Suppose I take the example of the cars in that car dealership over there. Suppose we both know they have been breaking down a lot.

Suppose that, while discussing the matter, we hear a rumor that possibly the car dealer's disgruntled son-in-law has been tampering with the cars in the showroom, causing them to break down a lot. As rumor has it, the possible tampering is both very effective and very hard to detect, because of the son-in-law's expertise.

Now look at these two statements about a particular car: "This car is a reliable car" and "This car breaks down a lot." What effect does the rumor have on my attempted proof that the second of the two statements necessarily falsifies the first?

It has the effect that, unless I rule out the rumored possibility of tampering, I am not entitled to claim the second statement is an guaranteed

---

[6] Mackie, "Evil and Omnipotence," 26.

falsifier of the first. After all, I am trying to prove that it is not even possible for a car that breaks down a lot to be a reliable car. But now there is a rumor to the effect that breaking down a lot is possibly not this car's fault, thus possibly not an indicator of unreliability in the car in its own right.

Notice, I am not trying to prove it is very unlikely that a car that breaks down a lot is a reliable car. We would all agree on that. I am trying to prove it is literally impossible. So, to succeed, I must rule out even a rumored or speculated possibility that something external to the car itself is the cause of the breakdowns. I must prove that, in its own right, the statement "This is a reliable car, even though it breaks down a lot," necessarily cancels itself out. I must prove there is no possible exception to the mutual incompatibility of the two ideas, reliability and breaking down a lot. I must prove that no mitigating circumstance is even a possibility. With this in mind as the measurement of success, let us return to Mackie.

Mackie told us that because goodness, in its essential nature, is opposed to evil, a good person eliminates evil as far as possible. And he told us that, in its essential nature, omnipotence means power without limits. (In developing his case, he mentions that he is prepared to accept omnipotence as meaning the power to do anything that is not logically impossible. This is the concept of omnipotence we discussed in the previous chapter. This qualification has no bearing on the success or failure of his argument, so we do not need to dwell on the difference between power without limits and power without logical limits. We will simply accept the second concept as the essential meaning of omnipotence.)

Suppose we combine the two points, first, that a good person eliminates evil as far as possible, and second, that an omnipotent person can do anything that is logically possible. Mackie's stated expectation is that any world issuing from a perfectly good and omnipotent person would necessarily contain no evil at all; no exceptions are even possible, so any rumored exception would be guaranteed to be false. On this reasoning, a three-way conjunction of omnipotence, perfect goodness, and evil is a logical impossibility.

Could there possibly be some additional relevant fact that could introduce the possibility of an exception, in the way that the rumor of the son-in-law may perhaps introduce the possibility of an exception in the case of the cars that are breaking down a lot? That is a key question. For if I do not rule out even the speculated possibility of tampering, then I fail to prove it is strictly impossible for a car that breaks down a lot to be, of its essential nature, a reliable car. Similarly, if Mackie does not rule out even the possibility of an exception, he will not have met his burden of proof, and his argument will fail.

## The burden of proof

At the conclusion of a trial, the judge explains the law to the jury, as it applies to the evidence they have heard. Their duty as jurors is to reach a verdict on the evidence, relative to the law as explained. Our situation here is broadly similar.

Mackie must prove there could not possibly be an exception which would make it possible for God and evil to co-exist. In order for him to fail to prove this, there does not have to be an exception in fact. An exception does not even have to be possible.

Of course, if there were either an actual or possible exception, then Mackie would certainly fail to prove his point that no exception is possible. An actual or possible exception would be sufficient for him to fail. But neither an actual nor a possible exception is necessary for him to fail. For he would fail to prove his point if his argument contained a serious flaw: some logical fallacy, for instance. If his argument had a serious flaw, he would fail to prove his point, even if his point were right. Once again, think of the Al Capone example in chapter 1.

The two essential ideas to keep in mind, as we estimate Mackie's burden of proof, are these: first, that he does not have to be wrong about the point he is trying to prove in order to fail to prove it; second, he does not have to be proved wrong about that point in order to fail to prove it. He could fail for reasons that are internal to his own argument itself. The burden of proof is on him to prove no exception is possible, and that is the only basis on which to judge his success or failure, in this first stage of his argument. This is a heavy burden of proof. But it is the right burden, rightly placed.

Suppose you are charged with a crime and brought to trial. Suppose the prosecution lays out its case against you. In response, suppose your lawyer emphasizes to the jury the correct legal point that, for you to be convicted, the prosecution must prove you are guilty. Suppose she says nothing further. That is, she makes no attempt to prove you are not guilty, and she does not even claim you are not guilty. Suppose she is content to let the jury decide whether the prosecution met its burden of proof, which is to prove your guilt beyond a reasonable doubt. Suppose the prosecutor fails to do that. Then the prosecution's case fails, even though the defense neither claimed nor proved anything to the contrary. Now, in a final twist on the example, suppose that, unknown to anybody but yourself, you did commit the crime with which you are charged. The prosecution might still fail to prove you guilty.

Now think of Mackie as like the prosecutor. The burden of proof is on him to prove that God and evil strictly contradict each other. He must prove it, not beyond a reasonable doubt, which, in itself, is a high order of proof, but beyond even the possibility of doubt. He must prove it beyond even the conceivability of an exception.

The burden is not on the theistic defense to claim an exception, or even the possibility of an exception. Nor does it have to prove there is an exception, or even that an exception is possible. The defense is not required to do anything at all.

### Good overall, and good in all respects

In the previous chapter, we settled on the idea that God would always and only do what is overall good. Here in this chapter, let us work with a weaker version of that idea. It is that, perhaps, it is possible that God would always and only do what is overall good. Now, is it logically possible that some overall good situation brought about by God might not be good in all respects? Mackie must prove that it is not possible.

Let us speculate about a possibility, both for context and for a concrete example. Perhaps it is possible that no world containing human beings could be overall good that did not make provision for justice. If so, then even omnipotent power would have to make provision for justice, in bringing about an overall good world containing human beings. But perhaps it is possible that restraint and correction are essential mechanisms of justice. If so, then possibly some amount of frustration or disappointment, for instance, would be an unavoidable byproduct of achieving justice.

But in themselves those are not good things. True, they may sometimes be good as means to valuable ends, that is, they may be instrumentally good. But they are not good as such. In themselves, they are evils. So perhaps it is possible that not even God could bring about an overall good world, containing human beings, without evil occurring in it.

We are not in a position right now to claim this as a possibility. Nor do we need either to claim it is a possibility or to prove that it is. The burden of proof is Mackie's entirely. Accordingly, it is up to him to prove there is no such possibility. Until he does, his claim about an implicit contradiction between God and evil is not proved. Until he does, it remains just a claim. And so far in his argument, Mackie has claimed there is no such possibility, but he has not proved it.

## III   Interim Verdict: 'Not Proved'

We must be careful not to overstate things. 'Not proved' is not the same as 'disproved.' And it does not imply it either. 'Not proved' means the burden of proof is not met.

But that does not mean the conclusion itself is false. That is a separate matter, unaffected by failure to prove it true. Nor does a failure to prove the conclusion true mean that it has thereby been disproved, that is, proved to be false. That too is a separate matter, requiring a proof of its own. To illustrate both points, recall Al Capone from chapter 1. Furthermore, it does not mean that the conclusion could not possibly be proved in some other way. All those possibilities remain open.

## Suggested Reading

Mackie, J. L. (1990) "Evil and Omnipotence," in M. M. Adams and R. M. Adams, eds, *The Problem of Evil*. Oxford: Oxford University Press. This 1955 article, now a classic, is widely available in anthologies.

# 4

# A Free-Will Defense of
# the Possibility that God Exists

In the first stage of his argument, J. L. Mackie failed to prove a contradiction between the idea of God and the fact that terrible things happen.
But his claim of logical inconsistency between them was not itself
disproved there either. So the question naturally arises whether it can be
disproved, or whether the argument fares better in its second than in its
first stage. In this chapter we take up those issues.

## The free-will theory of God and evil

Attempting to disprove Mackie's claim, Alvin Plantinga draws on the
resources of a venerable theory in the theistic tradition, the free-will
theory of evil in a world supposedly made by God. The theory figures
prominently in the work of St Augustine (354–430) and, almost 900 years
later, in the work of Thomas Aquinas as well. Later, we will see some
prominent contemporary theistic philosophers use it too.

## I  To Prove a Possibility

To disprove Mackie's claim, Plantinga must prove a possibility. This is
different from the situation in the previous chapter, when there was no
burden on the theistic defender to prove anything. Then, the prosecutor,
Mackie, was attempting to prove a contradiction, and the verdict –
'proved' or 'unproved' – turned solely on his success. But now the
defense is attempting to do something. It is attempting to prove that
Mackie's claim of a contradiction is itself false. Accordingly, the defense
now has a burden of proof of its own. It must prove the possibility that,
even though terrible things happen, God exists. Plantinga does not have

to prove that God actually exists, or that it is probable that God exists. Proving the mere logical possibility of it will do.

The premises, which is to say the statements of evidence, in an argument to prove a logical possibility do not themselves have to be true. They do not even have to be believed to be true. They do not have to be claimed to be true, or proved to be true. All that is required is that they could possibly be true, in the bare logical sense of possibility, explained in the previous chapter.

If you are now thinking that the burden of proof is a lot lighter for Plantinga's free-will-based defense than it was for Mackie, you are right. And that it is a lot lighter reflects the intrinsic natures of logical possibility and impossibility respectively, and the difference between proving the one and proving the other. We covered these points in the previous chapter, so I will not go through them again. This disparity between the requirements for success in the two cases does not reflect any bias or tilt in favor of theism over atheism. My thumb is not on the scale behind the scenes.

Let us look at the understanding of free will, that is, freedom of choice or decision, that is pivotal in Plantinga's defense against Mackie's argument.

## Freedom to choose

Writing this section of chapter 4, I have before me right now two alternative possibilities. I could begin the next paragraph with the word 'since,' or I could begin it with another word instead.

I could have gone either way. It was entirely up to me. Right now, it is entirely up to you whether you read on in this book or whether you stop. You could do the one thing or you could do the other. (As for me, I'm going to assume you made the right decision just now.)

Plantinga's understanding of free choice is reflected in those two examples. The core of it is the idea that, in various circumstances, it is entirely up to me or you to decide what to do. I will state Plantinga's understanding of freedom of choice more explicitly, to be sure we have it right, and available for use as we go on.

### Libertarian free choice

The essence of Plantinga's idea of free will, freedom of choice, is this. I have freedom to choose between courses of action only if, at the time of choosing, I have before me genuinely open alternative possibilities and it is entirely up to me which of them I choose. In philosophical discussion, this two-part understanding of freedom of choice is often called 'libertarian' freedom.

Consequently, I do not have libertarian free will on any occasion when I am caused or forced to choose or to do some action, or when, for whatever reason, there is no genuine alternative available to me. So, for instance, if my hormones made me do it, or my medication, or I did it at gunpoint or under hypnosis, then I did not have free choice on that occasion. And the same is true if my temperament, or my bad upbringing, or processes in my brain, or anything else made me do it, or if, for whatever reason, there was no other option available to me as a genuine alternative.

In Plantinga's view, if I do not have free choice of the sort just sketched, I am not morally responsible for my behavior. At face value, this libertarian view seems to reflect the commonsense understanding of freedom of choice and, for that reason, to be plausible, perhaps even obvious. For instance, think of a situation where you held people morally responsible for something they did or didn't do. You blamed or praised them because you thought they deserved it. And it seems to make sense for you to think that only if you also think they could have chosen or done something else instead. After all, it doesn't seem to make much sense to blame me for doing something if I genuinely couldn't help it, or to praise me for doing something if not doing it was never even an option for me.

Despite its initial appearance of obviousness, libertarianism is a controversial theory, with each of its two core points in dispute. Once again, they are: free choice means that I myself am the sole agent of choice; and free choice means there is a genuine alternative available to me at the time of choosing. Briefly, I will illustrate a disputed feature of each point.

Typically, when we make choices, we are aware of nothing in our brains, or temperament, or upbringing, influencing us. But we are all familiar with the saying "absence of evidence is not evidence of absence." That is, we are all familiar with the cautionary idea that, just because we are not aware of anything influencing the outcome in a particular situation, it does not follow that in fact there is nothing influencing the outcome in that situation. For instance, when I spoke on the phone a little while ago, answering a question from a friend, I had no awareness whatsoever of the processes in my brain or in the muscles and sinews of my throat, or of the movements of my tongue, without which I could not have answered the question at all. But, while unaware of all those things and much more besides, I do not doubt for a moment that they occurred, or that I could not have answered the question otherwise. Now, I obviously did not choose any of those occurrences. For one thing, I know next to nothing about most of them, and so could not have chosen them even if I had had a mind to.

All of those processes are cause–effect occurrences in parts of a physical thing, my body, and they are subject to the same forces and laws of nature as everything else in spacetime. Given that, how confident can we be that it is not, for instance, things happening inside our brains, things of which we have no consciousness and which we do not control, that are the real sources of our choices and decisions? Just because we are not aware of any causally determining processes behind our choices, how confident can we be that there are no such processes behind them? After all, absence of evidence is not evidence of absence. In addition, don't we need good reason to suppose that the forces and laws of nature stop at us, when we deliberate and make choices, while applying to everything else in the universe?

Now to the second libertarian claim. It is that, whenever I make a free choice, I recognize a genuine alternative which I could just as easily have chosen instead, even though everything else is exactly the same. In the 2004 presidential election in the United States, I voted for John Kerry. Could I have voted for George Bush instead? Or for a third candidate, or not voted at all? Was any of those a genuine alternative for me? Before you answer, consider that I believed it was very important to vote Bush out of office, that I considered Kerry by far the best of the candidates, and that I thought he would be a very good president. With all of that remaining exactly the same, could I really have just as easily voted for Bush as for Kerry, or voted for a third candidate, or not voted at all? Surely not. Nonetheless, I maintain that I voted freely for Kerry.

### Compatibilist free choice

The principal rival to libertarianism is the compatibilist theory of free will. It argues that the libertarian theory has unrealistically high standards for choices to be free. As its name suggests, the compatibilist theory characterizes freedom of choice in terms that are compatible with cause-and-effect processes.

The compatibilist theory does this by distinguishing between causes that are internal to me and causes that are external to me. Examples of the former would be my own desires and wishes, while our earlier references to acting under hypnosis or at gunpoint will do nicely as examples of the latter. Equipped with this distinction between internal and external causes or sources, the compatibilist then maintains that choices caused by my own internal psychological states, for instance, my own desires, wishes, preferences, and so on, are free choices. Even though they are caused, the compatibilist theory considers them to be free. The reason is that they have the right sort of causal pedigree.

Here is an example. Suppose you ask me why I walked home instead of taking the bus. I tell you that I chose to walk because I felt I needed the exercise, or because I wanted to enjoy the cool weather, or because I like to walk in the rain. I would be telling you that my choice issued from what I felt I needed, or from what I wanted or liked. On this point – classifying choices that issue from the chooser's own needs and desires and so on as free choices – the compatibilist theory further maintains that it is reflecting the commonsense view of the matter.

Furthermore, the compatibilist theory does not make it a necessary condition of free will that, all things being equal, I could always just as easily choose something else instead.

Compatibilism and libertarianism, then, disagree on both of the core claims in the libertarian theory.

There are serious philosophical difficulties in the compatibilist theory too. Very briefly, here are two, one for each of the foregoing points of difference. Earlier we had an example of choices made as a result of hypnotic suggestion. We saw that the compatibilist theory, like its libertarian rival, would classify such choices as unfree. Now, in order to facilitate a brief description of a problem facing the compatibilist theory, let us vary that example a little. Suppose now that, under hypnosis, I am told to have a certain desire when I wake up. For instance, think of people who go for hypnotic treatment to stop smoking, because their previous efforts have failed. Sometimes the treatment involves their being told, under hypnosis, to no longer want or desire to smoke when they wake up.

Notice that, in the modified example, I am not told to make a certain choice after waking up. Instead, I am told to have a certain desire. That is the difference in the example. Now suppose that I do have that desire when I wake up, and suppose it causes me to make a certain choice. Would it be a free choice?

It is not clear that it would be. Why not? The reason is that, while my choice came from my desire, my desire did not come from me, but from a source beyond my control. True, the hypnosis example dramatizes the point. But doing so serves to highlight the fact that, typically, my desires are caused by things over which I do not have control. For instance, my temperament seems to be among the causes of my desires, but I am not the cause or source of my own temperament.

The challenge to the compatibilist theory now is to justify isolating one segment in the unbroken chain of causes and effects – the segment that goes from desires to choices – and calling it free, while classifying the other segments in the same chain as unfree. And keep in mind, as you consider this challenge to compatibilism, that the word 'cause' has exactly the same meaning in the segment under consideration as it does in all other segments of that unbroken chain of causes and effects. And so does the word 'effect.'

The second problem arises concerning the compatibilist idea that, in order for my choices to be free, it is not necessary for me to have the option of choosing something else instead. Here, too, let our example be a situation where it is my own desire that is the source or cause of my choice.

Suppose I am a drug addict, and I choose to take this drug now. I do so because of my desire to take it. And, being addicted, I do not have the ready option of choosing not to take it. In this example, then, the condition of easily choosing something else instead is absent, but my choice does come from my own desire. Under the compatibilist theory, it seems we should consider my choice to be a free choice. But I think we would hesitate to do so. Why? The reason is that the addict's inability to avoid choosing the drug is part of the very essence of his addiction. And it seems strange to consider a choice to be free in such circumstances.

True, the example of addiction dramatizes the point at issue. But it does not change the essential nature of the point. Instead, it highlights the compatibilist idea that the ready availability of a viable alternative is not necessary for free choice or free will.

We cannot explore either theory here, or adjudicate the debate between them. For one thing, that debate is among the most vexing in the whole of philosophy. Fortunately, to assess Plantinga's use of libertarianism, we do not need to. That being so, and with the libertarian theory of free choice being an essential part of Plantinga's defense against Mackie, let us accept the theory for the sake of argument. Doing so permits us to examine Plantinga's defense on its own terms.

As we do so, it is worth noting that Plantinga's defense does not require the theory to be true. It requires only the logical possibility that it could be true. Accordingly, what we are accepting for the sake of argument is proportionately modest. It is that, possibly, the libertarian theory of free will is true. That stipulation in hand, let us now turn to Plantinga's argument, the aim of which is to disprove Mackie's point that there is an implicit contradiction between God and evil.

### A God-made world with the possibility of moral goodness

If God is perfectly good, then everything God does is done with good intentions. So, if God made the world, it was with the intention of bringing about an overall good world. Of course, we don't know just what a God-made world would be like, but it is possible that it would contain human beings, and possible that it would provide sufficient opportunity for us to achieve moral goodness.

But, given the correlation mentioned between freedom and responsibility, God could not just go ahead on his own and create a world with moral goodness built in. For, on that correlation, moral goodness can come about only as an achievement, by beings who have sufficient freedom, knowledge, responsibility, and experience.

Consequently, while a person's moral goodness can be nurtured from the outside, no person can be made morally good, or morally bad either, from the outside. Human beings could come factory-equipped, so to speak, with libertarian freedom of choice, but not with moral goodness. Moral goodness is an option, not standard equipment.

There is a downside to creating beings with libertarian freedom. Being omniscient, God would know it. God would know that a libertarian free choice is beyond the power even of omnipotence to bring about. That is because a caused free choice, in this sense of freedom, is a contradiction in terms on a par with an uncurved circle. So the inability of even omnipotent power to cause or bring about the free choices of beings possessing libertarian freedom does not negate divine omnipotence.

For various reasons, among them the compatibilist theory of free choice described above, you might hesitate to accept that last point. After all, compatibilism suggests an idea of freedom on which choices could be both free and caused. Given compatibilism, perhaps the failure of omnipotence to cause certain free choices, namely, good ones as opposed to bad, could be grounds to deny divine omnipotence or divine perfection, thus grounds to deny there is a God. And perhaps the compatibilist theory is right.

However, none of this is to the point. For, as we saw, all that Plantinga's argument requires is that his libertarian concept of freedom could possibly be true, not that it is true, or even plausible. And as we have stipulated the libertarian theory, we are agreeing for the sake of argument that there is no logical possibility of an externally caused free choice. Thus Plantinga has his crucial premise, which is that it is logically possible that the free choices of human persons are beyond the power of an omnipotent God to cause or bring about.

Perhaps you are unconvinced for a different reason. Perhaps you are thinking that, if circumstances called for it, God could over-ride libertarian freedom. That may be true. However, it is not cause to be doubtful about the idea of libertarian freedom itself. Indeed, it accepts libertarian freedom, just not in all circumstances. So it is not a doubt about the concept of libertarian freedom as such.

Nonetheless, the doubt highlights an important point in Plantinga's use of the concept of libertarian freedom. It is that his concept is of full-time libertarian freedom. It may be useful to think of it as like the full-time all-wheel-drive system in certain kinds of cars.

In essence, then, the logical possibility Plantinga is proposing is that God, consistent with his intentions in granting full-time libertarian freedom in the first place, could not subsequently interfere with it, control it, or over-ride it. This opens up the possibility of horrors like the Holocaust, the Pol Pot mass exterminations in Cambodia, the genocide in the Darfur region of Sudan, and so on. The possibility of moral evil is an unavoidable byproduct of libertarian freedom.

## Intending and foreseeing

How could a perfectly good being intend to bring about a world in which the Holocaust could possibly occur? It is a good question. There are two parts to the answer.

The first part of the answer itself makes two points. Point one is that such a world would have to be as good overall as, or better overall than, a world without the possibility of the Holocaust. Point two is that, possibly, either the occurrence of the Holocaust was necessary for the world to be as good as, or better than, any alternative world, or it is an unavoidable but regrettable byproduct of bringing about an overall good world.

Given Mackie's failure, so far, to prove a contradiction between God and evil, that two-part scenario has not been proved impossible. So, until we have proof to the contrary, we must keep an open mind on those logical possibilities.

The second part of the answer stresses the point that God, intending to bring about such a world, would not thereby have to intend to bring about the Holocaust itself, or any of the other evils in the world. This idea turns on a distinction between intending something and foreseeing that it will occur. God, being omniscient, may foresee the evils of the world. But God, being perfectly good, would not intend them to occur. That is, God would not select them for their own sake. So, even if they are a necessary part of the means of bringing about an overall good world, or an unavoidable byproduct of doing so, God could permit or tolerate them without intending them.

Consider an analogy. As the parent of a young child who broke his leg playing on the jungle gym, you hold the child's leg steady while the doctor sets the bone. You know this procedure will cause great pain to your child. And, of course, you do not intend your child to suffer. But you foresee that he will. Yet you allow the procedure to go ahead. For the greater good of the child is served by setting the bone now, painful as that is, compared to either not setting it at all, or setting it later. You foresee the pain, you permit your child to suffer it, but you do not intend it. What you intend or want is the proper healing of your child's leg. If an anesthetic had been available, you would have insisted on your child getting it, unless there was a good medical reason for the child not to get it.

On this analogy, then, the idea is that, possibly, God intends to bring about a world that is at least as good overall as any world without the evils that exist in the actual world. God might foresee that certain terrible evils are inevitable byproducts at various stages in the development of that world. But God would not intend or want those evils to occur, and would not choose them as such.

### Plantinga's free-will defense summarized

The basic ingredients of Plantinga's defense are now at hand. Let us put them together. It is possible that God intended to make a world that contains human beings and in which moral goodness could occur. It is possible that worlds like that are better overall than worlds not containing any moral goodness or any moral evil. But it is possible that worlds like that must contain freedom of choice. There are rival conceptions of free choice, but it is possible that full-time libertarian freedom is the only kind on which moral responsibility, thus moral goodness, can occur. But libertarian free choices are beyond the power of God to cause or bring about, even though that kind of freedom can result in very bad choices and actions. God would possibly foresee such outcomes, but would not intend them.

Consequently, it is possible that God could go ahead and bring about that kind of world, without any contradiction between those evils that could occur and divine perfection. On this chain of possibilities, God could justifiably bring about a world that, through the free choices of human beings, would contain terrible evils.

In this way, Plantinga claims to prove that the existence of God remains logically possible, even though the world itself contains evil. If he is successful, he will have disproved Mackie's claim to the contrary.

## II  Mackie's Response

Plantinga's argument is simple and powerful. But Mackie offers a simple and powerful response that puts this free-will defense in serious question. Plantinga himself describes the core of Mackie's response as "subtle and important."[1]

### Lifelong moral blamelessness

The first step in Mackie's response is to grant, for the sake of argument, all of the premises in Plantinga's defense. Even having done that, he then suggests an alternative, and far better, possibility that, it seems, would have been available to God.

The alternative would have been to create free human beings who, unlike us, would be known in advance to lead morally blameless lives. Looking back on this idea about twenty-five years after formulating it, Mackie called it the "central thesis" in his argument.[2]

---

[1]  Alvin Plantinga, *God, Freedom, and Evil* (Grand Rapids, Mich.: Eerdmans, 1996), 33.

[2]  J. L. Mackie, *The Miracle of Theism* (Oxford: Clarendon Press, 1982), 164, n. 14.

The core idea is that it is logically possible for a person to have full-time libertarian freedom, yet never make a bad moral choice. And if it is logically possible to have one such person, it is logically possible to have the entire world's population consist of such people. Thus, there could be full-time libertarian freedom of choice, moral responsibility, moral goodness, but no moral evil.

An example will bring the idea into sharp focus. But first, we need to bring something obvious out into the open. It is that there is some age at which human beings become mature enough to be morally responsible. I do not mean that there is some split second when we go through a transition from non-moral to moral status. All I mean is that there is some period in which we become mature enough to understand moral issues as such, and to make moral choices. The period does not have to be identical for all persons. Neither does it matter just what the age is. Perhaps it is seven years old, or eight, or ten; it doesn't matter. The point to focus on is that there is some such period. And surely there is. After all, when you were an infant you weren't capable of moral choices, but now you are. So, at some age between then and now, you got mature enough. Let us call it the age of moral maturity. With that idea in place, here is the example of what Mackie is proposing.

Suppose that, shortly after a child reaches the age of moral maturity, an issue comes up where a moral choice must be made. The child has full libertarian freedom to decide any way he or she wishes. Suppose the child thinks the matter over carefully, then freely decides on a course of action. Suppose the choice is a good moral choice. It makes no difference what concept of morality is in force, consequentialist, non-consequentialist, or something else entirely. Use any you wish. Then suppose that, the good choice having been made, the child dies. All of his or her moral choices, all one of them, have been for good.

In itself, this is enough to establish the point, which is that it seems to be logically possible for all of a free person's moral choices to be good moral choices.

The example works for longer lives too, which is not surprising, as it reflects the fundamental point that it is logically possible for all of a free person's moral choices to be good. Suppose a child comes to the age of moral maturity, a moral issue comes up, and the child, exercising full libertarian freedom, makes a morally good choice. Suppose that, later on, the second moral issue in the child's life comes up, and again the free choice is a good choice. Suppose further that, later on again, a third issue comes up, and then a fourth, and so on, and, in each case, a good moral choice is freely made. Suppose the child's winning streak continues through all occasions when moral issues come up. Then, suppose the child dies. The basic idea is that there seems to be nothing incoherent or logically impossible in the concept of a morally blameless person, regardless of the length of the streak of free and good moral choices.

To avoid a possible misunderstanding, we should distinguish that basic idea from a neighboring idea that might be confused with it. This different idea is that, because a first (or second, or third, or any individual) moral choice could be a good choice, all subsequent moral choices could be good choices too. That second idea involves an unjustified generalization. But the first idea, the basic idea in my examples of Mackie's central point, does not. For one thing, it does not involve any generalizing at all. It does not go from one choice or several choices to all choices or many choices. Instead, it is the idea, illustrated by the example of a person who makes only one moral choice in his or her whole life, that a morally blameless life seems to be a logically possible life for a person who possesses full libertarian freedom.

The concept of such a life is the core of Mackie's rebuttal to Plantinga's argument. Perhaps religious people have the idea that some icons of their faith actually led lives of that sort.

### God at pre-creation

Switching now from the human side of Mackie's scenario to the divine side, let us focus on omniscience. Following the majority view within the monotheistic tradition, let us stipulate on behalf of Mackie's counter-argument that omniscience includes knowing the future.

Now imagine God at pre-creation. Suppose, with Plantinga, that God intends to make an overall good world in which there will be full opportunity for moral goodness to emerge. Consequently, in time, this world will contain human beings possessing full libertarian freedom. But, at pre-creation, God has not yet begun to bring about the world according to those specifications. In particular, no human beings have yet been made.

Before making any human beings, God has to decide which ones to make. After all, God does not just make every person that there could possibly be. For instance, it is possible I could have had another sister, or a twin. But those possible persons were never actual.

Furthermore, God would be very interested in, and careful about, the life-histories-to-be of all possible persons he makes into actual people. After all, divine creation of actual persons would presumably involve more than God just hoping for the best.

For comparison, consider that, for instance, manufacturers of CD players, before committing themselves to a new model line, want all relevant information on performance projections, market demographics, advertising costs, and so on, for their yet-to-be-made CD players. And if projections over a certain period are not good enough, it is reasonable to suppose that production of that line of CD players will be halted at the research and development stage. Surely God is no less smart or conscientious than Sony. But God has a big advantage over Sony. God knows the future. So, before settling on which possible persons to bring about as actual persons, God knows their full life-histories in advance. No hunches or statistical projections are required before starting production.

Now, among the infinite number of possible persons that God might make are all those possible persons who, if they were actual persons, would freely lead morally blameless lives. And God, whose omniscience includes foreknowledge, knows at pre-creation who they would be.

### The essence of Mackie's rebuttal: controlling who gets libertarian freedom

So Mackie's rebuttal comes to this. Although God could not control libertarian freedom, God could control who gets it. No curtailment of freedom would be involved.

The essential idea in Mackie's rebuttal seems right. For instance, we would never grant total freedom to a person if we felt pretty sure that she would seriously abuse it and harm others. We would not leave the babysitter alone with the children, if we knew she would harm them. We wouldn't do it, even if we only had a hunch she might harm them.

Consider parole boards. They exist precisely to control who, from a certain population, gets freedom and who does not. The basic idea they operate on is that, if they think a convict will abuse his freedom, they withhold that freedom from him. For they know that, once the freedom is granted, it is beyond control for a time and up to a point, perhaps enough time for serious harm to be done.

At face value, then, understood in real-world or commonsense terms, what Mackie is suggesting about the sorts of people who would be good candidates for libertarian freedom, and the sorts of people who would not, looks right.

His challenge to the free-will defense of the logical consistency of God and evil, then, turns on the question of why God wouldn't give full-time libertarian freedom only to the people who would not abuse it. After all, it's what we would do, if we had the power and opportunity.

Morally blameless people are rare. So how could God populate the earth with sufficient people? Maybe it would be objected that, on Mackie's hypothesis, God could not meet necessary population targets, whatever they might be. So, maybe for that reason, God would have to lower his standards and so could not do what Mackie is proposing.

To examine this objection, suppose for the sake of argument that the current population of the earth, plus its population at all past and future times, is the desired population of morally blameless persons, or at least in the desired population range. Now it is true that this number, the total number of morally blameless persons, is only a tiny fraction of the total number of possible persons. But the total number of possible persons is infinite. So, no matter how small a percentage, or a fraction of a percentage, of the number of possible persons that number of morally blameless persons turns out to be, God would have a big enough pool of possible persons to choose from. So, God would have no population-shortage problem.

How could an omnipotent, omniscient, perfectly good God, intent on making a world with full opportunity for moral goodness, not choose this option? No murder, no rape, no lying or cheating, no death camps, no pogroms, no ethnic cleansing, no religious persecution, no religious bullies imposing their beliefs on others, no child abuse, no torture, no moralistic hypocrisy. Furthermore, not only would there be full libertarian freedom and full opportunity for moral goodness, but the net surplus of moral goodness over moral evil would be vastly better than in the actual world, assuming there is such a surplus in the actual world.

Consequently, all other things being equal, the possible world that Mackie is describing would appear to be far better overall than the actual world, while still containing human beings, all with full-time libertarian freedom. It is a powerful challenge to the free-will defense.

Mackie folds this response to the free-will defense into his original argument as follows: "Clearly, [God's] failure to avail himself of this possibility [that is, actualize only morally blameless persons] is [logically] inconsistent with his being both omnipotent and wholly good."[3]

The criticism seems to give powerful support to his original conclusion. A suspension of our interim verdict of 'not proved' seems warranted.

## III   Proving a Possibility

### First response: logical limits on the power of omnipotence

A crucial element in Plantinga's response to Mackie's rebuttal is the previously mentioned idea that bringing about a world containing moral goodness is necessarily a two-step process, with God controlling only the first step. Plantinga's conclusion from this is that God could not, strictly speaking, bring about a world which contains moral goodness, either with, or without, moral evil. Even if the world were to turn out to contain moral goodness and no moral evil, Plantinga's point is that God would not, because he could not, have brought that about.

To see why Plantinga thinks this, let us consider the two stages in world-making that he has in mind.

*Stage one*
In stage one of world-making, it is within the creative power of God to make the laws of nature, particles, the entire universe, including human persons with full-time libertarian freedom. Furthermore, God could make any persons he wished, within the limits of logical possibility.

*Stage two*
To simplify our consideration of the development of stage two out of stage one, let us suppose that God makes only one person in stage one. The number of people does not matter any more now than it did when we were examining Mackie's concept of a morally blameless life, so we may legitimately focus on just a single person to keep things simple. Let us suppose, then, that God brings into being one person with libertarian free choice, for instance, the child in the example of moral blamelessness. That is stage one accomplished.

---

[3]  Mackie, "Evil and Omnipotence," 33.

Now suppose a moral issue comes up for this person. It is entirely up to him or her what happens next. That is the essence of libertarian freedom. Consequently, whether he or she makes a right or wrong moral choice is not in God's control. It is entirely up to the person alone. That is how stage two is accomplished.

The point here is that God cannot bring about what happens next, once the moral issue comes up. Stage two, where moral choices get made for good or ill, is beyond the power of omnipotence to bring about. God alone does not have the power to bring morality into being.

How could God be omnipotent, yet be unable to do this? Plantinga's answer, which Mackie is committed in principle to accepting, is that God could not do this for purely logical reasons. For, to bring it about that a free person makes the right moral choice at stage two, God would have to bring about that person's free choice. But the essence of libertarian freedom is that no outside agency can be the cause of a free choice.

So, Plantinga concludes, there are worlds that, for purely logical reasons, God cannot cause or bring about. An example would be any world containing the conjunction of libertarian freedom and morality. Whether those worlds come to be or not is not fully within the power of God. After stage one is reached, what happens next is up to human freedom.

The world that Mackie described as a possibility, a world populated entirely by morally blameless people who exercise full-time libertarian freedom, is one such world. Therefore, for logical reasons that do not compromise either omnipotence or perfect goodness, Plantinga's conclusion is that God could not do what Mackie describes.

### Back to Mackie's challenge

Plantinga seems to be right about this. But it may not be the end of the matter. For perhaps Mackie's point could be recast as follows. Why wouldn't God facilitate the occurrence in stage two of moral goodness, without any moral evil? How? By making only the right people at stage one. It is what we would do, if we had foreknowledge at pre-creation. Who are the right people at stage one? They are those who are foreknown by God to go on to lead morally blameless lives. Being known to lead such lives freely, they would in fact go on freely to lead such lives.

Retooled, the challenge turns on the difference between bringing something about, in the sense of causing it to happen, and facilitating somthing. To facilitate something means to bring about the right conditions for the desired outcome to come about without further causal interference. It is a serious challenge, even granting Plantinga's point that God could not bring about a world containing moral goodness.

## The possibility of depravity

Plantinga's response to this recast challenge develops a rather bleak possibility. It is the possibility that, to some extent, human nature is essentially corrupt. 'Fallen' is the term used by some religious people for such a condition. The idea is that, possibly, human nature is such that, in exercising freedom, each human being goes wrong at least once. Plantinga calls it "transworld depravity."

The idea here is not that all people would inevitably go wrong at least once. After all, Plantinga is committed to libertarian freedom. It is the idea that, possibly, each person does in fact freely go wrong at least once.

This suggestion seems arbitrary, and perhaps your first response is complete disbelief. But let us recall two things: first, conditions behind the veil of ignorance; and second, the lightness of Plantinga's burden of proof.

First, behind the veil of ignorance, we do not know our individual religious preferences, but we retain our knowledge about religion. So we know about the Christian idea of original sin. Second, to succeed in proving a point to be logically possible, it is not necessary for that point to be true, or plausible, or believed, or even believable in any realistic sense. Indeed, it could be both disbelieved and massively implausible, and that would make no difference to the enterprise at hand. Recall the logical possibility of repeatedly surviving a 10,000-foot fall.

The possibility that Plantinga is relying on here, the possibility of a depravity inherent in human nature, is a gloomier version of the Christian doctrine of original sin. Here, from *Webster's Unabridged Dictionary*, is part of the entry for 'original sin.' It is, the dictionary says, "a tendency to sin and depravity which, in Christian theology, is held to be inherent in mankind as a result of Adam's sin of rebellion . . ."

Plantinga's concept is stronger than the notion of original sin. The difference is that the concept of original sin is the concept of a tendency to go wrong, whereas Plantinga's transworld depravity is the concept of each person actually going wrong.

In essence, then, Plantinga's response is that, because of the logical possibility that human nature includes this innate fallenness, God could not do what Mackie suggests. For, according to the 'depravity' hypothesis, no matter which people God brings about, each of those people will go morally wrong at least once.

What about the morally blameless child? Where is Plantinga's conjectured depravity in him or her? This is a natural challenge to Plantinga's hypothesis. But it is not sufficient to defeat it. For, granting the possibility of an essential depravity in human nature, the result is the possibility that there could be no such child. True, this seems very implausible and far-fetched, but, as we saw, implausibility has no bearing on what is logically possible.

We have already granted the possibility that God could not bring about a world with moral goodness and no moral evil. Now, granting the logical possibility of Plantinga's 'depravity' hypothesis, we must grant the possibility that God could not facilitate the coming about of such a world either.

The upshot is both that the existence of God is a logical possibility, despite evil in the world, and that Plantinga proves it. And so Mackie's claim about a contradiction between them is proved false.

### A second response to Mackie: the possibility of omniscience without foreknowledge

The foregoing response to Mackie's challenge involves finely sliced logical distinctions and technicalities, for instance, the strict meaning of 'bringing about.' A second, more commonsensical, response is also available to the theist. In presenting it, we depart from Plantinga, who does not endorse it.

The key to this second response is that, possibly, God does not know the future. Without foreknowledge, God could not know which possible people would be morally blameless. So, without foreknowledge, God could not know which people to actualize without risking evil behavior.

Is it logically possible that omniscience does not include foreknowledge? If the answer is yes, Mackie's rebuttal to the free-will defense fails, and so too his attempt to prove his original point by way of that rebuttal.

It is a disputed question within the theistic tradition whether omniscience could exclude foreknowledge. There were serious debates about it among philosophers and theologians of the Middle Ages, and the issue remains unsettled today. We saw in chapter 2 that one of the main reasons to think it is possible that God does not know the future is that the future does not at present exist. On this idea, there are simply no future facts to be known. True, there are other philosophical theories about the future, and about knowledge of the future, on which omniscience does include foreknowledge. But none of those theories has successfully proved that it would be logically impossible for God to be omniscient, if the future were unknowable.

So, absent that proof, it seems we must allow the logical possibility that God, while omniscient, does not know the future. But if it is possible that God does not know the future, then it is possible that God could not have done what Mackie is proposing in creating only people who will be morally blameless.

This response to Mackie may turn out to have some costly implications, as follows. It is a fundamental tenet of many believers' faith that God knows the future. Consequently, the possibility that God does not know the future may shake that bedrock idea and perhaps weaken the believer's confidence that things will turn out well in the end. Furthermore, the possibility seems to make the concept of God subject to the concept of time. After all, not knowing the future means not knowing now what happens later. And, for many theists, the concept of God is that of a being outside of time, and independent of it. For that reason too, then, the possibility may shake the believer's faith, by seeming to diminish the concept of God.

### Final verdict

Granting the logical possibility of so-called transworld depravity, our final verdict on Plantinga's specific version of the free-will defense is that it is successful in defending the possible co-existence of God and evil. This means that Mackie's claim is not just unproved, but disproved.

Similarly, and independently, if it is possible that omniscience does not include foreknowledge, then, for that reason too, Mackie's claim about a strict contradiction between God and evil is disproved.

About twenty-five years after the publication of his original argument, Mackie made the following concessions:

> We cannot, indeed, take the problem of evil as a conclusive disproof of traditional theism, because . . . there is some flexibility in its doctrines,

and in particular in the additional premises needed to make the problem explicit. There may be some way of adjusting these which avoids an internal contradiction without giving up anything essential to theism.[4]

The first sentence in this quotation suggests Mackie's acceptance that his claim is unproved. The second sentence suggests his acceptance that it is disproved.

For contrast, recall Mackie's original claim: "it can be shown . . . that religious beliefs . . . are positively irrational, that the several parts of the essential theological doctrine are inconsistent with one another."

## Compatibilism and the free-will defense

We have been discussing Plantinga's defense against Mackie on its own terms. Principally, this means we granted, for the sake of argument, the logical possibility that the libertarian theory of free will is true. But, for all we know, all formulations of that theory may in fact be false and some version of compatibilism may be true. Would that make a difference? In the present context, no.

The reason is that, as I noted earlier, the premises in an argument to prove a logical possibility do not have to be true. It is enough for them to be logically possible. So it makes no difference to Plantinga's defense if the libertarian theory is false, or even if it is known or proved to be false. To make a difference, the theory would have to be logically impossible. And being false, supposing for the moment that the theory is false, does not mean being impossible. For instance, it is false that John Kerry is the president of the United States, but his being the president is not impossible. As we saw, the burden of proof is very light when all that is being attempted is a proof of a mere logical possibility. So, even if Plantinga came to believe that libertarianism about free will is false and announced it, the position of Mackie's argument would not be improved. Later on, however, when we are examining arguments for and against the probability, as opposed to the mere logical possibility, of God's existence, we will find that the burden of proof is heavier for the libertarian theory of free will than it is here.

---

[4]  Mackie, *The Miracle of Theism*, 176.

## IV   The Logical Argument from Evil

Two loose ends need tidying away.

The first concerns the common description of the issue we have examined through this and the previous chapter. In philosophical circles, it is usually called the logical problem of evil, or the logical argument from evil. Those names are a bit inaccurate, inasmuch as all arguments are logical arguments.

The point in the name is that, in the core issues in dispute between Mackie and Plantinga, as well as in the wider debate on the topic, it is the fundamental concepts of logic that are decisive. Those concepts are logical possibility, logical impossibility, mutual consistency and inconsistency, necessity, and contradiction. It is on those that the give and take of arguments and counter-arguments in this and the previous chapter turned, and on which success and failure are decided.

So the names 'logical argument from evil' and 'logical problem of evil,' while a bit misleading, do point toward the concepts on which success and failure turn. Furthermore, the names are well-established by precedent. For both reasons, then, it would be confusing to replace them.

By contrast, in the arguments to which Plantinga's proof of logical possibility frees us to now turn, success and failure will depend on the comparative weight of probabilities. Nothing as clean as a contradiction will be in play. And nothing as broad and receptive as logical possibility will be enough to establish success.

The second loose end concerns the fact that, while Mackie's point was disproved, not all life was knocked out of the logical problem of God and evil. Mackie's point was quite general. It was that the idea of God and the existence of any evil at all, the very fact of evil as such, could never possibly co-exist. To disprove it required only proving the possibility of an exception. And Plantinga did, as does the detachment of foreknowledge from the concept of omniscience.

But just because it is possible that some evil (the exception) can co-exist with the idea of God, it does not follow that all the evils which actually occur in the world are logically consistent with the idea of God. So the possibility still remains that some particular amount of evil, or some particular kind or instance of evil, could be shown to contradict the idea of God. And if so, then the co-existence of God and evil would be proved impossible after all.

## Suggested Reading

Kane, Robert (2005) *A Contemporary Introduction to Free Will*. Oxford: Oxford University Press. This is a good introduction to libertarian and compatibilist accounts of free will.

Mackie, J. L. (1982) *The Miracle of Theism*. Oxford: Clarendon Press. See esp. ch. 9.

Mackie, J. L. (1990) "Evil and Omnipotence," in M. M. Adams and R. M. Adams, eds, *The Problem of Evil*. Oxford: Oxford University Press.

Plantinga, Alvin (1996) *God, Freedom, and Evil*. Grand Rapids, Mich.: Eerdmans. See esp. chs 4–8.

# Part III

# Design and Evil

# 5

# Natural Order, Natural Selection, and Supernatural Design (1)

We have a partial answer to our first question. We know the existence of God is a logical possibility, even though the world is obviously imperfect. That answer naturally prompts a follow-up question.

### Our second question

Would we be justified in upgrading our claim about God's existence from possible to probable? If so, it will be on the strength of facts in or about the world. The facts we are going to draw on are basic. They are that the world is complex, orderly, regular, and conducive to life, and that it contains living things whose experience includes pleasure and pain.

The argument for the existence of God we will examine is a probabilistic or inductive argument. Historically, most arguments for the existence of God have been deductive.

Briefly, an inductive argument aims to raise the probability of its conclusion. It may aim to raise it to the level of being more probable than not, or, short of that, to a level higher than before. In contrast, a deductive argument aims to establish that, given the evidence in its premises, its conclusion has to be true. Few philosophers nowadays think there is a successful deductive proof that God exists.

If we were to emphasize deductive over inductive arguments, then our second question would be whether we are entitled to upgrade our claim about the existence of God from possible to certain. Instead, our question is whether the idea of divine creation would be a reasonable conclusion to draw. In particular, would it be a reasonable conclusion for a person lacking prior acquaintance with that idea to draw?

In ordinary life, we say that a belief or a statement is reasonable when we think it could well be true, when it is plausible to think it is true. We think a belief or a statement is implausible when we think it is likely to be false, that is, improbable. Given this correlation between the terms 'probable' and 'plausible,' and between the terms 'improbable' and 'implausible,' I am going to use them in this and subsequent chapters as closely overlapping and virtually synonymous terms.

### Going further behind the veil of ignorance

For the right degree of impartiality, we must go further behind the veil of ignorance than before, almost as far as Rawls himself. Briefly, let us remind ourselves of what is in store for us.

At present, our make-believe is that we do not know if we are religious or not. But now we need to ensure that, if the concept of a supernatural explanation comes up in our investigation, it does so only on the strength of evidence. So, in addition to not knowing if we are religious or not, we imagine that we know nothing at all about religion, or about philosophy either. Furthermore, we exclude all supernaturalistic ideas from what we know at starting out. But we keep our general knowledge and our scientific knowledge. In true experimental spirit, we are receptive to any good explanations, including supernaturalist ones, on their merits.

## I   Order and Evolution

### Order, complexity, life, means, and ends

Nature is orderly and regular, at least above the level of sub-atomic particles. In addition, it is vastly complex. It is complex at both the microscopic and macroscopic levels. The two things, order and regularity on the one hand, complexity on the other, make a remarkable combination.

What best explains natural order, regularity, and complexity? Can natural science explain these things? Or does scientific explanation itself presuppose them? If it does, then we may wonder if science is in principle unable to explain the existence and nature of the universe in a fundamental way. And if that is so, then either there is no explanation or there is a non-scientific explanation.

But we are getting ahead of ourselves. Let us begin at the beginning, by looking at some aspects of the basic fact that the physical universe is orderly, regular, complex, and conducive to life. Later on, the fact of suffering and other evils will come in.

Order and complexity are evident in both organic and inorganic things. Let us focus here on the organic, the world of living matter. What best explains the emergence of life on this planet?

In organisms, as in the wider life-support systems to which they belong, complex order includes patterns and cycles of occurrences that we commonly describe in terms of outcomes. Over time the geranium plant bends towards the light, and photosynthesis occurs. The wild salmon return from the ocean to their spawning place upstream.

What accounts for this particular kind of regularity in nature, the means-to-ends order exhibited in living things? In our own case, means-to-ends behavior often reflects intention and purpose. I put the water in the kettle and the kettle on the stove in order to make tea. This raises the question whether means-to-ends activities outside human life also reflect intention and purpose.

The question is not whether the wild salmon are choosing to swim from the ocean to their destination upriver. The answer to that is no. It is the instinctual force of nature that accounts for their return. Furthermore, that is a far stronger force, less variable and more regular, than choice. For, as we know well from our own case, with choosing there come indecision and changes of mind. If the salmon had to plan a route, they might get lost. It happens to me often enough. But they are relentlessly successful, generation following generation. It is a process far too regular and successful for choice to be involved.

Instead, the question is whether there is purpose and choice behind the patterns of life in living things. Are they functioning as they do because they have been planned and organized, as part of a planet-wide ecological network? Or can the development of life and the ecology of this planet be satisfactorily explained another way?

### Survival of the fittest

The explanation of the development of living things given by Charles Darwin (1809–82) in his 1859 book, *On the Origin of Species*, is accepted in the scientific community as the best explanation. It is as well known as anything in science that life evolved, developing from primitive to complex forms, over enormous lengths of time.

The essential idea in Darwin's theory is that of a natural competition over time for the scarce resources necessary for survival. He called it natural selection. He explains the basic idea in the following passage,

A struggle for existence inevitably follows from the high rate at which all organic beings tend to increase . . . [A]s more individuals are produced than can possibly survive, there must in every case be a struggle for existence, either one individual with another of the same species, or with the individuals of distinct species, or with the physical conditions of life.[1]

Later on, he adds this point:

Let it be borne in mind how infinitely complex and close-fitting are the mutual relations of all organic beings to each other and to their physical conditions of life. Can it, then, be thought improbable that variations useful . . . in some way to each being in the great and complex battle of life, should sometimes occur in the course of thousands of generations? If such do occur, can we doubt . . . that individuals having any advantage, however slight, over others, would have the best chance of surviving and of procreating their kind? . . . This preservation of favourable variations and the rejection of injurious variations, I call Natural Selection.[2]

Strictly speaking, there is no selection in natural selection. Instead, organisms adjust over long periods to changes in their environment. And those adjustments, in minuscule and incremental stages over vast amounts of time, bring about changes both in those organisms themselves and in their descendants.

In addition to no choices being involved, no reasons are involved. The geranium does not turn towards the light for a reason, in the way that you ordered the Caesar salad for a reason. The plant is responding to causal forces. It is not acting out of any motive or desire or for any purpose.

Natural selection in Darwin's theory is natural adaptation or natural adjustment. Think of the flow of a river adjusting over time to erosion in parts of the river bed and banks – and vice versa, too, for the river bed and banks adjust to the water flow. The adaptations, or selections, in evolution are more like those adjustments than they are like your selection of the Caesar salad from the menu.

The changes that come about in these ways are inherited by the descendants of those adapting organisms. In time-spans much shorter than

---

[1]   Charles Darwin, *On the Origin of Species by Means of Natural Selection* (London: John Murray, 1859), 63.
[2]   Darwin, *On the Origin of Species*, 80–1.

those involved in evolution by natural selection, we see the same phenomenon play out in agriculture and horticulture. Breeders of animals and growers of plants mix and select for various traits in the animals they breed or the plants they cultivate. They do so to maximize reproductive success in animals and plants with the desired characteristics. Some obvious examples are seedless grapes and cucumbers, lean pigs, cockapoos, and so on.

Darwin theorized that something similar is afoot in the natural world. The big difference, of course, to repeat the point, is that natural selection is not deliberate or chosen. But the basic idea of the gradual dominance by certain traits over others holds good. Which traits? In the competition for survival in the natural world, the answer is, those traits that work best for the survival of the individual, the species, or perhaps the individual's genes. Hence the term 'survival of the fittest.'

Behind the veil of ignorance, we know of the well-established credentials of this theory. We know it is the basis of modern biology. We know that the fact it is called the theory of evolution does not mean it is only a theory. It is as well established as Einstein's theories in physics. We know that the word 'theory,' in the sciences, means a well-established piece of science that is the basis for additional research and discovery.

### The Dover case

We know too that, as in any developed area of science, there are loose ends, open questions, and disagreements among researchers on important points to do with evolution. That is normal science. But we know as well that, especially in some places in the United States, there is opposition to Darwin's theory as such. This opposition disputes its basic ideas themselves, namely, that life developed from non-living matter, and that, just as all other organisms do, highly developed primates like us share a family tree with more primitive ancestors. But we also know that, within the community of science itself, such opposition is rare. And we know that in other developed countries there is, for all measurable purposes, much less opposition to Darwin's theory as such.

The thrust of the opposition in principle to Darwin's theory is that the development of life cannot be fully explained in wholly naturalistic terms. We, behind the veil of ignorance, know of this opposition, but we do not know that it is rooted principally in certain religious communities. This ignorance does not compromise our grasp of the essence of the opposition view, however, for that view insists that Darwin's theory fails on strictly scientific grounds. The issue came to a head in a recent (2005) case in US federal court in Dover, Pennsylvania.

At the Dover trial, the American biochemist Michael Behe provided testimony central to the opposition's view of Darwin's theory as unable adequately to explain the development of life. Behe argues that certain systems in organisms are 'irreducibly complex,' and that incremental adaptation – the core concept in the theory of evolution – cannot in principle account for the fact of irreducible complexity.

The important word is 'irreducible.' Behe's example for laymen, now well publicized, is a mousetrap. A mousetrap is a simple but efficient device. Visualize one with a wooden base, a metal spring, a metal arm. Behe's claim is that, absent any of the pieces, the resulting combination cannot function. Indeed, it is hardly a mousetrap at all. All of the pieces must be present and integrated with one another, or the whole cannot work. His essential point is not that, missing a part, an irreducibly complex system will work badly. It is that it will not work at all.

Behe likens the mousetrap to an irreducibly complex feature in a micro-organism. He argues that, on Darwin's theory, there will inevitably have been a period in the past when not all of an irreducibly complex micro-organism's features are present. His conclusion from this is that, by definition, the system is at that period non-functional. In his view, such systems, which he maintains are plentiful in nature, represent all-or-nothing situations. Either all the parts are present and integrated, or the system simply does not function at all. Consequently, he reasons, such micro-organisms cannot have come to their present state through gradual functional adaptation.

He concludes that, because of its essential incrementalism, Darwin's theory of natural selection fails in principle to explain the very thing it is supposed to be explaining, that is, the development of life. That is the essence of his opposition to Darwin's theory as such.

Contrary to Behe, the American philosopher of science Michael Ruse, reflecting the view of the scientific community, maintains that there are many instances in cell biology of complex processes and organisms coming about through gradual adaptation or selection. Accordingly, at this stage in the history of the theory of evolution, the reasonable view is that it is fundamentally right.

This does not mean that the theory is infallible. No scientific theory claims that. But it means we have no good scientific grounds to suppose

Darwin's theory is in principle not up to the job of explaining the development of life.

The judge in the Dover case agreed. Citing overwhelming scientific evidence, he ruled that there are no scientific grounds to support the view that Darwin's theory is not well-established science. Thus he ruled that there are no grounds to restrict the teaching of it as such in the Dover school system, and no grounds to caution the students in those schools to be wary of it.

## III Evolution and Creation

Richard Swinburne, one of the foremost theistic philosophers, accepts Darwinism. In his words, "This [Darwinian] explanation of the existence of complex organisms is surely a correct explanation . . ."[3]

But two deeper questions remain. What explains the basic laws of nature? What explains the fact that the universe is conducive to life? These are natural and obvious questions. They are the questions set out at the start of this chapter. To pursue them, let us invoke the near-precedent that, in chapter 1, we found in Thomas Aquinas, and invite Swinburne behind the veil of ignorance.

### Explaining the basic laws of nature

To frame our questions, let us continue the quotation begun just above: "This [Darwinian] explanation of the existence of complex organisms is surely a correct explanation, but it is not an ultimate explanation of that fact." Swinburne goes on: "For an ultimate explanation we need an explanation at the highest level of why those laws rather than any other ones operated."

Darwin's theory presupposes that organisms and their environments interact in lawlike ways. Similarly, it presupposes that adaptive changes within organisms, and in the generation of their offspring, are also lawlike. The whole of nature seems to work in ways described in the laws of nature – universal laws above the quantum level of sub-atomic particles, statistical laws at that level. Swinburne condenses the point into

---

[3]   Richard Swinburne, *Is There a God?* (Oxford: Oxford University Press, 1999), 60.

the following analogy: "If all the coins found on an archeological site have the same markings, or all the documents in a room are written with the same characteristic handwriting, we look for an explanation in terms of a common source. The apparently coincidental cries out for explanation."[4]

The point covers organic and inorganic things equally. When we ask why the laws of biology are what they are, we push back to the laws of chemistry and finally to the basic laws of physics. But when we ask for explanation of the basic laws of physics, there are no more basic scientific laws to provide it.

Swinburne maintains that expecting natural science to explain the basic laws of nature is a waste of time. For, in the last analysis, scientific explanation is explanation in terms of those very laws, whose own explanation we are now seeking. His point is that a scientific explanation of the basic laws of nature would be circular. It would involve using those laws to explain themselves.

## Explanations and causes

It will be useful to distinguish between explanations and causes. Here is an example to establish and illustrate the difference.

On September 22, 1979, in the Indian Ocean near Prince Edward Island, a spy satellite, programmed to detect nuclear explosions, detected a flash that lasted about one thousandth of a second. That is the duration of the initial flash characteristic of the explosion of a plutonium bomb. The satellite was very reliable, with a perfect record up to that point. The suspicion was that either South Africa or Israel, or both jointly, had tested a plutonium bomb. But there was no subsequent corroboration of a nuclear explosion. No eye-witnesses were ever found, and no radio-active fallout was detected. A panel of experts was convened to look into the matter.

After investigation, the experts concluded that South Africa was not involved. Furthermore, Israeli responsibility seemed unlikely, for the site was both at sea and far from Israel. Jeremy Bernstein, writing about this still-unsolved puzzle in the May 25, 2006 issue of the *New York Review*, said, "As far as I can tell, the prevailing opinion is that the Vela satellite observed something else, although it is not clear what this was."

---

[4] Swinburne, *Is There a God?*, 50.

Let us begin with the obvious. Something happened in the Indian Ocean on that night in 1979 to cause the flash that the satellite detected. And something else caused the event that caused the flash. They didn't just happen. They had causes. But nobody knows the precise natures of those events or what caused them. There is no explanation of what happened.

Essentially, the difference between an explanation and a cause is this. An explanation is relative to us, it reflects our understanding of something. But a cause is whatever occurrence in the world brings about something else, some simultaneous or subsequent state. Causes happen. We think up explanations to try to understand them and their effects. Causes are part of the workings of the universe, including the workings of our bodies and brains. Causal explanations come from thinking and talking about causes and their effects.

Let us apply the distinction between explanations and causes to our two basic questions: What explains the basic laws of nature? What explains the conditions in the universe at its origin? We can do this by asking a third question: What caused or brought about those laws and conditions? Or, to refocus the question, what caused or brought about the universe itself? If and when we figure that out, we will have our explanation.

### A finite or infinite universe?

So far, we have been assuming that the universe is finite, that it had a beginning, thus a cause, in the first place. But there is another possibility too that physicists take seriously. It is that the universe is infinite, that it had no beginning, that there never was a time before anything existed.

Nowadays the consensus among physicists is that the universe is finite. The standard model of the universe is that it began in the Big Bang, almost fourteen billion years ago. On that consensus, our question is: What caused the Big Bang and the initial conditions in the infant universe, as well as the basic laws of nature that physicists find in it?

But perhaps the universe is infinite. Even if it is, the essential point in our basic questions remains the same. It is that, if life were eventually to emerge in an infinite universe, both the laws of nature and the underlying conditions would have to be right. And then the question would be: What explains those?

The laws of nature are part of the basis of all scientific explanation. We saw Swinburne maintain that, consequently, a scientific explanation of why those laws exist rather than others would be circular. He maintains that an ultimate explanation must be couched in terms of a source or cause outside those laws themselves. But the laws of nature apply to the entire physical universe. So Swinburne concludes that what explains them must be a cause outside the physical universe.

### The odds against life

The second of our questions about evolution looks for explanation of the fact that conditions in the very early universe were right for the eventual evolution of life. In his 1988 book, *A Brief History of Time*, the famous English physicist Stephen Hawking tells us that, "If the rate of expansion [of the universe] one second after the Big Bang had been smaller by even one part in a hundred thousand million million, the universe would have recollapsed before it ever reached its present size."[5] That 1:100,000,000,000,000,000 reflects awfully long odds; yet if the rate of expansion in the first second of the Big Bang had been off by even so tiny an amount, conditions would have been wrong for the eventual development of life as we know it.

Some physicists and philosophers of science, for instance, the American philosopher of science, Ernan McMullin, do not subscribe to Hawking's assignment of a numerical value to the probabilities involved here.[6] But this does not change the basic point that, insofar as the eventual evolution of life is concerned, the constraints on the initial conditions in the universe were very severe.

So what best explains the fact that, against very long odds, conditions were right in this way? What caused them to be so? Essentially, three kinds of explanation compete to answer the question.

#### The chance hypothesis
Perhaps it is just a matter of chance. After all, the initial conditions in the seconds after the Big Bang had to be some way. But this is not a very appealing explanation, for the odds are very long, much longer than the odds against winning the lottery. It is a possibility, to be sure, that chance is the explanation. But we can hardly judge it a probability.

---

[5]   Stephen W. Hawking, *A Brief History of Time* (New York: Bantam, 1988), 121–2.
[6]   Ernan McMullin, "Anthropic Explanation in Cosmology," *Faith and Philosophy* 22: 5 (2005), 610.

*The multiverse hypothesis*

A hypothesis taken seriously by some influential physicists – the afore-mentioned Stephen Hawking, for instance, as well as the famous Russian physicist Andrei Linde – is that there are multiple universes, not just one. On that hypothesis, the odds on conditions in one of a vast number of universes being those very conditions in our universe are not so long. This is often referred to as the multiverse hypothesis, sometimes as the megaverse hypothesis.

Here is an analogy. Suppose you have 100 dice and are wondering about the likelihood that they will all simultaneously turn up 6. The odds are pretty long. But suppose you throw the dice 500,000 times. The odds get a lot better that, one time, all the dice will turn up 6. It is still a matter of chance that all 100 dice come up 6 at one time, but now the difference is that the chance is a lot better than before.

With world-renowned physicists taking the multiverse hypothesis seriously, we are not in a good position here to dissent. But, if we extend the supposition that the universe is finite to the multiverse hypothesis, the question comes up: What is the cause of the multiverse? Absent an answer, the multiverse hypothesis may explain the occurrence of the initial conditions in this particular universe; but it would leave unanswered our two basic questions: What caused the laws of nature across the multiverse? What caused the initial conditions in those other universes?

*The personal explanation hypothesis: the design hypothesis*

Against this background, Swinburne suggests an explanation of both things at the same time, the laws of nature and the universe's suitability for life. He sees it as a naturally arising answer to the basic questions we are investigating. In addition, he claims for it the virtue of simplicity. Echoing the principle of explanation, Ockham's Razor, that traces to the medieval philosopher William of Ockham (*c.*1285–1349), Swinburne maintains that "the simpler a theory, the more probable it is."[7]

For that combination of reasons – comprehensiveness plus simplicity – he thinks his explanation has more plausibility than either the chance

---

[7]  Richard Swinburne, "Prior Probabilities in the Argument from Fine-Tuning," *Faith and Philosophy* 22: 5 (2005), 644.

hypothesis or the multiverse hypothesis. In addition, he claims it is probable in its own right. He sees its probability coming, in part, from its strong roots in a kind of explanation that we commonly use in daily life. He calls it personal explanation.

Swinburne distinguishes between two kinds of explanations, impersonal and personal explanations. He maintains that, in context, each can be a form of ultimate explanation.

Suppose I ask you why your hair is wet today. You tell me that you were outside just now when it started to rain. The explanation of your wet hair, then, is the rainfall. This is an impersonal or non-personal explanation. If we wished, we could track back through all the previous stages of cloud formation and so on. The result, suitably tracked backwards in the sequence of events, would be an ultimate explanation of your wet hair. In theory, no further questions about it would remain.

Suppose I ask you why your hair was also wet yesterday. You tell me your sister had poured a glass of water over your head. We ask her why. She tells us you were being self-important, and she felt like dousing you. And, she adds, she also did it for the fun of it. Enough said. Now that we have her motives and reasons in hand, we have no further question. In Swinburne's view, we have an ultimate explanation. This time it is a personal explanation.

In keeping with this distinction, Swinburne offers the hypothesis of a personal agent to explain both the basic laws of nature and the conduciveness of the universe to life. He sees the alternative as our having no explanation for the laws of nature. Recall his earlier point that, as all scientific explanation is ultimately explanation in terms of the basic laws of nature, a scientific explanation of the basic laws of nature themselves would be circular. In addition, he maintains that his proposal is a more satisfactory explanation of the evolution of life than either the multiverse or the chance hypothesis. The core of his idea is that the laws of nature and the initial conditions in the universe are what they are on purpose.

This is a version of the hypothesis of design, a line of thought with a long life in the theistic intellectual tradition – although we do not know this behind the veil of ignorance, and consequently are not influenced by the idea's pedigree. Nowadays the hypothesis of supernatural design is sometimes called the 'fine-tuning' hypothesis.

As we saw in chapter 2, design occurs only by the intention of a designer. By definition, design is not accidental. Accidental order is possible, but accidental design is not. So, if there is indeed design behind the basic laws of nature, there must be a designer. Furthermore, for reasons previously mentioned, this conjectured designer must be separate from the physical universe and not subject to its laws or forces.

Our understanding of design comes entirely from our own case: human design, as found in cars, laptop computers, picture frames, mousetraps and so on. What does design in our own case require? First and foremost, there must be a mind of the right sort, with the mental capacity or imagination to foresee outcomes. In addition, it must have the mental capacity to figure out how to achieve foreseen outcomes, and the perseverance to see the process through from concept to realization. Then, on top of design, there is execution, which requires the practical and theoretical knowledge to bring a design into existence as the object designed.

If there is indeed a designer of the universe, our best understanding of the concept of design means that the conjectured designer will be supposed to have those traits. Considering that it is the universe itself that we are now supposing might be designed, perhaps it would be reasonable to think that the mind of its designer, although similar to ours in the ways mentioned, would be vastly superior to ours.

## IV  Evaluating the Rival Hypotheses

Three rival explanations of natural order and of initial conditions at the Big Bang have come up. One: This is the only universe, and both natural order and the initial conditions at the Big Bang are due to chance. Two: This universe is one of many; thus the chances of those things coming about are greater. Three: The universe exists by design; thus order and conditions at the Big Bang were intentional. Each of these hypotheses offers a substantive explanation.

In addition, there is a fourth hypothesis, which declines to offer an explanation. Its point is that here, on these matters, our questions have outrun our ability to answer. This fourth idea recommends an essentially skeptical or agnostic stance on explaining the basic laws of nature and the fact that the universe is suitable for the evolution of life. In essence, it is the supposition that there is no explanation more basic than explanation in terms of the laws of physics.[8] It does not deny that natural order or initial conditions at the Big Bang had causes, although it does not affirm that either. Its point is that, in principle, no explanation of either phenomenon is available to us. In addition, it calls into question our justification for supposing that the three substantive hypotheses mentioned are the only possible explanations.

This fourth option is attractive. But we must be careful not to over-interpret it or to be misled by it about the other three. For skepticism about an ultimate explanation of natural order or the initial conditions at the Big Bang does not compel us to be silent about the three substantive hypotheses. In particular, it does not mean that we cannot rank them relative to one another. Here is a mundane example of the underlying point.

Suppose you are buying a car and you have narrowed the options down to three. Suppose you have researched each one, and taken it out for a test drive. Suppose, however, you are not persuaded that any of them is the right car to buy. Does that mean you think all three cars are equal? Probably not. You may still think the Volkswagen is better overall than the Toyota, but inferior overall to the Honda. So, while you may rank the Honda the best overall of those three cars, you are not sufficiently persuaded of its merits to buy it.

The same is true of theories and explanations. Perhaps we cannot judge one of the three substantive hypotheses more probable than not. Perhaps we are not persuaded to 'buy' any of them. But that does not mean we think all of them occupy the same place on the scale of probability. Consequently, even if we incline to skepticism, we may still be able to rank the substantive candidates in relation to each other. Considering the enterprise in this book, let us approach that 'comparing' task with a focus on the design idea.

There are significant difficulties in the chance and multiverse hypotheses: the long odds in the former case, the unexplained existence of the multiverse in the latter. Are there difficulties in the design idea too, and if so, how do they compare with those difficulties?

---

[8]   It is important to distinguish between this idea and a restrictive theory that is often called scientism. Scientism is the idea that, in the last analysis, only scientific explanations are genuine explanations.

Swinburne rightly describes Darwin's hypothesis as not an ultimate explanation. And he argues that we can legitimately ask for the source of the basic laws of physics. By the same logic, then, we ask whether the design hypothesis is an ultimate explanation. If it is not ultimate, then something beyond or behind the conjectured designer brought about that designer, granting for the sake of argument the essential point that there is a designer. But if the design hypothesis is an ultimate explanation, the sequence of causes and effects originates in the conjectured designer.

If we pick the first option, that something else caused the conjectured designer, the very same question will come up about that further cause. What caused it? And so on endlessly. So the design hypothesis will be useless as an ultimate explanation unless the second option is true. But what is there to recommend that option? And, more specifically, what is there to recommend that option uniquely? After all, even if there is reason to suppose the sequence of causes and effects in the universe originates in the conjectured designer, perhaps there is also reason to suppose it originates in the Big Bang.

Does the sequence of causes and effects in the universe originate in the Big Bang? Once this question is asked, an obvious and sensible response to it would seem to be another question. That is: What caused the Big Bang? But then, by the same logic, isn't it just as obvious and sensible to ask about the cause of the conjectured designer? With these questions, we arrive at the nub of the debate on the designer hypothesis.

"The simpler a theory, the more probable it is." That is the key to Swinburne's thinking on the questions now before us. The fine-tuning or designer hypothesis proposes that the vastly complex universe originated in a single mind, which itself has no external cause. The idea offers simplicity plus comprehensiveness. But what are we to make of the idea that a thing has no external cause? Such a thing would not have been caused by something else, and neither would its cause be some earlier stage or state of itself. Can we make sense of this, the bedrock idea in Swinburne's design argument? We will take up that question in the next chapter.

## Suggested Reading

Behe, Michael J. (2007) "Molecular Machines: Experimental Support for the Design Inference," in N. C. Rauhut, ed., *Readings on the Ultimate Questions*, 405–19. New York: Penguin.

Kitcher, Philip (2007) *Living with Darwin*, ch. 4. New York: Oxford University Press.

Ruse, Michael (2005) *The Evolution–Creation Struggle*, ch. 12. Cambridge, Mass.: Harvard University Press.

Swinburne, Richard (1999) *Is There a God?*, chs 4 and 5. Oxford: Oxford University Press.

# 6

# Natural Order, Natural Selection, and Supernatural Design (2)

## I  The Simplicity Conjecture

### A simple being

The idea has come up of a supernatural person as the original source of the universe. It includes the conjecture that this person has no external cause. In the spirit of impartial experimentation characteristic of life behind the veil of ignorance, suppose we let our imagination run, in order to feel out the idea.

Perhaps if something had no beginning, it would have no external cause. So we conjecture it to exist eternally, thereby giving it neither beginning nor end. But what would keep it going? Consistent with our conjecture, we have to imagine it not needing a cause in that way either. So we conjecture an eternal and self-sustaining person. We conjecture a personal being who is dependent on nothing internal as well as nothing external. By contrast, this laptop computer is dependent, among other things, on its battery working, on its memory pack, and so on. So, to make our conjecture work, perhaps we need to suppose this supernatural person having no parts or internal relations, and so not being dependent on the proper functioning and arrangement of those parts. Let us suppose it is a completely simple being.

We suppose it has no dimensions, thus no size, shape, duration, and so on. We suppose that, having no duration, in addition to having no beginning or end, it is timeless. We suppose it to have no boundaries, no limitations, no constraints. In effect, our conjecture about absolute simplicity brings up the conjecture of an infinite being.

We are far out on a speculative limb. We console ourselves with the thought that, sometimes, scientists make startling conjectures in order to try to comprehend puzzling observed features of the universe. For instance, since it first came up in the early 1960s, the theory of quarks has become widely accepted among particle physicists. Another startling example is the idea that almost all of the matter in the universe is beyond direct observation, being so-called dark matter.

These theories earn their keep by helping to explain otherwise incomprehensible phenomena. In addition, the scientific community holds out the hope that one day there will be direct empirical confirmation or disconfirmation of them. Does the idea of a simple, uncaused, supernatural mind earn its keep too, either by better explaining the origin of the universe than its chance or multiverse rivals, or, in its own right, by giving an explanation that is more probable than not?

### Puzzling simplicity

The idea is that the universe exists by choice of this alleged person. We have lots of experience of choices, so let us apply that experience to the conjecture.

I choose this seat in the auditorium, and I put my coat on the empty seat beside it. Those are two different choices. Each is different from my hope that the play will be good, from my thoughts and feelings as it progresses, and from my opinion at the end.

If the conjectured supernatural being chooses to bring about the Big Bang with initial conditions suited to the eventual evolution of life, then, on the analogy to ourselves, let us think of that as one choice. As such, it is different from some other choice, the choice of the basic laws of physics, say. But, on that understanding, this conjectured being no longer seems to be radically simple. For now there seem to be parts in it: this choice, that choice, this expectation, that judgment, this memory, and so on.

In short, when we look into the idea, it is far from clear that the simplicity conjectured of this being squares with the concept of the being as a maker of choices. But the essence of the personal explanation hypothesis is that the universe was brought about by choice. And absolute simplicity seems a prerequisite for the idea that the chooser is dependent on no cause. So the difficulty in understanding this conjecture of an absolutely simple being as the original cause of the universe persists.

## II   Problems about Consciousness and Causation

### Felt consciousness

What is the substance of this conjectured entity? Of what stuff is it made? Considering the stipulation that the basic laws of nature cannot apply to it, because it is represented as having no physical properties at all, what positive characterization is to be given of it?

Behind the veil of ignorance, what resources are available for an answer? Perhaps an answer can be found in terms of felt consciousness, that is, in terms of how being conscious feels to us. Our awareness of pains and feelings and so on is not awareness of brain processes or any physical processes or states as such. In addition to pains and feelings, felt consciousness includes the experience of having intentions, making choices, and so on.

But there is strong reason to think such an account of the substance or nature of the alleged non-physical designer would not do. For, while felt consciousness does not present to us the physical base of our aware-ness as such, the fact is that we have no acquaintance whatever with conscious beings not having such a base. Every conscious being we know of has a body. And there is no reason to suppose that fact is just a coincidence. Instead, there is good reason to think that a physical base is a necessary condition of consciousness in the first place. Both our common experience and the scientific literacy we retain behind the veil of ignorance strongly support the point.

The upshot is that, at best, a description in terms of felt conscious-ness might represent how it feels to be a non-physical mind, but it would not tell us anything at all about the stuff of which such a mind is composed.

### Tolerable gaps in otherwise good theories

Theories have gaps. Sometimes they even have big gaps at a basic level, especially novel theories. In contemporary physics, for instance, the string theory of the ultimate nature of matter has gaps and no definitive experimental confirmation, yet it is taken seriously by many physicists. Let us extend the same courtesy to the supernatural design idea, and not press too hard for a positive description of the substance of the alleged non-physical supernatural mind, or read too much into the absence of such a description.

But there is another gap that appears to be quite serious. It comes in the problem of understanding the nature of the causation that the design idea supposes to operate between the choice or intention of the conjectured non-physical supernatural mind and the occurrence of the Big Bang. By definition, it cannot be any kind of causation that would be within the jurisdiction of the physical sciences. Likewise, the conjectured choice or intention to bring about the universe cannot be covered by any laws of nature. Consequently, the kind of choice or intent attributed to this conjectured supernatural being must be understood in terms of the libertarian theory of free will, discussed in chapter 4.

## The problem of causation

The problem that the design hypothesis was devised to solve is essentially a causal problem. What is the ultimate source or cause of the universe?

But if we characterize the ultimate cause of the universe as intrinsically non-physical, an obvious question comes up. It is, How can something with no physical properties at all, no mass, volume, density, specific gravity, surface, and so on, bring about something, all of whose properties are physical properties? How is causation supposed to work here? What concept of causation is supposed to be in play? It cannot be physical causation. For physical causation seems to require a physical source, but that is ruled out in this case by definition.

Neither of the following suggestions solves the problem. But their failure helps to bring the magnitude of the problem into perspective.

### First failed solution
You ask about the arrangement of pictures and other things on those shelves. I tell you that I arranged them, thinking they would look good this way. That is, I imagined the arrangement, I decided on it, I then actually arranged the photographs, clock, and so on accordingly. Causation here is explained in terms of a prior decision.

This is an example of what we saw Swinburne call personal explanation. Doesn't it happen all the time? So, why not likewise with the conjectured supernatural designer? That is, the designer thinks up the physical laws and initial conditions in the universe, then decides to implement them, then actually arranges things in nature accordingly.

But this won't work here. Why not? Because we still have no experience of disembodied consciousness, let alone of disembodied consciousness with causal power. We have no experience of decisions that are not based in brains. All our experience of the causal power of decisions relates to decisions whose base in reality is a functioning brain in a living animal, a physical thing subject to the laws of nature. So the first suggestion won't get us out from under the basic laws of nature. It gives us no reason to think of causal action from an essentially non-physical source.

*Second failed solution*
Maybe we could take comfort in what is sometimes called the hard problem of consciousness. Essentially, that is the problem of explaining how the brain, roughly three pounds of spongy matter, brings forth the whole world of awareness and meaning. That remains one of the biggest unsolved problems in studies of the brain.

With that unsolved problem in mind, perhaps we should view the problem of original causation as a more-or-less parallel case. Maybe we could call it the hard problem of causation, or of existence, and not read too much into failure to solve it.

Where exactly is the suggested parallel? It is in the idea that there may be a parallel absence of necessary concepts. The hard problem of consciousness is hard because we don't have concepts adequate to it. Indeed, some eminent thinkers who work on the problem have suggested that, because of the nature of our brains, we may be incapable of coming up with adequate concepts. We may be as unable to solve the hard problem of consciousness as dogs are of solving problems in algebra. But the suggested parallel won't do. Among several reasons, here are two.

First, we know that the brain does in fact give rise to consciousness. The hard problem is explaining how. But we do not know that a supernatural, intrinsically non-physical, thing gave rise to matter. That is, the problem the supernatural design hypothesis presents to us is not just a 'how' problem.

True, the problem is sometimes phrased in a way that makes it seem to be a 'how' problem. But that is misleading. To be a 'how' problem, it would first of all have to be a settled fact that the physical universe did originate in a non-physical mind. But we do not know that is a fact at all. It is precisely the hypothesis now under investigation. So, any suggested parallel to the hard problem of consciousness would appear to commit the fallacy of presupposing the very thing that needs to be proved.

But the reality is even stronger. The reality is that all of our relevant experience points the other way: to matter, specifically the brain, giving rise to mind or consciousness, not to mind originally giving rise to matter.

Second, a related reason the suggested parallel won't work is that, in the hard problem of consciousness, there is no presumption that what needs explaining is the connection between something intrinsically physical and something intrinsically non-physical. That is, the problem in the hard problem of consciousness is not due to the concept of a mysterious, non-physical stuff. But the current problem with the design hypothesis is. It is: How can a conjectured non-physical object be thought to bring physical stuff into existence?

## The magnitude of the problem

If the designer hypothesis is unable to provide a good account of how this conjectured causal action from an intrinsically non-physical source to a physical effect works, then we are in danger of having the designer hypothesis evaporate before our very eyes. For the hypothesis is first of all a causal hypothesis. So, if the concept of cause in it is not understood and cannot be explained, then the hypothesis itself is not understood and cannot be explained. And if that is so, then it does not enable us to understand the fact that the universe came to be the way it is.

Perhaps it is the concept of causation itself that is the problem. If we look carefully at our experiences of causal action, maybe all we really find is sequences of occurrences, which we then, out of habit, gloss as causes and effects. So, perhaps the reason we cannot account for causal connection between the conjectured supernatural mind and the physical universe is that we truly cannot account for causal connection anywhere, merely glossing before-and-after sequences as cause-and-effect sequences.

Although, now far behind the veil of ignorance, we do not know it, this is essentially David Hume's description of what experience tells us about causes and effects. If we incline to this view, then, in effect, we will be trading in the hard problem of consciousness for a different hard problem of causation.

Swinburne himself would not do so. For it would undercut the supposition that the basic laws of nature, along with the universe's conduciveness to life, have a cause. Thus it would short-circuit the enterprise of seeking that cause. Anyway, apart from that implication, this skepticism about causation would contribute nothing to understanding the nature of the conjectured supernatural person.

## Cause–effect proportionality

At this point in our investigation, with the nature both of the supposed original cause and of original causation open and unsolved problems, we have good reason to suspend the supernatural designer idea altogether, pending adequate repair. However, let us postpone that step. Let us give the designer hypothesis every benefit of the doubt and probe it further.

Plausibly, the following commonsensical idea would come up, back here behind the veil of ignorance. It is that there is proportionality in what we are justified in thinking about unseen causes, based on experience of their effects. For instance, if I see the arm of a balance scale which contains a ten-ounce weight tip up, I am entitled to conclude that the weight on the other arm is more than ten ounces, even if I do not see that other arm. But I would be unjustified, on that basis, to judge that the counterbalancing weight was more than twenty ounces.[1] Let us apply this commonsense idea to the hypothesis of a supernatural, mental cause of the laws of nature and of the universe in which they are manifest.

### No headway towards omniscience
If there is a designing mind behind the universe, how much knowledge and mental capacity are we entitled to say it possesses? The answer is, enough to produce the material universe. How much knowledge and mental capacity is that? We don't know. But let us suppose for the sake of argument it is a lot. Does this give us any reason to suppose it is an infinite amount, whatever that is? No. That idea would not come up behind the veil of ignorance, except perhaps in our earlier speculation about radical simplicity.

### No headway towards omnipotence either
Can we say how much power would be required to bring about the basic laws of nature and the Big Bang? Would it have to be a lot? We don't know. But, even if it would, would it have to be infinite power, the level

[1]   David Hume, *Enquiries Concerning Human Understanding and Concerning the Principles of Morals*, ed. L. A. Selby Bigge, rev. P. H. Nidditch (Oxford: Oxford University Press, 1995), 136.

of power in omnipotence? We have been given no reason to think so, apart from the speculation about radical simplicity.

Behind the veil of ignorance, then, a conjecture about knowledge or about power sufficient to bring about the universe would not develop into a conjecture about infinite knowledge or power.

### Regular, like a robot

"[N]ot merely are there enormous numbers of things, but they all behave in exactly the same way. The same laws of nature govern the most distant galaxies we can observe through our telescopes as operate on earth, and the same laws govern the earliest events in time to which we can infer as operate today."[2]

Nature is massively orderly and regular, at least above the level of sub-atomic particles. We see it for ourselves all the time, and Richard Swinburne reminds us of it in those lines.

We know from our own experience that our minds are often fitful and quirky, innovative and exploratory, intuitive, not always logical in a linear way. That our minds are not always strictly logical, but often jazzy and loopy, especially when imaginative, is no defect. On the contrary, it often reflects creativity.

Now, wouldn't that make you wonder whether, even if the massive orderliness and regularity in nature do reflect the workings of a mind, it is more like the 'mind' of a robot than that of a person like us? For instance, unlike us, computers never 'tire' of running the same programs in the same way, or of ploughing on and on through the same calculations, the endless sequence of pi, for instance.

### Teamwork

The universe is huge and complex, so let us take for comparison some enormous and complex artifact, say the super-conducting, super-colliding particle accelerator that CERN, the European organization for nuclear research, operates in Switzerland. Clearly, a vast amount of mind-power goes into it – into both its design and construction, on the one hand, and its operation on the other. Or consider the reconstruction

---

[2]  Swinburne, *Is There a God?*, 49.

of Dresden and other European cities after the end of World War II, another enormously complicated undertaking. In the context of our investigation here into the ultimate source of natural order and initial conditions at the Big Bang, the important point about these big enterprises is that they involve teamwork and proceed by trial and error.

But aren't there also great and complex things that do not come from teamwork, but from a single mind? Yes. For instance, there was the proof not too long ago by the Princeton mathematician Andrew Wiles of one of the great problems in mathematics, Fermat's last theorem. There is Einstein's theory of special relativity, Shakespeare's *Hamlet*, the music of Mozart or Beethoven, the art of Cézanne or Picasso, and so on. So, our experience of creativity seems to be a mix of teamwork and solo achievement.

However, while not undercutting the genius of creative individuals, we know that their creativity plays off, and in some cases uses, work already done in a tradition. That is, the creations of even the most creative geniuses are not literally from scratch. True, Wiles's proof or Einstein's theory or Picasso's paintings are not teamwork, but they are not completely separable from past work in their respective fields either. That is, they are not completely separable from intellectual, cultural, artistic, and social contexts, and as such they remind us of the fundamental fact that we are not solitary minds, but intrinsically social and cultural beings. That idea is central in the thought of Aristotle (384–322 BCE), in ancient times, as well as of two of the most influential philosophers of recent times, Ludwig Wittgenstein (1889–1951) and Martin Heidegger (1889–1976), although those names ring no bells of recognition back here behind our veil of ignorance.

Behind the veil of ignorance, we have no ulterior motive to prefer a single great-mind hypothesis to a consortium of minds, great or not so great. Back here, our golden rule of procedure is to prefer the best explanation.

So, once the concept of mind-power comes up as a possible explanation of the preconditions of life in the universe, it seems more plausible to develop that concept in terms of teamwork, or in terms of progressive development, rather than in terms of a single mind, creating literally from scratch. After all, we have no experience of such a thing. Even when we scale back from big projects to smaller ones, you know very well that no one person designed and built the little box that your iPod came in. You know it was teamwork, or progressive improvement on past efforts, all the way. And you know as well, marvelous and original as your iPod itself is, that its development was only possible because of the state of development of the electronics, computer, and plastics industries, among others.

The upshot is that Swinburne's idea of a radically and intrinsically simple being is not well supported by our experience of creativity or originality.

A related point comes up when we ask how the idea of a radically simple person fits with our actual experience of persons. Dovetailing with the earlier point about creative genius, our experience of persons seems to show us that we are by nature social and cultural beings, and shows us no example of the kind of radically solo person that Swinburne's theory proposes. True, there is Robinson Crusoe, and there is Tom Hanks in the movie *Castaway*; but neither represents the kind of self-containedness that Swinburne has in mind. For both were users of language and makers of plans long before they washed ashore on their respective islands.

This sketch of what experience does and does not show is not sufficient reason to deny either the actuality or possibility of such a person as Swinburne is conjecturing. But it adds to our previous reasons to be skeptical or suspicious of the concept. It adds to our reasons to see it as a very puzzling idea.

## Proportionality and disproportionality

Life is known to exist only on this planet. The universe is known to be so vast it can scarcely be imagined, containing billions of entire galaxies that are accelerating away from each other. The earth is a minor planet, even in its own solar system, thus very minor indeed in comparison to its galaxy. So, considered in size relative to the entire universe, even to imagine it as a single grain of sand relative to the Sahara desert would be an exaggeration of its size.

So the question naturally comes up: All of that for this? It seems, if intentional, monumentally disproportionate. And that naturally triggers a further question about the value-system of a mind that might think there was a proper proportionality between means and end here.

A related question comes up about time. The almost fourteen billion years since the Big Bang is an awfully long time. Compared to it, the mere hundreds of thousands of years since the emergence of *Homo sapiens* is so little time as to be tantamount to the last few days relative to the last several hundred years. So again the question comes up: All of that for this?

True, given what we know about the initial conditions at the Big Bang, and given evolution, the universe would have to be this old in order for conditions to become right for supporting human life on this planet. But, considering the vastness of the universe, it is very difficult to grasp the outlook of a being who would judge our eventual existence a good return on so massive an investment of galaxies and planets and, on this planet, of species that have gone extinct.

### Other long odds

There were very long odds against the initial conditions at the Big Bang being right for the eventual evolution of life as we know it. The design argument we are examining says those odds are simply too long to be credibly explained as mere chance. That point is fundamental in the development of this design argument. If that point is wobbly, then so is the hypothesis of design.

But it seems to be a fact that, by chance, lots of things occur against very long odds. For instance, I don't know what the odds were against that particular sperm fertilizing that particular egg on that occasion, but I'm pretty sure they were very long. Yet if it hadn't happened, that fertilized egg would not have gone on to be me. Furthermore, those long odds were themselves made possible, among other conditions, only because certain particular sperms and eggs of my grandparents had previously come together just so, and so on back in time. The odds, surely, were enormous. Yet here I am.

How best to explain the fact that I exist? Let us take inspiration from our discussion of how best to explain the fact that the initial conditions at the Big Bang were right for life eventually to evolve on this planet. That is, let us compare the explanations we get from chance and from design, respectively.

At face value, chance seems an appealing explanation of my existence. After all, if just a few circumstances had been different, my parents would never have met, to say nothing of all the previous circumstances involving two sets of grandparents, great-grandparents, and so on back. In addition, the chance hypothesis has the appeal of simplicity, and we are heeding Swinburne on the value of simple explanations that are adequate to the known facts.

But, on the other hand, perhaps I was meant to be. Let us consider that option. First of all, it is a different idea from the idea that human life was intended or designed from the universe's beginning in the Big Bang. For now the idea is that this particular member of the species, me, was meant to be. A similar idea would apply to you and all other people too, of course, but just for now let my life stand for all lives.

If a being who is able to turn intentions into results intended me to exist, then things were arranged from the start so that, in due course, I came about. But, over and above the foregoing points about very long odds, this explanation of my existence seems to conflict with the libertarian theory of free will. We saw in chapter 4 that the libertarian theory is essential to Plantinga's defense against Mackie. And we saw earlier in the present chapter that the libertarian theory is essential to the concept of choice or intention in the designer hypothesis now under discussion. Furthermore, as we will see later on, it is also an essential part of the defense that Richard Swinburne and others make against the idea that the enormous amounts of seemingly pointless evils in the world show the existence of God to be improbable. Clearly, then, the supernatural designer hypothesis can endorse no point that would conflict with the libertarian theory of free will.

Where does the conflict seem to be? According to the libertarian view, my parents had full-time libertarian free will, which, presumably, they exercised in choosing each other, as well as in making all those other choices, without which they would never have met in the first place. And the same would be true of my grandparents and so on back. If my father's father had not left Ballyvourney for Cork, then he would never have met his second wife, and the rest would have been a different history. But if my existence was arranged or inevitable from the start, almost fourteen billion years ago, then he had to leave that town, my parents had to choose each other, and so on. If so, then those choices were not free in the libertarian sense of freedom. Those choices could still perhaps be deemed free choices on the compatibilist idea of free will that we discussed in chapter 4, but not on the libertarian concept.

The upshot now seems to be that, unless we hold a compatibilist theory of free will, we cannot hold a design theory of my existence. So, unless we are compatibilists, we are left with the 'chance' explanation of my existence.

But we agree that, on the libertarian theory, the odds against things being just right for my existence are enormous. So, if we are content with a 'chance' explanation of the fact that I exist, even in light of those odds, why not likewise with the explanation of the initial conditions at the Big Bang being just right for life eventually to develop on this planet? Furthermore, when we consider that I am but one of the approximately three and one-third billion people now alive, the odds against all of us existing here and now are stupefyingly enormous, given libertarianism. If we accept a 'chance' explanation, notwithstanding such odds, why baulk at a 'chance' explanation of conditions at the Big Bang? True, the odds that Hawking mentioned, 1:100,000,000,000,000,000, are very long, and their initial effect is to make the 'chance' hypothesis seem fantastically improbable. But in light of other long odds, as well as of difficulties in understanding key points in the designer hypothesis itself, perhaps the 'chance' hypothesis now seems less out of the question than it did at first.

Still in pursuit of a comparative ranking of the three substantive hypotheses, let us now fold into the mix the fact that terrible things happen.

## III   Conditions at the Big Bang, the Design Hypothesis, and the Occurrence of Terrible Things

The world is a place where terrible things happen for no apparent good reason. This is as obvious a fact as the facts that the world is complex and orderly, and that conditions at the Big Bang were right for the eventual evolution of life on this planet. Those facts of complexity, order, and suitability for life led us to speculate about their ultimate cause or source. Let us now add the facts of seemingly pointless evils to the basis on which we have been speculating about the original source of the universe.

### Omniscience without foreknowledge again

Perhaps it would be objected that the facts of evil should not be included in the data on the basis of which we speculate about the original source, if any, of the universe. For perhaps it would be suggested that, while complex order and suitability for life were intended by the conjectured designer, seemingly pointless evils were not. What might support this suggestion?

Let us recall that, in chapter 4, we acknowledged the logical possibility that the conjectured supernatural designer would not know the future. Wouldn't this pre-empt any problem arising from the occurrence of terrible things? For possibly the conjectured supernatural designer would not have known that such things would occur.

This idea would have a huge cost in arbitrariness. The reason is that the central idea in the fine-tuning hypothesis is that conditions at the Big Bang were intended for the future evolution of life. Consequently, some significant anticipation of the future is central in the hypothesis. Even granting that this foresight might fall short of strict foreknowledge, the supernatural-designer hypothesis is only plausible at all when it is assumed that the foresight was pretty solid and reliable.

Without gross arbitrariness, that cannot be denied or ruled out now, when a different fact is the focus of our attention. Consequently, if it is reasonable to suppose that certain conditions in the first instant of the Big Bang were anticipated to lead to the evolution of human life almost fourteen billion years later, then certainly it is reasonable to suppose that the supernatural designer could and would have anticipated the occurrence of terrible things. So we can dismiss the objection to including the fact of seemingly pointless evils in the data on the basis of which to speculate about the original source, if any, of the universe.

## Rationality plus

To this point, we have concentrated on the cognitive and active sides of the conjectured supernatural mind. We have concentrated on its knowledge, its capacity for planning and for making decisions, as well as its capacity to act on those decisions. But the introduction of this new dimension of evidence, the fact that terrible things happen, points us towards other features of mind and behavior.

It is an intrinsic feature of our minds that we have feelings as well as thoughts. Furthermore, our feelings contribute at least as much to our essential nature as does our rationality. Pain and pleasure, sympathy, compassion, kindness, frustration, love, desire, encouragement and discouragement, and so on contribute at least as much as our rationality to the kinds of beings that we are. We are evaluative beings, whose choices and actions reflect values. Our choices and actions do not just turn out well or badly, they are often self-consciously made as choices for good. A sense of fairness or justice, a feeling of respect, and so on, are reflected in our outlook, and show the character of our minds, at least as much as logical skill.

The upshot is that, if we are entitled to speculate from our experience of deep order, together with the long odds against life emerging in the universe, that maybe a mind is behind it all, then, from our experience of seemingly pointless and un-balanced-out pain and suffering, loss and destruction, we are just as entitled to speculate about the moral status and the value-system of such a mind. What would we come up with?

## Four hypotheses

Maybe the mix of good and bad things in the world reflects a mix of good and bad traits in the designer mind itself. That's one supposition. Let us call it the mixed mind hypothesis.

But the notion of a mixed mind naturally triggers the contrasting idea of a mind without such a mix. So we might speculate that the designer mind was good only or bad only, that is, intrinsically and completely good or intrinsically and completely evil, respectively. Let us call these the perfectly good and the perfectly bad mind hypotheses.

Then there is a hypothesis which is at odds with all three of the previous ones. It is the hypothesis that there is no value-system at all in the supposed designer mind, that the mix of good and bad occurrences merely reflects chance, or blind causality. Let us call this the indifferent or value-free mind hypothesis.

With the evidence available to us, we can quickly dismiss the hypotheses of the perfectly good and the perfectly bad minds. This is not to deny the logical possibility that the designer of the universe, supposing there might be such a thing, could be either perfectly good or perfectly evil. But the evidence available to us is mixed. As such, it is no basis on which to conclude that its source is unmixed, either perfectly good or perfectly bad. In thinking about that point, recall the distinction we made in chapter 1 between believing something and concluding something. The point right now is that it would not be justified, on the mixed evidence of good and bad in the world, to conclude that the mind-source (if any) of the world is perfectly good or perfectly bad.

The evidence available to us is a mix of good and bad. Perhaps, then, any mind-source of it is similarly mixed, or perhaps there are several sources that are in conflict with one another. The latter idea borders on the earlier idea about teamwork.

The forces of nature do not respect the good or the innocent. The sea will drown saints as readily as sinners. Cancer does not discriminate between the virtuous and the wicked. Hurricanes kill or maim all who happen to be unlucky enough to be in the way. As we take stock of the forces of nature, we see clearly that nature seems to have "no more regard to good above ill than to heat above cold, or to drought above moisture, or to light above heavy."[3]

The indifference reflected in this state of affairs is not indifference in the moral or culpable sense of the term. That is the sense of the term applying to someone neglecting a thing that he or she ought to care about or attend to. Instead, it is the indifference of a snowfall to the subsequent slipperiness of the roads, or the indifference of a dog to that painting by Roy Lichtenstein. The second sense of the word reflects a fact that experience makes plain to us. It is that, so far as the forces of nature are concerned, there seem to be no 'oughts' or 'ought nots.' There is only what happens.

Noting the mixed evidence of good and evil in nature, the complete lack of systematic correlation between virtue and good fortune and between wickedness and bad fortune, the only reasonable and plausible conclusion, from among our four hypotheses, is either the mixed mind hypothesis or the indifferent mind hypothesis.

Suppose we had stopped short of the hypothesis of a supernatural mind as the original source of natural order. Suppose we had stopped at the Big Bang. Then we would have before us a picture of the universe as, from its inception, indifferent to us, our pains and our pleasures, our lives and deaths.

Either way, then, whether we push on to entertain the idea of a non-physical, supernatural source or stop at the Big Bang, a hypothesis that seems well fitted to the mixed evidence of good and evil, pain and pleasure, is a hypothesis that nature itself, as well as any original source it may have, is simply indifferent to us and to all other forms of life.

This provisional judgment does not mean that the four versions of a mind-source of natural order that we considered – the mixed mind, the indifferent mind, or either of the 'pure' minds – are the only possible hypotheses about the moral status of an original mind-source of order in the universe. Nor does it mean that either the hypothesis of indifference or the mixed mind hypothesis is more likely to be true

[3]  David Hume, *Dialogues Concerning Natural Religion*, ed. J. C. A. Gaskin (Oxford: Oxford University Press, 1998), 114.

than not. For, after all, even though they might be the most probable
or plausible of those four, they themselves may not be more probable
than not. That is, the probability of each of them may itself be under
50 percent.


## IV   Verdict

### *An answer to one of our two questions*

Does the world provide us with good evidence to conclude that God
is its source? Does it give us good evidence to conclude that its source
is a perfectly good, omniscient, omnipotent, supernatural person? We
conducted a religiously neutral investigation to try to find out. The basic
facts in the investigation are the deep orderliness in the universe, the
occurrence at the Big Bang of the right conditions for life to evolve,
the mix of pleasure and pain experienced by some living things, and the
apparent pointlessness of much of that pain. For the reasons discussed in
this chapter, our investigation indicates that the idea of God would not
come up as the overall best explanation.

The idea of a personal cause, beyond the natural world, might plausibly
come up on the strength of some of the basic facts in question. But the
idea of God, as such, would not come up, either on the basis of those
facts or on the basis of all of the evidence we considered.

Does the world provide some reason to consider the idea of a source
outside of the natural order? To this weaker question, I think our investigation answers 'yes.'


### *The message in the difficulties*

Concentrating on the facts of natural order, complexity, and the universe's
suitability for life, we judged that any hypothesis of a supernatural
mental source which those facts might justify as a candidate explanation
would not go far enough to arrive at the idea of God. Perhaps such a
hypothesis would go some of the way there, but not all of the way.

But the mix of good and evil carries a different message. Now the
problem is not that of falling short of a conclusion that God is probably the original source of the universe. It is that the occurrence of
terrible things is sufficient evidence to block that conclusion. Although

we would not know of their author behind the veil of ignorance, the following words aptly reflect the point at which we have arrived: "however consistent the world may be . . . with the idea of such a Deity, it can never afford us an inference concerning his existence. The consistence is not absolutely denied, only the inference."[4] To infer a perfectly good creator from the mix of good and evil in the world would be as unjustified as inferring a perfect cook from a mix of excellent, terrible, and mediocre meals.

In the thirteenth century, at the hands of Thomas Aquinas, and in most attempts since to infer a divine source of the world, the data considered have been restricted to various physical facts, especially natural order and causation throughout nature, or to the fact that human beings develop systems of moral evaluation. But the fact that there is a vast amount of seemingly pointless suffering and waste of life in the world is usually not included in that database. That fact is typically treated as a second-order fact, to be subsequently squared with the God supposedly inferred from those other facts. We may well wonder what justifies such selectivity and ranking.

The selectivity is the stranger in that it seems to preordain the failure of attempts to infer God from the facts of order, complexity, and suitability for life. The reason is that the sought-for conclusion, the proposition that God exists, is about a personal being who is represented to have knowledge, power, and goodness. But unless there is a basis for all of those properties in the evidence, we know before starting that the attempt will fail. We know before starting that some parts of the conclusion, the moral component in the concept of God, say, will not be underwritten by the selective evidence considered.

The facts of order and conduciveness to life are insufficient to warrant the conclusion that their original source is an infinitely good, powerful, and knowing God. The fact of evil blocks a conclusion that the original source of natural order is perfectly good. Thus it blocks a conclusion that God is that source. But this does not mean, or prove it probable, that such a source is not perfectly good. Something can be so in fact, even though we cannot prove it likely. Once again, let us recall Al Capone, and be careful not to over-interpret the point at which we have arrived.

---

[4]  Hume, *Dialogues Concerning Natural Religion*, 107.

## Suggested Reading

Hume, David (1998) *Dialogues Concerning Natural Religion*, ed. J. C. A. Gaskin. Oxford: Oxford University Press. In Parts IV and V, there is a very good discussion of the idea of modeling a supernatural mind on a human mind. In Part XI, there is an excellent discussion of how the facts of seemingly pointless evil block a conclusion that a supernatural mind, if any, might be God. As I mentioned previously, any edition of the *Dialogues* will do.

# Part IV

# Evil and Design (1)

# 7

# Is the Existence of God Improbable?

Does the idea of God square with the facts of terrible evil in the world, or do those facts give us reason to think there is probably no God? This question returns us to the first of our two investigations.

We come back to it against the background of a win and a loss for the core theistic idea. We saw it proved that the existence of God is logically possible. But we saw an impartial attempt to explain order and life in the universe fail to settle on the idea of God as their explanation.

That failure does not mean there is no God. Nonetheless, it is natural to wonder if the fact of evil blocking inferences to God might also be rational ground to think there is no God.

We remain behind the veil of ignorance, but less far back than in the last two chapters. Now we suppose our knowledge of philosophy and of religion comes back to us, but we continue not to know our individual religious orientation or preference.

## I   The Problem in Focus

### Eight points about justified evils

When it is justified to cause or permit a person or animal to suffer pain, loss, or harm, the justification usually comes from one or more of the following things.

1   The evils are either necessary or unavoidable in bringing about an outweighing good outcome, or in preventing an equally bad or worse outcome.

Consequently,

2    there is either a logical or a causal connection between the painful
     means and the good end achieved, or the evil end avoided;
3    the amount of evil involved is proportionate to the amount of good,
     and is not excessive;
4    the benefit is to the victim himself or herself, or the victim is among
     the beneficiaries.

Let us pause here briefly to add a clarification to point 4. The clarification involves distinguishing between benefits of suffering, as such, on the
one hand, and benefits of whatever causes the suffering, on the other. The
crux in point 4 is that the victim benefits from whatever causes the suffering, for instance, surgery to remove a tumor, not from the suffering
itself. For if we think the victim benefits from the suffering itself, we may
lose our motivation to relieve suffering. Now back to our list.

5    The victim consents, or would consent, or a responsible person con-
     sents on behalf of the victim and for the benefit of the victim.

Then there is

6    self-defense. We can view self-defense either as an instance of point 1,
     that is, as something unavoidable in bringing about an outweigh-
     ing good or in preventing something equally bad or worse, or as a
     new kind of circumstance. The newness comes from the fact that,
     typically, the person harmed in self-defense is not innocent. A similar
     situation is when
7    the pain or harm is inflicted in appropriate punishment for wrong-
     doing. Punishment may be in retribution or deterrence. Deterrence
     is a form of benefit to others, so this points us to other situations,
     sometimes controversial, where
8    the benefit is to a person or persons, or animal or animals, other than
     the victim. All things being equal, this point is not controversial if,
     for example, the victim is quarantined because he has a contagious
     disease. But it is controversial if, for example, the victim is forced into
     a medical experiment intended to benefit others.

Apart from one side of the last item, the foregoing points are broadly
uncontroversial. Furthermore, in the absence of good reason to suppose
otherwise, it is reasonable to think they would apply to a God-made world.

Against that background, then, it is natural to wonder, for instance, how the deaths of the children in the Pakistani earthquake contribute to a greater good that is otherwise unachievable, or how they prevent a greater evil that is otherwise unavoidable. It is equally natural to wonder how those deaths benefit those children themselves.

### Two approaches to establishing that the existence of God is improbable

Nowadays there are two influential arguments, each of which reaches the conclusion that the great abundance of seemingly pointless evil in the world makes the existence of God improbable. One is a direct argument, developed by William L. Rowe; the other is indirect and comes from Paul Draper. Both arguments appeal to our reasonable expectations about a world designed and brought about by God. Those arguments are the subject of this chapter. We will examine responses to them in the next four chapters.

## II  Draper's Indirect Argument

### Hume's four hypotheses

Assume for the sake of argument there is something which is the original source both of natural order and of the initial conditions in the universe that made the universe conducive to the eventual evolution of life. In the previous chapter, we came up with four hypotheses about the moral nature of that conjectured source.

One hypothesis is that the source is simply indifferent to considerations of good and evil. Another is that it has a mix of good and evil qualities. Those were the hypotheses we judged the best fit with our evidence. The two other ideas that came up were that the original source is good through and through, and that it is evil through and through. We dismissed that pair right away. On the strength of our evidence, there was simply no impartial way to conclude that either of them was likely or plausible.

Those four hypotheses closely match four suggested by David Hume. They are: the theistic idea of an infinitely good God; the polar opposite idea of an infinitely evil supernatural being (think of René Descartes's 'evil genius' hypothesis from another context); the Manichaean idea from the third century CE of a cosmic war between two more-or-less evenly matched supernatural forces, one good, the other bad; and finally the idea that the original cause of order in the universe, whether natural or supernatural, is indifferent to the conditions of things, indifferent to pain and suffering, for instance.

In examining Draper's argument, our emphasis will be on the first and the fourth of Hume's four hypotheses. That is, our emphasis will be on the theistic idea of God as the source of order in the universe and on the indifference hypothesis, the idea that there is no caring being behind the natural order of things.

### Reasonable expectations, and three questions

If I believe you are a good and decent person, I expect you to behave in certain sorts of ways. Furthermore, I think it is probable that you will behave in those ways. Both of these things are plausible and reasonable. Believing you are a good and decent person, I think it is very improbable that, all other things being equal, you would leave a young child to drown in a shallow stream. I would be very surprised to learn that you did. But I would not be surprised that a horse that was grazing nearby did nothing to help. Likewise, obviously I would have no expectations of help from that tree in the corner of the field. The horse and the tree would have been, and would have been expected to be, completely indifferent to the child and his fate.

Generalize from them to the whole of the natural world, apart from human beings. On the indifference hypothesis, there is no value-system at work behind the scenes, no force for good or evil, no altruistic concern for others working through the basic natural forces. There is just cause and effect.

Broadly speaking, there are two interpretations of the idea that there is no value system at work behind the scenes. The first is that the physical universe is the totality of what exists. This view is often called naturalism. The second is often called deism. Its core idea is that any supernatural source of the universe there may be is unconcerned with the fates of living things.

Considering the fact that there is a vast abundance of terrible things in the natural world – diseases, birth defects, tsunamis, earthquakes, and so on – ask yourself a question. Do you find their occurrence surprising on the indifference hypothesis?

The answer, surely, is no. It is not surprising at all. On that hypothesis of a completely indifferent universe, it is what you would expect and predict. That is the naturalistic reading of the indifference hypothesis. But the deistic reading of the hypothesis yields the same unsurprisingness. If our hypothesis is that there is a mind behind the universe, but a mind that is completely unconcerned about happenings after the Big Bang, then the occurrence of seemingly pointless terrible things will be no surprise. On the naturalistic idea of a completely indifferent universe, we would be no more surprised by the absence of any effort to prevent the occurrence of seemingly pointless evils than by the indifference of the tree to the drowning child in the example above. And on the deistic idea of a completely indifferent mind behind the universe, we would be no more surprised by the absence of effort to prevent the occurrence of seemingly pointless evils than by the indifference of the horse in that same example. It makes no difference to our expectations whether we give a naturalistic or a deistic interpretation to Draper's (or Hume's) indifference idea.

Now ask yourself a second question. In asking and answering, keep in mind that, behind the veil of ignorance, any religious or irreligious preference you may have is unknown to you. On the theistic hypothesis of a loving, all-good, and all-powerful God, do you find those very same things surprising – the seemingly pointless diseases, suffering, deaths, and so on? Can you say, on this hypothesis, that you would have expected or predicted such things? Surely not. Surely, on the basis of the theistic hypothesis, you do find the fact of such occurrences surprising. Otherwise, what does that hypothesis mean? For instance, ask yourself if you would be surprised to hear that a person you considered good and decent stood by while a young child drowned.

And now, ask a third question. It is a comparative question, presupposing neither of the foregoing questions or answers. It is: On which of the two hypotheses – the indifference hypothesis and the theistic hypothesis – do you find the facts of indiscriminate suffering and waste of life the more surprising? To help you get your bearings in this question, ask yourself this: In the earlier example of the child left to drown, do you find it as surprising that the horse or the tree did nothing to help as you do that the decent person did not help?

The third question takes us to Paul Draper's point. Draper suggests that the facts of seemingly pointless suffering and waste of life are far more surprising on the idea of a loving God than on the idea of indifference.

Using surprisingness as a rule of thumb to guide us in estimating relative probabilities, Draper suggests that the theistic hypothesis is less probable than the indifference hypothesis.

## The surprise principle

Let us call this rule of thumb the surprise principle. The essence of it is that, within the range of ordinary human experience, surprisingness is a useful guide to judging probability. It is a rule of thumb that applies to occurrences in the natural world as well as to people's behavior.

In the famous story by Franz Kafka (1883–1924), "Metamorphosis," the main character, Gregor Samsa, transforms overnight into a giant insect. Against the backdrop of Kafka's story, consider the two following questions. Are you expecting your best friend to wake up tomorrow as a giant insect? How surprised would you be if he or she did? (In both questions, I am assuming that an insect is not your best friend to begin with.) If you're at all like me, your answers will be, "no" and "very," respectively. Actually, "very surprised" is far too mild to do justice to my reaction if that were to happen.

Because you would be very surprised if your best friend turned into an insect overnight, it seems safe and reasonable to say that you regard the probability of that happening as exceedingly low. For all practical purposes, you have no expectation whatsoever that it will happen, and you would think it was completely mad to take out insurance against the eventuality. Perhaps the best that can be said for it is that it is logically possible, perhaps as a miracle brought about by Descartes's evil supernatural being. You would be surprised if it happened, because you attach very low (if any) probability to its actually happening. And you are not surprised in the least that it does not happen.

Why do you judge the probability to be so low? One reason is that you know of no actual case of such a transformation. The surprise is not because of some special quality your friend has that would make it especially improbable that he or she, of all people, should transform into an insect. You would be just as surprised if your mother or Bob Dylan woke up as an insect.

Suppose you buy a single ticket for the New Jersey State Lottery. Let us say you know that many millions of tickets have been sold. You know, therefore, that there are very long odds against your winning. Presumably you would not be at all surprised if you didn't win, and very pleasantly surprised if you did. Why no surprise at not winning? Because, with odds of one against many millions, it is very improbable that yours is the winning ticket. True, the probability of your winning is equal to that of any other single-ticket holder, so a win for you would be no more surprising than a win for any other person who has only one ticket. Nonetheless, it is very improbable that you will win. So you cannot reasonably be expecting to win and not expecting to lose. You cannot reasonably be surprised when you lose, and you would think it was completely mad to take out insurance against the eventuality of not winning.

## The surprise principle, and reasonable and unreasonable expectations

Suppose we put the two following facts side by side. The first is the fact that there is a vast amount of seemingly pointless pain and suffering in the world. The second is the fact that, approximately forty-two light years away, in the constellation Puppis, three large planets are orbiting a sun-like star.

Apart from the trivial fact that the two things are mentioned together on this page, and so are linked together in that way, what bearing does the one have on the other? And what expectations do you have about either one in relation to the other? To both questions, surely, the answer is "none." At the very least, it would be eccentric to expect either of the two things to be affected by the other.

Now let us make the same comparison, and ask the same questions, about these two things. The first, again, is that there is a vast amount of seemingly pointless pain and suffering in the world. The second this time is the idea that God exists.

Now, it is not at all eccentric to see a substantial connection between the two things, and to expect the one to have a significant bearing on the other. Why? It is because the concept of God is that of a supernatural person, an infinitely good, infinitely knowing, loving, powerful, designer and creator of the world. And, as we have noted, there is an essential connection between being a good and loving person and doing something, or at least wanting or trying to do something, about pain and suffering. Then, when we add in the idea of God as having infinite power, it seems reasonable to expect a high degree of correlation between God's wanting to do something about pain and suffering and God's succeeding in doing something about them.

By contrast with the distant planets question, the point seems to be that it would be eccentric not to have expectations of action by a good and powerful person who is aware of great suffering. At the least, that idea seems reasonable and plausible at face value. But if we think the original source of the universe is indifferent to pain and pleasure, and to good and evil generally, then the eccentricity would be in having expectations of that source to mitigate or eliminate evil, and to promote good. That idea too seems reasonable and plausible at face value.

The cornerstone of Draper's argument is the contrast between each of those ideas' fit with the facts of evil in the world.

### Draper's indirect argument

Judging on the enormous amounts of seemingly pointless evils, Draper finds the idea of God more surprising than the indifference idea. On the basis of such evils, then, he concludes that the idea of God is more improbable than the indifference idea. That is, he uses surprisingness as his guide to improbability. And from that judgment of comparative probabilities he concludes that the idea of God, in its own right, seems to be improbable, that is, seems less probable than not.[1]

Notice that the third of those conclusions is carefully qualified. It is that the idea of God, judged in its own right, seems to be improbable. Why the qualification? Why does Draper limit himself to concluding that the idea of God seems improbable, instead of concluding that it is improbable? The reason is that there may be some outweighing factors that offset or undercut the force of the evidence provided by the abundance of seemingly pointless evils in the world. For instance, there may be a successful proof that God exists, albeit not the design argument we considered in the two previous chapters. Or there may turn out to be some satisfactory explanation for the existence of evils that, right now, seem to be just pointless. Or, short of a satisfactory explanation of those evils, some satisfactory defense may be found against Draper's argument. For instance, some serious defect may be discovered in his argument. In upcoming chapters we will examine the possibility of a successful defense or

---

[1]   Paul Draper, "Pain and Pleasure: An Evidential Problem for Theists," in William L. Rowe, ed., *God and the Problem of Evil* (Oxford: Blackwell, 2001), 183.

a successful explanation. In light of all those open possibilities, then, Draper hedges his overall conclusion.

I noted that Draper's argument for the improbability of theism is indirect. Its indirectness comes from the fact that the main thrust of the argument is towards showing that, judged on the facts of evil in the world, the theistic hypothesis is less probable than the rival indifference hypothesis. Then, everything else being equal, the conclusion that the theistic hypothesis seems to be improbable is picked up as a consequence of that comparative point.

## Comparing probabilities

For the present, let us keep the various qualifying factors out of the picture, and examine Draper's argument only on the terms that have come up so far. As just mentioned, we will examine defenses and explanations in subsequent chapters. In that restricted context, now, suppose Draper is right about the theistic idea being less probable than the idea of indifference. If he is, then the improbability of theism itself in that context will logically follow.

To see that, consider this parallel case. Suppose that several mutually inconsistent hypotheses are offered to explain some phenomenon, say the mysterious flash detected near Prince Edward Island in 1979 that I referred to in chapter 5. For purposes of the example, it does not matter how many rival hypotheses are involved. So, to keep things simple, suppose there are just two. And suppose that all other factors are the same for both hypotheses.

Suppose that, just like theism and the hypothesis of indifference, those hypotheses are mutually inconsistent. That is a crucial point. It means that, if one is true, the other is false.

Now, suppose that, following a thorough investigation, one of those hypotheses is rightly judged more probable than the other. Let us say it is simpler and fits better with background knowledge. Let us call the better hypothesis Hypothesis A, and its rival Hypothesis B.

We know that Hypothesis A has higher probability than B, although we do not know the actual probability score of either one, or A's margin over B. But we know enough to know that the probability of Hypothesis B is less than 50 percent, that is, that B is less probable than not. How?

We know it like this. The negation or denial of Hypothesis B follows from Hypothesis A, for, being mutually inconsistent, if either is true, the other is false. So the probability that Hypothesis B is false is the same as the probability that Hypothesis A is true. But the probability that A is true is higher than the probability that B is true. Consequently, the probability that B is false is higher than the probability that B is true. And that is to say that Hypothesis B is less probable than not, which means that its probability is less than 50 percent.

### The relative probabilities of the theistic and indifference hypotheses

Let us bring the same logic to bear on the comparative analysis of the theistic and indifference hypotheses. In doing so, we keep in mind that they are mutually exclusive. So, if the hypothesis of God has lower probability than the rival hypothesis of indifference, then, everything else being the same, the probability of theism has to be lower than 50 percent. But probability lower than 50 percent means that the odds on being false are better than the odds on being true. All other factors being equal, Draper does judge the hypothesis of God to have lower probability than the indifference hypothesis. So, all other factors being equal, his conclusion is that theism is more likely false than true.

But the qualifying phrases, 'all other factors being equal,' 'everything else being the same,' and so on, are important. Without examination of the total picture, a probabilistic argument such as Draper's will at most establish that the idea of God is improbable, relative to a certain segment of the relevant factors. Hence, Draper's conclusion is that, all things considered, the existence of God seems to be improbable.

In this respect, probabilistic arguments for the non-existence of God are quite different from arguments such as the one from J. L. Mackie that we examined in chapters 3 and 4. For, if Mackie or anybody else succeeds in establishing a strict contradiction between the idea of God and some fact in the world, then, regardless of any other factors, the non-existence of God will have been proved without qualification. Any idea or hypothesis that is a strict contradiction of a fact has to be false.

Doubling back for a minute to our investigation in the two previous chapters, we can tack on a further point, as an addendum to the conclusion we reached in chapter 6. It is that, if Draper's conclusion is justified, then we have further reason not to conclude that an all-powerful and all-good God is the probable explanation of the universe. This is because, if Draper is right that the idea of God is less likely than the idea of indifference, then, everything else being equal, we are not entitled to conclude that God is the more-probable-than-not explanation of the universe.

### Draper's limited commitment to the indifference hypothesis

Draper's argument does not commit him to accepting the indifference hypothesis in its own right. His use of it for the purpose described, and his judgment that it appears to be more probable than the theistic hypothesis, do not mean he thinks the indifference hypothesis itself is more probable than not. He may think that, or he may not. The point right now is that his indirect argument does not require him to think it.

Consequently, his argument does not commit him to a naturalistic, as opposed to supernaturalistic, theory of the origin of the universe. Nor is he committed to deism, perhaps the supernaturalistic hypothesis having the best fit with the idea of indifference. His commitment is to rejecting one particular version of supernaturalism, namely, theism.

## III   Rowe's Direct Argument

Since the first version of William L. Rowe's argument was published almost thirty years ago, his position on God and evil has been influential and much discussed. By contrast with Paul Draper's indirect argument for the improbability of God's existence, Rowe's approach is direct. Like Draper, Rowe grants from the outset the logical possibility that God exists and that all evils are justified. Like Draper, Rowe focuses his attention on probability, not bare logical possibility.

### Looking for probable justification among great goods we know of

No matter how hard we try, we cannot seem to conceive of anything that could ever justify many of the terrible evils that occur in the natural world, as well as many of the terrible things that trace back to human responsibility. For instance, what justifies the destruction, the loss of life, the terrible suffering, caused by the Indonesian tsunami or the Holocaust? Or, on a smaller scale, what justifies the torture and dismemberment of a four-year-old child, the beheading of an infant because he was born into a rival tribe, or the protracted agony of a fawn, badly burned in a forest fire caused by lightning, lying unseen for days before dying?

What could ever convince us that, overall, it was better for the child to be tortured, the infant to be beheaded, or the fawn to suffer? Wouldn't we think it monstrous of someone to suggest that, overall, or on balance, those things were better than not?

Broadly speaking, we permit bad things to happen when we think a greater good would otherwise be lost, or when we think an equal or greater evil could not otherwise be prevented. That is the over-arching idea in the list of eight points about justified evils with which I began this chapter. Now let us think of some great goods and some great evils. Among the good things, surely, any reasonable person would agree to include genuine and permanent peace, cures for various terrible diseases, and eternity in the presence of God (supposing God to exist). Among great evils, we would include the torture of thousands of children, a plague with effects worse than all the effects of cancer combined, and eternity apart from God (supposing God to exist).

Now ask: How might the suffering of the fawn trapped by the fire, or the torture and dismemberment of the child, or cancer, contribute to the coming about of any of the aforementioned great goods? Or how might they contribute to the avoidance of the aforementioned great evils? How might the one be causally or logically necessary for the achievement, or the avoidance, of the other? We cannot think of any remotely plausible connection. If we were to substitute other great goods or great evils, we would fare no better.

But maybe that judgment is hasty. After all, what about this? The terrible treatment of the dismembered child, for instance, issued from libertarian free will, libertarian free will is of great value to morality, and morality has great intrinsic value. The train of thought in the suggestion is that it is necessary for God to permit the possible occurrence of such a terrible thing in order to achieve the great overall good of a world that includes morality.

Let us grant the suggestion for the sake of argument. But an obvious question that the suggestion prompts is this: Why are there no exceptions? Likewise with the Holocaust. Why is there no exception for Hitler? Why did he not have a quiet, or not-so-quiet, death in his sleep? Why would God never intervene? Granting, for the sake of argument, the great value of libertarian freedom overall, why is it without exception or restriction in certain extreme cases?

Part of the very concept of moral maturity is judging when to make exceptions. On the supposition that God exists, the absence of any exceptions suggests here, as did the robot-like regularity of natural laws we considered earlier, that, even if there is a mind behind the universe, it is perhaps not much like a human mind at all. And it may not be the kind of mind, or reflect a kind of value-system, that we would admire.

Suppose we did find a plausible reason for the fact that, as far as we can tell, there are no exceptions to the evil exercise of free will. And suppose we did find a plausible way of seeing libertarian freedom, with or without exceptions, as either necessary or unavoidable in the achievement of some great overall good or the avoidance of some great overall evil. Even if we made those large suppositions for the sake of argument, there would still remain the vast amounts of pain, suffering, waste of life, destruction, and so on that do not issue from the exercise of freedom at all.

The overall point is that, try as hard as we can, we cannot seem to come up with any justifying correlation between the great goods we can think of, on the one hand, and many of the terrible things that happen in the world, on the other. Any connections we might come up with seem remote and far-fetched, as remote and far-fetched as any we might imagine between suffering here on earth and conditions on those planets forty-two light years away in the galaxy Puppis. And the same holds true for the equal or greater evils that we can think of.

Since none of the justifying or compensating good things that we have experience of, or can conceive of, even remotely seem to justify or balance out many of the terrible things that happen often in the world, the reasonable conclusion is that probably there is no justification for such things, and no balancing out either. And a parallel point applies for equal or greater evils.

But if God exists, surely there would be such justification, or such *ex post facto* balancing out. Considering the very idea of God, it seems plausible to think there would have to be. Furthermore, it seems plausible to think we would have some idea, or at least some inkling, of those justifying or balancing factors. But we don't. So the reasonable conclusion is that probably there are none, which in turn means that probably there is no God.[2] That is the essence of Rowe's argument.

---

[2]  William L. Rowe, "The Problem of Evil and Some Varieties of Atheism," in M. M. Adams and R. M. Adams, eds, *The Problem of Evil* (Oxford: Oxford University Press, 1990), 128.

### Appearance and reality, and thinking realistically

Rowe's argument turns on a relationship between appearance and reality. Its central idea is that, for many terrible things, the way things seem to be is probably a good guide to the way things are. And the way things often seem to be is that many such things have no justification or no balancing or outweighing benefit. So the reasonable conclusion seems to be that this is the reality too. The reasonable conclusion seems to be that many victims are just unlucky.

Rowe's line of argument reflects the kind of thinking we employ day to day. We recognize that, within limits, anything is possible. However, in talking with the plumber or the doctor or the flight attendant, we are not guided by remote possibilities. In those situations, we have a robust and realistic sense of what is plausible or implausible. In those situations, we are not usually tempted by a far-fetched possibility, when options that do not strain credulity are open to us.

Suppose that, time and again, your friend ignores you when you are in need of help. Suppose, over and over, he or she is silent in the face of your suffering. Suppose, time and time again, your friend does not even try to help when, to all appearances, he or she could. Which of these would it then be the more reasonable and plausible for you to believe – that he or she is a good and caring friend to you in your need, or that he or she is not a good friend at all, but indifferent to your need?

True, this person may be withholding help, comfort, compassion, or solidarity for your own long-term good. And, true, he or she may have a very good reason to keep that fact secret from you. It may be that, for instance, he or she cannot help you on any occasion when you are in need, or speak tenderly to you, because his or her secret undercover life might then come to light, endangering you, your family, and many more people too. After all, anything is possible, within the limits of logical possibility. And so, it may be for your own, or for the overall, good that your friend lets you suffer, when to all appearances he or she could help. Likewise, the fact that he or she never once offered sympathy or consolation or encouragement may be for your own overall good.

But now, ask yourself, absent any evidence, with only the suggestion of that possibility to go on: How impressed are you? How much credibility would you be inclined to give to the suggestion, in the actual, concrete situation when your friend ignores your need for help? None, I imagine.

Rowe's argument, in essence, reminds us to bring the foregoing standards of judgment to the issues of good and evil in a supposedly God-made world. His point is that, when we do, we see it is a reasonable and well-supported judgment that, probably, there is no God. Are those standards appropriate to the issue? We would need a good reason to think they are not.

### *Rowe and Draper on possible explanations, and the indifference hypothesis in two strengths*

We left Draper's argument with the jury still out, so to speak, not having reached a verdict. Judging on the basis of terrible things that occur with no apparent justification or good reason, and with only the indifference hypothesis and the theistic hypothesis in the picture, Draper rated the former more probable than the latter. But he conceded that, before a final verdict could be issued, other factors would need to be taken into account. After all, there might be plausible theistic explanations of seemingly pointless evils. Or there might be defects in his reasoning. Or there might be a successful proof of God's existence.

By contrast, Rowe's direct argument for the improbability of God incorporates references to possible theistic explanations of evil right from the start. Consequently, the conclusion he draws is not provisional, in the sense of waiting for consideration of the main theistic explanations. However, like Draper's argument, Rowe's argument would fail if a serious defect were discovered in its reasoning or if a successful proof of God's existence were developed. For those reasons, then, our verdict on Rowe's argument too must, for the present, be provisional.

Put into the language of indifference, the gist of Rowe's position is that it is reasonable to conclude that the universe, apart from us, is indifferent to good and evil. As we saw, this is the core of naturalism. Naturalism embodies a full-strength version of the hypothesis of indifference. The gist of Draper's thinking is that, on the basis of seemingly pointless evil, the hypothesis of indifference is more probable than the theistic hypothesis, with the consequence that theism appears improbable. But this line of argument does not commit him to the further idea that the original source of the universe, if any, is probably indifferent to evils such as pain and suffering.

Looking at Rowe and Draper side by side, then, we see that, for Rowe, the probability is that the indifference hypothesis is true, whereas we are not entitled to attribute the same view to Draper. In Draper's case, we may not go farther than to say he thinks that, judging from the evidence of evil in the world, the indifference hypothesis is more probable than the idea that God exists.

Should believers be troubled by these arguments? Yes. For both arguments raise questions that reflective theists will want to ask and answer for themselves.

## Suggested Reading

Draper, Paul (2001) "Pain and Pleasure: An Evidential Problem for Theists," in William L. Rowe, ed., *God and the Problem of Evil*. Oxford: Blackwell.

Lewis, David (2007) "Divine Evil," in Louise M. Antony, ed., *Philosophers without Gods*. Oxford: Oxford University Press. Over and above the evils discussed by Draper and Rowe, and by Mackie (see chapters 3 and 4 above), those all being evils that God does not prevent or eliminate, the influential American philosopher David Lewis emphasizes evils that he describes as being caused by God.

Rowe, William L. (1990) "The Problem of Evil and Some Varieties of Atheism," in M. M. Adams and R. M. Adams, eds, *The Problem of Evil*. Oxford: Oxford University Press.

The essays by Draper and Rowe are widely available in anthologies.

# 8

# Skeptical Defenses

There are two main sorts of defenses against the arguments set forth in the previous chapter. I will call them technicality defenses and substantive defenses respectively.

Technicality defenses probe for weaknesses in the arguments themselves. The legal analogy is a defense that aims to trip up the prosecution's case by showing that it fails to meet its burden of proof. Such defenses aim to achieve either a pre-emptive dismissal of the case or a verdict of 'not proved.'

By contrast, substantive defenses take up the challenge of trying to explain the occurrence of so much seemingly pointless suffering and waste of life, as well as other terrible things, in a world supposedly made by God. Their aim is exoneration. The legal analogy is a defense aimed at showing that the accused person did not commit the offense, that he or she is innocent. Think of situations when an accused person wants more than acquittal. Sometimes he or she wants a verdict in the court of public opinion, as well as in a court of law.

We will examine the most prominent technicality defenses against Rowe's and Draper's arguments in this and the next chapter, leaving substantive defenses for chapters 10 and 11.

The technicality defenses deployed against Rowe and Draper are skeptical defenses. The essential point in them is that, insofar as the relationship between belief in God and the existence of evil is concerned, we lack access to crucial information. According to these skeptical defenses, the information in question is crucial, because without it we cannot reach a justified verdict on the relationship between belief in God and the occurrence of enormous quantities of seemingly pointless evil.

I will give a fuller description of those skeptical defenses shortly. For the present, let us note that they continue a long skeptical tradition in philosophy, a tradition stretching back to the fourth century BCE. Briefly, philosophical skepticism reflects an outlook that calls into question our capacity to know various sorts of things. For instance, the idea that we cannot know the future is a form of skepticism. Recall that the point came up in chapter 4, while we were examining responses to J. L. Mackie's argument that the joint existence of God and evil is a strict logical impossibility.

In the philosophical literature on these topics, it is common to distinguish between defenses and theodicies. Alvin Plantinga is prominent among those making the distinction. In his sense of the terms, what I have been calling a substantive defense is pretty much the same thing he and others call a theodicy. At the end of the next chapter, I will qualify this point with an exception. What I am calling a technicality defense is part of what he and others call simply a defense. In the interest of simplicity, I shall not use the terminology of defenses versus theodicies here. Instead, I shall continue to speak of technicality and substantive defenses.

## I   How Much of a Bad Thing Is Too Much?

How much of a bad thing is too much? The question is asked by the American philosopher Peter van Inwagen. It is an obvious question, and, at face value, a simple one. Yet answering it is difficult – perhaps, in lots of contexts, impossible. The question raises an important issue, relevant to the assessment of the arguments put forward by Draper and Rowe.

### The Goldilocks problem

What are the proper requirements for a grade in my Introduction to Philosophy course? Why not three of four short essays instead of two of three? Why not nine author-recognition questions instead of ten? I have no answer that rules out those alternatives as obviously wrong. They sound pretty reasonable. Indeed, I can't point to any set of requirements as being just right. If there is such a set, I don't know what it is. And I have more than twenty years' experience.

Van Inwagen's point is not just that, in many cases, it is difficult to say what amount is just right. His point is that, in many cases, there is no such amount. Suppose a parking fine in a particular town is $25.

But $24.95, or $24.99, would work just as well, and so would $25.05. Furthermore, perhaps there is no amount of frustration or disappointment that is just the right amount to allow a child to suffer for his or her own good.

Now apply van Inwagen's point to the underlying idea in Draper's and Rowe's arguments. Rowe's core idea is that much evil in the world is random and pointless. His basis for judgment is that we know a lot about good ends and evil means, but that no good end we can even conceive of would justify the vast amounts of evil in the world. Draper's core idea is that it is more surprising to find so much evil if God is responsible for the world than if God is not. It is the idea that the actual amount of evil goes far beyond what we would expect in a God-made world.

But the idea that such-and-such is either pointless or excessive presupposes that there are levels which are appropriate. Furthermore, to suggest that such-and-such is excessive presupposes some way of measuring what the appropriate level, the 'just right' amount, is. Likewise, the idea that such-and-such is random and pointless implies that there is some measure of what serves a purpose. Let us think of the problem of specifying the amounts or levels that are just right as the Goldilocks problem. In the story, remember, she found Baby Bear's porridge and bed to be just right, in contrast to those of his parents.

Given those ideas, van Inwagen is challenging Draper and Rowe to justify their assumptions and claims about excess, randomness, and pointlessness. He is challenging them to justify their depiction of the evils in the world as unexpected and surprising, if the world is God-made. It seems to be a perfectly reasonable challenge. After all, it seems reasonable to think that, unless and until they convince us that such-and-such is the measure or benchmark, they are not in a good position to convince us that the actual amounts are in excess of it.

Both the Goldilocks problem and the surprise principle that was our rule of thumb in the previous chapter seem reasonable. But discussing whether the vast amounts of terrible occurrences in the world make the existence of God improbable pits them against each other.

Implicit in van Inwagen's challenge is the idea that arguments such as Rowe's and Draper's must meet an initial burden of proof. It is the burden of clearly marking out the border between excessive and non-excessive amounts of evil in a God-made world. At first sight, the prospects of success appear to be discouraging.

### Finessing the Goldilocks problem

However, there may turn out to be less to van Inwagen's challenge than meets the eye. Let us apply common sense to the problem.

Take my Introduction to Philosophy class. I have certain expectations for achieving a grade, but I don't know the 'just right' expectations. And there may be none. But nevertheless, I do know, don't I, that the following standard is excessive, even for an 'A' grade – three papers accepted for publication in first-tier philosophy journals like *Mind*, *Nous*, or *The Philosophical Quarterly*? Likewise, we can't find the relevant difference between the $25 and the $24.95 parking fines, but we do know, surely, that public hanging is too much. To suppose otherwise is fanaticism or madness.

I do not know the 'just right' punishment for my child who dashed across the road right now, without looking left and right. Is no television after dinner throughout the weekend enough, or too much? How about gouging out an eye? If I can't solve the Goldilocks problem in the abstract, does that mean I cannot rank those two punishments, and reasonably choose one over the other? Of course not.

Even though there may be no solution in the abstract to the Goldilocks problem, it can't be reasonable to think that, in a God-made world, anything goes. Surely there is some level of misery, pain, suffering, waste of life, and destruction of all sorts that would be too much. Because we can't specify the cut-off point, are we wrong to think something is, or could be, excessive? William L. Rowe observes: "Surely there must be some point at which the appalling agony of human and animal existence on earth would render it unlikely that God exists."[1] To suppose otherwise, he maintains, is "unreasonable, if not absurd." Peter van Inwagen himself agrees that failure to solve the Goldilocks problem does not mean that anything goes.[2] In short, even if we cannot solve the Goldilocks problem in the abstract, it seems we can reasonably finesse it or bypass it.

---

[1]    William L. Rowe, "An Exchange on the Problem of Evil," in William L. Rowe, ed., *God and the Problem of Evil* (Oxford: Blackwell, 2001), 157. The other contributors to the "Exchange" are Michael Bergmann and Daniel Howard-Snyder.

[2]    Peter van Inwagen, *God, Knowledge and Mystery* (Ithaca, NY: Cornell University Press, 1995), 16–18.

The points about public hanging, eye-gouging, and college freshmen publishing in *The Philosophical Quarterly* seem to show the triumph of common sense over the potential for extremism implicit in the Goldilocks problem. Nonetheless, doesn't fairness in argument require us to be specific, if we are going to lay out an indictment of theism on grounds of excessive evil? Doesn't an indictment of anything require specificity? Here are two reasons to drive home the point in our present context.

First, by its very nature, the context of argument is different from, and is stricter than, the context of daily behavior. If I am making a case to support a conclusion that something is excessive, don't I have to be at least reasonably precise about the standards I am using to judge excess? Isn't that reasonable as an initial burden of proof? Think of how the issue might play out in a court of law.

Second, Rowe's and Draper's respective arguments are about the probability or improbability of God, which is something very different from the routine items of daily life, for instance, parking fines, standards of excellence in an introductory-level university course, and so on. Because the topic of the arguments is so distant from the mundane run of daily life, don't we need a pretty clear guideline in forming conclusions about it? That is, don't we need a solution to the Goldilocks problem to either formulate or assess arguments like Draper's or Rowe's, even if we don't need to solve it for day-to-day living?

This point disputes the idea that the undoubted reasonableness of finessing the Goldilocks problem in daily life translates over to a context of philosophical reflection on things remote from daily life. As we are no longer ignorant of philosophy behind the veil of ignorance, the point takes us back to David Hume.

Early in Hume's book *Dialogues Concerning Natural Religion*, the character who, more than any other, seems to speak for the author advises us to "become thoroughly sensible of the weakness, blindness, and narrow limits of human reason . . . even in subjects of common life and practice." A little further on, that character, Philo, develops the thought in this direction:

> When we carry our speculations into the two eternities, before and after the present state of things; into the creation and formation of the universe; the existence and properties of spirits; the powers and operations of one universal spirit, existing without beginning and without end; omnipotent, omniscient, immutable, infinite, and incomprehensible; We must be far

removed from the smallest tendency to scepticism not to be apprehensive, that we have here got quite beyond the reach of our faculties.[3]

If we do not set down specific criteria appropriate for judgments about supernatural things, how can we be sure that we haven't gone far "beyond the reach of our faculties"? It is a good question, providing good support to van Inwagen's Goldilocks principle. And if we think it is reasonable to specify such criteria, the next question is: What are they? This follow-up question provides further support to van Inwagen's principle.

## Being specific about a better world

Van Inwagen asks for greater specificity in another area too. He asks for a description of the laws of nature that would operate in a world where, supposedly, God could have prevented or eliminated various terrible evils, without sacrificing any great good. In addition, he requests a description of the (presumably different) initial conditions at the Big Bang, of the subsequent evolution of life, and so on, in such a world. In his words,

> One should start by describing in some detail the laws of nature that govern that world. (Physicists' actual formulations of quantum field theories and the general theory of relativity provide the standard of required "detail.") One should then go on to describe the boundary conditions under which those laws operate: the topology of the world's spacetime, its relativistic mass, the number of particle families, and so on . . . Finally, one should tell the story of the evolution of life . . . Unless one proceeds in this manner, one's statements about what is intrinsically . . . possible . . . will be entirely subjective, and therefore without value.[4]

The essential point is that, in putting forth the suggestion of a better world that God could have brought about instead of the actual world, Rowe, Draper, and others of like mind are not entitled to a free pass on

---

[3]   Hume, *Dialogues Concerning Natural Religion*, 36–7.

[4]   Peter van Inwagen, "The Problem of Evil, the Problem of Air, and the Problem of Silence," in William L. Rowe, ed., *God and the Problem of Evil* (Oxford: Blackwell, 2001), 213–14 (and in Daniel Howard-Snyder, ed., *The Evidential Argument from Evil*. Bloomington: Indiana University Press, 1996); also Peter van Inwagen, *The Problem of Evil* (Oxford: Oxford University Press, 2006), 117.

providing a reasonably detailed picture of the alternative world they are envisioning.

It seems to be a fair point. After all, in chapter 6, when we were discussing the hypothesis of fine-tuning, we asked for specificity about the substance of the conjectured fine-tuner and about the nature of the causation supposedly at work. Since those requests for more specificity were legitimate, then, by the same token, it would seem that so are van Inwagen's in the present context.

It is Hume's comparison between the indifference hypothesis and the theistic hypothesis that supplies the foundation for Draper's argument. And it is Hume's comparison between reasoning about things in daily life and about things involving supposedly supernatural beings that is the basis for the foregoing skeptical challenge to that argument. In effect, Hume is an expert witness for both sides. This is ironic, as he was not much in favor of the theistic hypothesis.

## II  Unreasonable Expectations

Let us now bring a second technicality defense into our discussion. Like van Inwagen's Goldilocks defense and his demand for design specifications of a conjectured world with less evil than the actual world, it is essentially skeptical in nature. It turns on claims about things beyond our capacity to know.

### A "noseeum" defense

The most famous and influential of the skeptical defenses of theism comes from Steven J. Wykstra. He calls it a "noseeum" defense. He takes the name from his background in the American midwest where, he tells us, "we have 'noseeums' – tiny flies which, while leaving a painful bite, are so small you 'no see um.'"[5]

The aim of Wykstra's defense is to undercut what he sees as over-reaching in arguments claiming that the abundance of terrible occurrences in the world tips the balance of probabilities against the idea of a perfect God. In particular, Wykstra's target is the expectation in such arguments

---

[5]  Stephen J. Wykstra, "Rowe's Noseeum Arguments from Evil," in Daniel Howard-Snyder, ed., *The Evidential Argument from Evil* (Bloomington: Indiana University Press, 1996), 126.

that, if the many evils in the world were ultimately justified, we would
be able to discover the justification, at least to some extent. But in many
cases we can discover no justification. If we then conclude that probably
there is none, we are assuming that how things appear to us to be
reflects how they probably are. In the previous chapter, we saw that was
the essential idea in Rowe's argument. Not surprisingly, Rowe's argument
in particular is the target of Wykstra's defense. If the idea that appearance is a good guide to reality is not justified in this kind of case, then
arguments such as Rowe's will fail. And the aim of Wykstra's defense is
to establish that, here, appearances are not reliable.

The basis of the defense is essentially the point made by Hume in the
lines quoted earlier. It is that, in thinking we can judge a supernatural
reality from a base in how things appear to us in the natural world, we
are stretching far "beyond the reach of our faculties."

As we saw, the step from appearance to reality in Rowe's argument
is not crude. It is not based on the obviously false idea that how things
seem to be is always how they are. Like you and me, he knows that is
not true. Consequently, his argument is not affected by the observation
that sometimes appearances are misleading.

Sometimes the ways things seem to be is indeed a good and reliable
guide to how they are. You and I operate on that supposition most of the
time. Right now, it seems to you and me that there are words in English
on the page in front of us. And like me, you don't doubt that at all, or
hesitate to act on it. When you are driving your car or playing tennis,
you take it for granted that, for the most part, how things seem to be is
indeed how they are.

Rowe's point is that we have quite a lot of experience and knowledge
about ends justifying means. We know that sometimes cures or treatments
for diseases are painful, so we know that the good of the cure cannot be
achieved without the painful treatment. Furthermore, we have a lot of
experience and knowledge of proportionality between the painfulness
of the treatment and the expected outcome. We weigh ends and means.
We juggle the combinations to try to find a good balance, and then we
decide as reasonably as we can.

But when it comes to the great amounts of awful things that happen
in the world, we cannot even remotely come up with what might be a
justifying reason for vast amounts of them, or a proportionality between
them and the occurrence of good things. Rowe's conclusion is that in
natural disasters, as well as in many other cases of seemingly pointless

suffering and death, the reasonable interpretation is simply that there is no point to them.

## Useless experience

In response, consider the following situations.

Suppose you are looking for a three-foot-square marble table. You are sent to look in a storage shed the size of a hangar built to hold a jumbo jet. That enormous shed is crammed with stuff. It is packed from the floor to within a few inches of the ceiling. You cannot even get into the shed, it's so full with old washing machines, tires, car doors, bicycles, beds, and so on. You stand at the doorway looking in. You do not see the table you're looking for. Should you conclude that the table you're looking for is probably not in the shed? Should you let appearances be your guide to the probable way that reality is in this case?

Suppose you are wondering if there are fleas in the garage. You stand there in the doorway of the garage looking in. You see no fleas. Should you conclude that probably there are no fleas in the garage?

Suppose your doctor wonders if this previously used hypodermic needle contains germs. She holds it up to the light and looks. She sees none. Should she conclude that, as no germs are apparent to the naked eye, probably the needle is germ-free? Would you feel OK to now be injected with that needle, or, for that matter, to continue as this doctor's patient?

Life has never been discovered on any planet other than the earth. Despite extensive searches, no signs of life elsewhere in the universe have been found. Should we conclude that probably there is no life elsewhere in the universe?

We should not draw any of those conclusions about the reality of things, based on the appearances of things. Why not? There are two main reasons. One is that we do not have enough information in any of those cases to justify a conclusion. The other is that the information we do have is not the right sort of information, or, in the space-exploration example, we cannot be confident that it is the right sort. In each case, with the information mentioned, we are not in a good position to make a judgment. To judge on the information available would be no better than blind guesswork.

Sometimes appearances are a good guide to reality. But other times they are not. Wykstra, Rowe, you, and I all agree on that. You look in the refrigerator to see if you need to buy milk. You see no milk there. Are you entitled to believe that you are out of milk and need to buy more? Probably, yes.

Now, which situation best resembles our failure to find reasons to justify God's permitting the many horrors in the world to occur? Is it the situation of failing to find the milk? Or is it failing to find germs in the hypodermic needle?

Wykstra's suggestion is that our viewpoint, relative to the truth about God and evil, is much more like the no-germs-visible-on-the-needle situation than it is like the no-milk-visible-in-the-fridge situation. And so his point is that we do not have a sufficient basis to draw a conclusion one way or the other. That is the essence of his skeptical defense.

### Motion to dismiss

When defense lawyers think that the prosecution is not entitled to introduce crucial information at trial, they will ask the judge to dismiss the charges against their client, for lack of evidence. In essence, that is what Wykstra is asking us to do here.

Here is an example. When defense lawyers think that the police have taken potentially incriminating documents from their client's house without a search warrant, or beyond the scope of the search authorized by the warrant, they will petition the judge to exclude those documents from the evidence against their client. And if the case against their client relies crucially on the information in those documents, they will ask the judge to dismiss the charges altogether.

Now, the basis of Rowe's argument is that no God-justifying reason to permit the vast amounts of pain, suffering, waste of life and so on is apparent to us among the many good things we know of. Wykstra does not disagree. But he denies it is a basis for concluding that, probably, there is no justification for those things. Emphasizing the enormous differences between us and an infinite supernatural being, if there is one, Wykstra maintains that we cannot justifiably go from how things look to us to how things might look to God. In a term sometimes used in legal circles, his point is that our failure to find a justifying reason has no probative weight or value. It is information right enough, but it is not evidence. Consequently, his defense is that, for lack of evidence, we ought to dismiss Rowe's argument and others like it, along with the charges reflected in them.

## III   A Third Kind of Skeptical Defense

### Van Inwagen again

Peter van Inwagen develops a second skeptical defense, in addition to the Goldilocks problem, although the Goldilocks problem remains an important part of that second defense. Aside from the Goldilocks problem, the skepticism in this second defense is similar to that in Wykstra's noseeum defense. It is David Hume's already cited point that, in venturing to make judgments about supposed supernatural objects, we extend far beyond the reach of our faculties.

In other respects, this defense is unlike Wykstra's. The essence of the difference is that this second proposal of van Inwagen's includes a possible explanation of why God might permit vast amounts of seemingly pointless evils. In effect, it is a combination of technicality and substantive defenses, whereas there is nothing of the latter in Wykstra's argument.

The substantive portion of van Inwagen's defense is a two-part story that, he maintains, is true for all we know. One part of it covers evils occurring since the origin of the human race, several hundred thousand years ago, while the other part covers evils before that time. Let us call the latter pre-historic evils. Obviously, none of them trace to human responsibility, whereas those evils covered in Part One of this defense will be both natural evils and moral evils.

### Part One of van Inwagen's two-part conjecture

The first part is a Garden of Eden story. In Christian mythology, the Garden of Eden is where Adam and Eve lived, in happiness and contentment, before they gave in to temptation and ate the apple that God had forbidden them to eat. In a variation on that story, van Inwagen conjectures that at some time in the distant past the human race was quite small, with all its members living in one area. He conjectures that the human race at the time lived in happiness and contentment, that it was immune to disease and death, and that people had paranormal powers. In his words,

> Because they lived in the harmony of perfect love, none of them did any harm to the others. Because of their . . . [paranormal] . . . powers, they were able somehow to protect themselves from wild beasts (which they were

able to tame with a look), from disease (which they were able to cure with
a touch), and from random, destructive natural events (like earthquakes),
which they knew about in advance and were able to escape. There was
thus no evil in their world. And it was God's intention that they should
never become decrepit with age or die.[6]

Perhaps, like me, you don't believe a word of this. However, for van
Inwagen's purposes, that doesn't matter. His purpose in making this conjecture does not require belief or even believability. He says of himself
that he doesn't disbelieve any of it. His point is that, if God exists, this
story could be true for all that anybody knows.

What does the requirement of being true for all we know mean?
The expression is not an exact term, and van Inwagen does not define
it. Nonetheless, it seems pretty clear that its intended meaning falls
somewhere between probability or plausibility, on the one hand, and mere
logical possibility, on the other. For instance, in Part Two of this defense,
he says that to succeed in establishing that his conjecture is true for all
we know, he does not have to establish that it is plausible or probable.[7]
So, 'true for all we know' is a weaker standard than plausibility.

The key to the concept appears to be the skeptical idea that we are not
in a position to say with justification that something is false. After all, if
there is a supernatural being who is omniscient, omnipotent, and perfectly good, who are we to say for sure what is and is not in fact true?

This amount of description of the term's meaning will be enough
for setting forth van Inwagen's second skeptical defense, although not
enough for reaching a verdict. For that, we will need to see how close to
mere logical possibility the concept goes. We will come back to that in
the next chapter. (A side note before proceeding: van Inwagen overstates
things a bit in the lines quoted. For he describes the Garden of Eden as
without evil, even though animals still suffer and die there.)

Van Inwagen's conjecture goes on to suggest that, for whatever reason,
those early human beings "abused the gift of free will and separated
themselves from . . . God." The result was "horrific." Among other things,
"they now faced destruction by the random forces of nature, and were subject to old age and natural death." In essence, van Inwagen is telling a
hell-on-earth story about the horrors of separation from God.

[6]   Van Inwagen, *The Problem of Evil*, 86.
[7]   Van Inwagen, *The Problem of Evil*, 120.

Next, he speculates that, in response, God devised a rescue operation. The goal of the operation is to provide opportunity for human beings to see the error of their ways, to atone for going wrong, and to once again love God. But atonement requires knowledge of wrongdoing, and both atonement and the kind of love in question require free will. The upshot is that the rescue is possible only when human beings recognize that they need to be rescued. And that recognition will only come from seeing the terribleness of life separate from God.

All this being so, if God were to cancel out the horrors of the world, he would be depriving human beings of opportunity to see both the true awfulness of separation from God and the error of their ways. But if he did that, he would be depriving people of opportunity to achieve the bliss of union with God. So, if God canceled the horrors of the world, he would be guaranteeing the failure of his own rescue plan. But God could never do anything self-defeating. Consistent with his rescue plan, then, God could not cancel the horrors of the world. But this inability of God's does not subtract from his omnipotence. For, as we saw in chapter 2, omnipotence does not include the power to do logically impossible things, and van Inwagen's idea is that God's canceling the horrors of the world would be logically incompatible with his own rescue plan.

Even so, couldn't God cancel some of those horrors without compromising his plan? Yes, it seems he could. Van Inwagen would not dispute it. But he would remind us that this idea takes us back to the Goldilocks problem. For, granting that there is no 'just right' amount of horror needed for human beings to see the error of their ways, and thus for the rescue plan to be feasible, there might always be some left-over horrors that could have been eliminated, without compromising the plan. And, for all we know, perhaps the horrors in the actual world fall into that 'left-over' category.

In order to be clear on van Inwagen's point about possibly 'left-over' horrors that perhaps could be eliminated, it may be useful to recall the example of the $25 parking fine. The point in the example is that some of that amount – say 5 cents – could be eliminated without compromising the effectiveness of the remaining $24.95 as a deterrent. Van Inwagen's point now is that perhaps some of the horrors in the world fall into an equivalent '5-cent' category, relative to everything else going on in the universe.

If so, then van Inwagen would agree that some horrors could be eliminated without compromising any divine plan there might be, say the 'rescue' plan he conjectures. So, why would God not eliminate them? It is an obvious question. But so is this: Why would the town council not eliminate the 5-cent difference between $25 and $24.95, and adjust its parking fine to the lower rate? Suppose the council did. But then the same question comes up about the difference between $24.95 and $24.90. And likewise, van Inwagen is arguing, with eliminable horrors in the world.

His point here is not just that we do not know the cut-off point, below which the parking fine would no longer be as effective as before. His point is that, for all we know, there is no such cut-off point. For the thrust of his Goldilocks argument that we examined earlier is that, in many situations, there is no definitive answer to the question: What is the 'just right' amount? In many cases, there may be an objective vagueness. The fact of the matter may be that $24.90 would work just as well as $24.95, which would work just as well as $25, which would work just as well as $25.05.

Let us bring this back now to van Inwagen's point about eliminable evils in a supposedly God-made world. The main idea is that, for all we know, there may be no amount of evil such that any amount greater than it would automatically be too much and any amount less than it would automatically be too little, relative to any divine plan there might be. So his point is that, no matter what the state of the world might be at any given moment, there may always be evils that could be eliminated without compromise to any such plan.

When we take the Goldilocks idea into consideration, we do not blame or condemn the town council for keeping the parking fine at $25, even though the fine would probably work just as well at $24.95. And the thrust of van Inwagen's argument is that we should think about God and eliminable evils in the same sort of way. In essence, then, his position on eliminable evils comes down to two points. The first is that we should acknowledge that we have no reliable way to measure whether any particular horror is too much in a God-made world. And the second is that, therefore, we are in no position to say of any particular horror, no matter how bad, that it is evidence that probably there is no God.

An example with bigger numbers than those in the parking fine may help in understanding his position clearly. After all, the universe is vast and has been expanding rapidly for almost fourteen billion years, and there is an enormous amount of terrible things here on earth. Very briefly, then, here is a version of a 'big numbers' example that van Inwagen uses.

Suppose the penalty for some particular crime is ten years in prison, with no parole. Factoring in two leap years, that makes 3652 days. Suppose the purpose of the prison sentence is a combination of punishment and deterrence. Would the sentence be less effective at 3651 days? Surely not. So the extra day is not needed for the sentence to be just as effective as it would be at 3652 days, and could be eliminated. Suppose it is eliminated and the sentence is cut back to 3651 days. Now you know what the next question will be. Wouldn't the sentence work just as well at 3650 days, and so on? If you have the time and inclination, run the same sequence of questions in terms of hours, starting at 87,648, then in terms of minutes and seconds. The start-up numbers in those cases are 5,258,880 and 315,532,800, respectively. And then there are nanoseconds, where the starting number is a billion times 315,532,800.

For all we know, there are no cut-off points below which the parking fine or the prison sentence or the quantity of evil would no longer be just as effective as before, or above which they would be excessive and should be eliminated. But, without a cut-off point, it seems we have no principled way to say of any particular amount of evil that it is too much or too little. That is van Inwagen's point. A distinction is a principled distinction when it is neither arbitrary nor just tailor-made to fit some particular circumstance, without being able to fit other circumstances which are not different from that particular one in any significant or relevant way.

The conjecture of a Garden-of-Eden story and of a subsequent rescue plan, together with continued reliance on the Goldilocks problem, is the first part of van Inwagen's mixed substantive–technicality defense. The second part covers evils in pre-historic times. By definition, none of those trace to human responsibility.

## Part Two of van Inwagen's two-part conjecture

Let the sufferings of pre-historic animals stand for all evils not covered by Part One of van Inwagen's story. This is a bigger category of evils than those addressed in Part One. After all, there have always been many more animals than people, and the span of time in question is far longer than that since the emergence of *Homo sapiens*, millions of years compared to hundreds of thousands.

Couldn't God have prevented the sufferings of pre-historic animals? For instance, couldn't God have intervened in nature to prevent such things? Van Inwagen would grant the possibility that God could have done so, inasmuch as God's power is sufficient for the task. But his conjecture goes on to speculate that such interference with the normal course of nature might have caused massive irregularity in nature. He suggests that such irregularity might have been an overall bad thing, perhaps as bad as, or even worse than, the badness of all pre-historic animal suffering combined.

Van Inwagen's next point is that, for all anybody knows, the foregoing conjecture is true. We are not in a position justifiably to say it is false. That is the essential skeptical point. And, if it is true, God, being omniscient, would know it. So, for all we know, God's justification for not preventing pre-historic animal suffering was his wish to prevent an equally bad or worse situation.

Van Inwagen's aim is not to advocate the two-part rescue and disruption hypothesis as being the truth. His aim is to establish the skeptical point that we are in no position to make an informed decision either way. And likewise in any side-by-side comparison with a rival hypothesis, for instance the indifference hypothesis. Why not? Because a justified, well-informed verdict would require capacities and powers, as well as access to information, that we simply do not have. Thus, like Wykstra, van Inwagen is arguing that Rowe's and Draper's respective conclusions must be set aside as not proved. In effect, this two-part defense is the basis of a motion to dismiss those conclusions.

## IV   Interim Verdict on Draper and Rowe

There may be no solution in the abstract to the Goldilocks problem. Nonetheless, that does not justify concluding that there is no evil-based case for the believer to answer. To conclude that defies reasonableness, for it seems to mean that, in a God-made world, anything goes.

The situation is different with the two other skeptical defenses. Although different in their details, Wykstra's noseeum defense and van Inwagen's second skeptical defense overlap in challenging the idea that commonsense standards of reasonable judgment apply to the problem of God and evil. Each of those defenses emphasizes that our limited, finite perspective may not be a good basis for a judgment of probability or improbability, insofar as an infinite, supernatural being is concerned.

At this point in our investigation, both of those defenses look strong enough to block the arguments of Rowe and Draper respectively. Accordingly, our interim verdict is that one or both of those defenses seems to succeed, and that the existence of God has not been shown to be improbable.

## Suggested Reading

Van Inwagen, Peter (1996) "The Problem of Evil, the Problem of Air, and the Problem of Silence," in Daniel Howard-Snyder, ed., *The Evidential Argument from Evil*. Bloomington: Indiana University Press.

Wykstra, Stephen J. (1990) "The Humean Obstacle to Evidential Arguments from Suffering: On Avoiding the Evils of 'Appearance,'" in M. M. Adams and R. M. Adams, eds, *The Problem of Evil*. Oxford: Oxford University Press. This article is available in many philosophy-of-religion anthologies.

Both of these works are a bit technical in places, but a non-specialist will still be able to get the gist of them. By contrast, Peter van Inwagen's most recent work on the problem of evil is quite accessible to a non-specialist readership. It is:

Van Inwagen, Peter (2006) *The Problem of Evil*. Oxford: Oxford University Press.

# 9

# Evaluating Skeptical Defenses

Suppose you are leaving your young child at the babysitter's, or your dog at the kennel. Your friend says to you that, whether the babysitter is good or not, or whether the kennel staff are good or not, should have no bearing on the service you expect. You would think that was complete nonsense, wouldn't you? And Stephen J. Wykstra would agree.

But we should not be surprised to find the world being the way it is if God exists, and we should not be surprised to find the world being the way it is if God does not exist. Either way, we should not be surprised. We should not expect God to make a discernible difference. We should not expect commonsense standards to work when we think about God and evil. That is the essence of Wykstra's noseeum defense.

To see that it is the core of his defense, go back to the hunt for the marble table in the cluttered shed as big as the biggest airplane hangar. The table is either in there or it is not. But you should not be surprised to find things looking the way they do, if the table is there. And you should not be surprised to find things looking the way they do, if the table is not there. Likewise with the doctor looking for germs, and the same with the other examples used to introduce the noseeum defense. Either way, you should not expect things to look any different. And so you should not be surprised by how things look, no matter how they look. The conclusion in each of those examples is right. Of course the huge shed would look the same to you either way, and so would the hypodermic needle, and so on.

As we saw in the previous chapter, the key question is whether those examples are good analogies for our capacity to form a justified opinion about God and evil, based on our experience. If they are good analogies, then, insofar as the occurrence of terrible evils and the existence of God is concerned, we must give up the idea that the world can enlighten us one way or the other.

# I  Side-Effects of Wykstra's Noseeum Defense

Dr Wykstra is prescribing strong medicine, and sometimes strong medicines have negative side-effects. Let us see if there are such side-effects here.

### *'Anything goes' versus the Goldilocks problem*

The essence of the noseeum-style examples is that, sometimes, how things seem to us is not a guide to how they are. Rowe's response is that, on the noseeum defense, then, anything goes:

> what [the noseeum] view comes to is this. Because we cannot rule out God's knowing goods we do not know, we cannot rule out their being goods that justify God in permitting any amount of evil whatever that might occur in our world. If human and animal life on earth were nothing more than a series of agonizing moments from birth to death, the [noseeum] position . . . would still require [us] to say that we cannot reasonably infer that it is even likely that God does not exist . . . But surely such a view is unreasonable, if not absurd. Surely there must be some point at which the appalling agony of human and animal existence on earth would render it unlikely that God exists. And this must be so even though we all agree that God's knowledge would far exceed our own.[1]

It is hard to see how a theist could think that anything goes. Yet to deny that anything goes is implicitly to grant that some amount of evil would be excessive. But then the theist, no less than Draper or Rowe, must solve or get around the Goldilocks problem.

However, to attempt to specify amounts of seemingly pointless evil that would or would not be excessive is inconsistent with the forms of skepticism advocated by Wykstra and van Inwagen. Attempting such specificity implies that we are in a position to tell, however roughly. But both of their skepticisms are based on denying that very point.

---

[1]  Rowe, "An Exchange on the Problem of Evil," 156–7.

Consequently, the dilemma for both seems to be: either accept that, for all we know, anything goes, or solve the Goldilocks problem. In essence, Rowe's accusation that, on the noseeum defense, anything goes, seems to cause the Goldilocks problem to boomerang.

What if the theist, unwilling to go all the way to 'anything goes' and unable to solve or finesse the Goldilocks problem, pleaded ignorance? What about a skeptical theistic response to the dilemma of choosing between those two inhospitable options? This would mean saying that he or she doesn't know whether anything goes or not. For all we know, maybe it does or maybe it does not.

This implies accepting that maybe, for all we know, anything goes in a God-made world. But this is no less odd than coming right out and accepting that, for all we know, anything does go. Either way, there is the very same problem of reconciling that thought with the concept of a perfect God. The 'maybe' does not diminish the oddity. So it does appear that Rowe's 'anything goes' challenge presents the theistic skeptical defender with a serious dilemma.

## The cost of bulletproofing

The noseeum defense aims to bulletproof theism. But a bulletproof theory or hypothesis may be less of a good thing than it seems initially.

The philosopher of science Karl Popper (1902–94) famously characterized scientific theories as essentially falsifiable. In his view, a theory is not a scientific theory unless, in principle, there is something that could happen, or be discovered, that would disconfirm the theory or prove it false. If there is no such thing, then nothing that happens or could happen makes any difference to the theory. And so the theory cannot be telling us anything definite or specific about how things are, or will be, in the world. If it is compatible with anything and everything that could happen, then it is not identified with telling or predicting that some specific thing happens, or will or won't happen.

True, the theistic ideas that God exists, made the world, watches over it with loving care, and has a plan that is working itself out in the world, do not combine into a scientific theory. And that is not a fault in those ideas, or a criticism of them.

But while the essential theistic claims about God are not scientific claims, neither are they just 'feel-good' claims, or claims devoid of overlap with, or implications for, the physical universe. Instead, they are claims that reflect a definite and specific view of the universe itself: for instance, that it was designed and brought about by God, who is an infinitely good and powerful person. In effect, the core theistic idea is a bipolar idea, with one of its two poles inside the domain of our experience.

That being so, is it reasonable or unreasonable to think that, at least in principle, acquaintance with one of the two supposedly related poles could give us something to go on in forming a concept of the other pole, or of the relationship between the two? The core idea in Rowe and Draper is that it is reasonable.

They are not the only ones to think so. Many influential thinkers of the theistic tradition itself, Thomas Aquinas and Richard Swinburne for instance, agree. Their respective arguments for the existence of God testify to it. And a very large cohort of theistic believers, perhaps the majority, hold some sort of similar view. At face value, it is a reasonable and plausible view.

In the lines quoted above, Rowe asks: What if all human and animal life from start to finish were uninterrupted agony? Suppose some of the victims are theists who accept Wykstra's defense. Consistent with that defense, it would be unreasonable for them to wonder if the world squared with the idea that a providential God designed it, brought it into being, and watches over it with loving care. Notice we are not talking about the outcome of the wondering, just the reasonableness of wondering in the first place.

Without suggesting that theism is a scientific theory, for of course it is not, we may wonder if it is really a plus that theism, on the noseeum defense, would be immune to question on the basis of our experience of evil. Nor does wondering this require or imply endorsement of Popper's theory of science.

Why might such immunity not be a plus? The reason is that, if an idea is compatible with literally anything that happens or might happen, as well as with anything that doesn't happen, then we have good grounds to think it may be completely vacuous.

Here is an example of too much immunity. Suppose you are the pitcher in a baseball game, and you consider throwing a fastball to the next batter. Suppose I am the catcher on your team, and you ask me what I think will happen if you throw that pitch. Suppose my answer is, "Something." I say to you that something will happen. And suppose I leave it at that. Well, come what may, my answer will stand up. Why? Because it is without specific content.

Let us run a further test on Wykstra's defense hypothesis. Suppose we apply his skeptical defense to the idea that the original source of the universe is an infinitely powerful, but also infinitely evil, being.

On this hypothesis of a perfectly evil source, what would be a reasonable expectation about the world? Before hearing of Wykstra's defense, I think we would have thought that things would be pretty bad, much worse than they are. Before hearing of his defense, I expect we would think there would be even more diseases, accidents, natural disasters, death camps, and so on, than we actually find to be the case. But on Wykstra's defense, those expectations would be illegitimate.

Suppose you were asked if it would be reasonable to expect the world to be the very same, whether brought about by an omnipotent evil being or by an omnipotent good being. Pre-Wykstra, I think you would answer no, that it would be reasonable to expect the nature of the creator to make a discernible difference in the creation, especially if the creator is supposed to have infinite power and so on. But post-Wykstra, if we accept the noseeum defense, we are committed to answering that, as far as we could expect to be able to tell, there would be no difference.

Perhaps you don't agree with me on this. Perhaps your view is that it's a mistake to expect to detect a difference. The next point may be a useful means of testing that idea.

## Moral indecision

We often try to do good rather than evil. We try to lead good moral lives, as we understand the concept. In this regard, theists often see themselves as acting in accordance with what God wants and values. But now, on the noseeum defense, it seems that theists would have just as good reason to think that, in doing an apparently good deed, they are actually furthering an overall evil outcome, intended by an omnipotent, infinitely evil creator, as they have good reason for thinking they are furthering the will of God.

I imagine a believer's initial response to this suggested implication of Wykstra's defense will be that the suggestion is nonsense. Yet the thrust of the noseeum defense is that the world gives us no guidance at all in grasping God's intentions. For all we know, doing this apparently good deed, saving the child who fell in the stream, may be completely at odds with what God wants. But whatever God wants is overall good.

So, for all we know, doing this apparently good deed may be completely at odds with what is overall good. Keep in mind that the core of the noseeum defense is that, in regard to our capacity for drawing justified conclusions about God, the ways that things appear to be cannot be assumed to be a good guide to how they really are. Consequently, the noseeum defense seems to turn a central precept in the moral outlook of many religious people, namely, that doing good is doing the will of God, into a recipe for moral indecision. It seems to make religion useless as a moral compass.

## Noseeum defenses and equilibrium in the concept of God

The theistic concept of God is of a being at once alien and familiar. On the one hand, it is the concept of a being beyond the physical universe, a personal being who is intrinsically non-physical, infinite in goodness, power, and knowledge, a being who is eternal and present everywhere simultaneously, a being who is essentially simple, which is to say, not composed of parts or dependent on anything for its existence.

In their own right, these are strange ideas. The words may be familiar, because of the prevalence of religion, but the ideas are strange nonetheless. It is very hard to understand what they mean. And it is even harder to grasp the idea of a single thing possessing all of those traits at the same time. That reflects the alien side of the concept of God.

But, on the other hand, there are familiar features in those concepts too. They are the features that reflect our own experience. Among them are the concepts of being a person, of goodness, power, knowledge, and mind. Once we take away the notion of infinity attaching to those qualities, they become graspable.

It seems to be an important feature of the theistic concept of God that the familiarity of some of its constituent features mitigates the strangeness of the overall picture, at least up to a point. For instance, infinite and perfect knowledge is gestured at, inasmuch as it is supposed to be like our knowledge, just a lot more. And the same thing applies to the ideas of infinite power and infinite goodness, respectively.

We think of goodness in our own case – being fair, kind, honest, trustworthy, compassionate, charitable, helping those in need when and as much as we can, and so on. Then we think of persons better than we are in those respects. Then we imagine the goodness that is the common content of our own and those better persons' goodness raised by an immense factor. In doing that, we suppose ourselves to be gesturing, by analogy and in a tolerably meaningful way, towards the idea of perfect or infinite goodness.

Now bring the noseeum defense into the picture. Doing so upsets the balance of the familiar and the strange in the concept of God. On the noseeum defense, we are not in a position to have any opinion at all on whether a world with horrible diseases, natural disasters, murder, rape, child abuse, plagues, sudden infant-death syndrome, torture, and so on, or a world with none of those things, is the better fit with the theistic concept of God. Either way, the noseeum defense forbids an opinion that would be drawn from our experience of things here and now. For all we know, it could be the one or the other, or some third thing that we cannot even imagine.

Let us briefly develop the point about the risk to the comprehensibility or intelligibility of the theistic concept of God, with respect to the idea of goodness.

### Noseeum defenses and the concept of moral goodness

For the sake of argument, let us grant the noseeum defense its central point. It is that we cannot legitimately expect to discover God's justification for permitting the many terrible things that happen and that, as far as we can judge, could have been prevented by God. It seems that God permits them, but we do not understand why.

But how, then, are we to understand the concept of divine goodness? For we cannot even imagine thinking that a human being who permitted such things, while having knowledge and power to prevent them, could be good. Among the side-effects of the noseeum defense, then, is a serious unbalancing of the theistic concept of God, and of the concept of divine goodness in particular. For, on that defense, the concept of divine goodness seems to become unfamiliar to the point of incomprehensibility. It seems profoundly different from what we consider human goodness to be.

That unfamiliarity then calls into question the theist's concept of God as the exemplar or model of moral goodness for us. For if we cannot understand how the concept of divine goodness compares to human goodness, the idea that the one could be the exemplar for the other is undermined.

Nonetheless, perhaps the noseeum defender will want to stick with the traditional theistic idea that divine goodness does reflect the true nature of moral goodness. But doing so creates problems of its own. The reason is that, given the apparent dis-analogy between divine and human goodnesses that we noted above, we cannot trust our judgment that things such as caring for the sick are really good after all. This brings back an earlier point about moral indecision. For instance, to us, fallible human beings, it seems that preventing child abuse is a very good thing. Likewise, alleviating animal suffering, or helping the sick or the elderly, seem to us to be good things. And similarly for prevention of torture, rape, diseases of all sorts, and so on. Who could possibly think otherwise?

But divine goodness, the goodness of a being with access to infinitely more power and knowledge than we have, never, as far as we can tell, prevents such things. So, our conventional supposition to the contrary notwithstanding, maybe it is not really good in the overall scheme of things to prevent child abuse or animal suffering, or to care for the sick or the old, and so on. In the complete and eternal scheme of things, perhaps doing nothing about such things is best. Perhaps doing something about them furthers an overall bad outcome or delays or interrupts an overall good outcome. Perhaps the reality is that, in doing what we think is good, we are fools rushing in where angels fear to go.

I'm sure most theists do not believe this at all. I'm sure they think the idea is simply preposterous. Nonetheless, theists who accept the noseeum defense will not be entitled to believe that doing something about terrible evils furthers an overall good outcome or to disbelieve that it furthers an overall bad outcome. For them, an open mind on the issue is part of the cost of accepting the noseeum defense's skepticism about appearances and reality. And to see how acute a problem this would be for them, put yourself in their place and imagine yourself saying, "I really can't say if preventing child abuse is overall a good thing or not."

The noseeum defense also seems to cut against arguments that try to establish the existence of God on the basis of various facts about the world, for instance the fine-tuning argument that we discussed in chapters 5 and 6. The strength of the noseeum defense is its refusal to allow experience to be a basis for opinions about anything supernatural, and that includes inferences of a conjectured supernatural source of natural order and of the universe's suitability for life.

## II    Verdict on Noseeum Defenses

The cumulative impact of the various side-effects we have been talking about is that the noseeum defense seems to put the concept of God well beyond our comprehension. In addition, it seems both to undercut any theistic foundation for moral thinking and living and to undermine any inference of God, based on experience of things in the world. In essence, then, Wykstra's prescription for combating the arguments of Rowe, Draper, and other like-minded thinkers seems to come down to fighting the case for the improbability of God by implicitly building a case for the incomprehensibility of God. At the least, this high cost testifies to the power of the problem of seemingly pointless evil in a supposedly God-made world.

### *Inclining towards fideism*

In chapter 2 we came across fideism, the 'faith alone' conception of religious belief. It rejects in principle any significant role for reason or evidence in the justification of faith. Now, in light of our examination of Wykstra's noseeum brand of skepticism, it is natural to wonder if his defense takes him close to fideism.

True, he engages in argument. But, in the last analysis, it is argument aimed at denying access by reason to any opinion on divine agency that is based on our experience of the world. In the end, his defense is a way of disallowing evidence that, if not disallowed, might threaten the belief that God exists. And that is an essential trait of fideism.

Perhaps the fideistic understanding of religious faith is the right one. That is not the issue now. What is in focus now is what seems to be the direction of Wykstra's defense, and the cost to theists of accepting it. If this suggestion about fideistic leanings in the noseeum defense is right, then theists inclined to accept or use it would need to examine the conceptual neighborhood to which that acceptance or that use may be relocating them.

## III    Evaluating van Inwagen's Second
## Skeptical Defense

The core idea in Wykstra's noseeum defense is that our here-and-now experience is not a reliable guide to the supernatural. Van Inwagen's point in his second skeptical defense is related, but different. Unlike Wykstra's defense, Van Inwagen's permits speculation, as well as the formation of hypotheses, about the vast amounts of seemingly pointless evil in the world. An obvious case in point is his own hypothesis of a Garden of Eden and a subsequent rescue plan. But, while we may come up with hypotheses to cover evils, his essential skeptical point is that we are in no position to then evaluate and pass final judgment on them. In his view, we are not able to get at the facts necessary to justify a final verdict on the various rival hypotheses.

Very briefly, let us recall the hard problem of consciousness, referred to in chapter 6. Essentially, it is the problem of explaining how the brain generates consciousness. Some thinkers, sometimes called mysterians by themselves and others, argue that the problem may be, in principle, beyond our capacity to solve. That is, there is a problem which we more or less understand; we think about possible solutions to it and come up with theories; but in principle we cannot discover the truth. Some mysterians about consciousness are distinguished philosophers, Colin McGinn for instance. Now, allowing for the different subject matter, van Inwagen's second defense seems to amount to a similar kind of mysterianism, insofar as the problem of God and evil is concerned.

In van Inwagen's view, this mysterianism favors the defender of theism. For, if the truth of none of the competing theories can in principle be established, then Rowe, Draper, and others cannot establish their respective conclusions about the improbability of God. Of course, by the same logic, the theist cannot establish a conclusion about the probability of God either. But, for purposes of defense, that does not matter. Given the nature of a defense, and especially its relatively light burden of proof, Wykstra's and van Inwagen's respective defenses are not required to establish that the theistic idea itself is true or probably true. For instance, a defendant in a criminal trial does not have to prove lack of guilt in order to get off. 'Not guilty' is the default position in that context, and the burden of proof rests on the prosecutor.' Similarly, Wykstra and van Inwagen claim defensive success, if neither Rowe nor Draper establishes his conclusion about the alleged improbability of God.

There is also another similarity between the two defenses. It is that, insofar as efforts to prove the existence of God, based on facts in the natural world, are concerned, the same side-effect applies to both. Like Wykstra's, van Inwagen's second skeptical defense does not marry with efforts such as Swinburne's design argument, or Aquinas's arguments in the thirteenth century, to conclude that God exists, based on facts about the natural world.

### Looking for a comparative verdict

The essential point in both Wykstra's and van Inwagen's defensive strategies is that, lacking adequate access to the decisive facts, we cannot definitively judge any of the rival hypotheses true or probably true. Indeed, we cannot even definitively judge that those are the only viable hypotheses. After all, the truth may be something we have never even imagined.

We found ourselves in a similar position before. In chapters 5 and 6, thinking about the origin of the universe, we examined various rival hypotheses. The principal ones were the multiverse hypothesis, the chance hypothesis, and the design hypothesis. We didn't know enough to make a definitive judgment that would settle the question, or even enough to know that those hypotheses are the only candidates. Nonetheless, we saw that we could still rank them. Our example at the time was that of buying a car. Even though we may not judge any of the cars we test-drive good enough to buy, and even though we may discover later on that a car we had not even considered is better than any we examined, we can still justifiably rank as better and worse those cars we do consider. Let us apply the same thinking to Draper, Rowe, and van Inwagen. That is, while accepting that we cannot definitively judge any of their respective hypotheses true, and while we cannot be sure that those are all the viable hypotheses, we may still be able to reach a verdict by comparing and ranking them.

In pursuit of a verdict in this indirect way, let us bring forward another idea from that earlier discussion. It is that, everything else being equal, we should prefer the simplest hypothesis that adequately covers the data we have. Let us begin this comparative evaluation with Draper and Rowe, and then bring in van Inwagen.

Both Draper's and Rowe's hypotheses cover the data pretty well, and both are simple. The essential idea in Rowe's hypothesis is that there is no caring being behind the universe, that there are only the blind laws of nature, utterly indifferent to pleasure and pain, happiness and misery, good and evil. Draper's hypothesis differs from this in certain ways, but in none that matters at present. Draper's version of the indifference hypothesis is open to a deistic as well as a naturalistic interpretation, as we saw before, whereas Rowe's is naturalistic through and through. As such, Rowe's version is the simpler of the two. Furthermore, while Rowe endorses the idea of indifference, Draper does not go beyond using it comparatively. True, neither of them can solve the Goldilocks problem in the abstract. That is, while each of them maintains that the amount of evil in the world seems excessive for a supposedly God-made world, neither is able to specify how much evil would not be excessive. Neither of them is able to quantify the amount of the alleged excess.

However, as Rowe points out, it surely cannot be the theistic position that just anything goes, that no amount is too much. A thousand Holocausts, twenty tsunamis a month, a plague of cancer; surely not just anything goes, in a God-made world. But if that is the theistic position, as surely it must be, then, as we saw, theists too need a solution to the Goldilocks problem. For they too acknowledge a concept of excessive evil in a God-made world. The upshot is that the Goldilocks problem seems to favor neither side above the other, and so seems not to be decisive. Accordingly, a motion to dismiss Rowe's or Draper's arguments on that basis is not warranted.

Let us now bring van Inwagen's hypothesis into the picture. As we saw in the previous chapter, there are two parts to it. Part One is a Garden of Eden story plus a divine rescue plan. Part Two covers pre-historic evils. Its conjecture is that preventing them might have caused other evils as bad as, if not worse than, those evils themselves. In now evaluating van Inwagen's hypothesis, I will concentrate mostly on Part One.

## The Garden of Eden

Van Inwagen speculates about the human race originally not being subject to the failings of old age or to death. He speculates about people having paranormal powers in the Garden of Eden: for instance, power to tame wild beasts merely by looking at them a certain way, to cure disease merely by touch, and to know when and where natural disasters were about to occur, thus giving themselves opportunity to escape injury or death in them. Before turning to the 'rescue' portion of the conjecture, let us examine the situation just summarized.

There doesn't seem to be much point in asking van Inwagen for greater specificity regarding natural processes in the Garden of Eden. For

instance, there doesn't seem to be much point in asking about the bio-
logical processes at the level of the cell, in beings who were not subject
to the effects of aging, or in diseased tissue that was cured by touch. There
doesn't seem to be much point in asking, for we can anticipate his
response would be a conjecture that God was working miracles in the
Garden of Eden.

It seems plausible to think he might make this response. For one thing,
the concept of miracle-working is in his story already. Expressing doubt
about some aspects of the theory of evolution, van Inwagen speculates
that God "miraculously ... [raised] ... to rationality" the immediate
ancestors of *Homo sapiens*, thus making them human persons like us (apart
from those paranormal powers and so on, of course).[2]

In order to shed additional light on the concept of miracle-working
in the Garden of Eden, let us switch briefly to a question about Part
Two of his hypothesis. The question is: If human beings, with just a
look, could avoid being killed or injured by animals, and if they could
cure disease with merely a touch, and so on, without causing massive
disruption in the process, why couldn't or wouldn't God have worked
similar miracles to prevent pre-historic evils? Van Inwagen's answer, as
we know from the previous chapter, is his conjecture that the scale
of miracle-working that would have been required would have created
a situation just as bad as, if not even worse than, the pre-historic pain
and suffering itself.

That idea in hand, let us switch back to Part One. Van Inwagen's conjecture about the massive disruption that pre-historic miracles would have
caused suggests that the conjectured level of miracle-working in the
Garden of Eden is less than a level that would cause massive disruption
in nature.

### A new Goldilocks problem

But if that is his position, then a new Goldilocks problem seems to
come up. For to be justified in saying that a particular level of miracles
is less than the amount that would trigger massive disruption, it
seems necessary to be able to specify the tipping point, the level of
miracle-working that would be too much. If van Inwagen were to propose that the level of miracle-working in the Garden of Eden was below

---

[2]   Van Inwagen, *The Problem of Evil*, 85.

the tipping point, then presumably he can tell us where the tipping point is. It seems just as reasonable to ask for specificity about this as it was in the original Goldilocks problem, when van Inwagen himself asked it of Rowe, Draper, and others of like mind.

Perhaps van Inwagen would respond as follows. Perhaps he would seek to either finesse or neutralize the point by emphasizing the smallness of the human population at the time. Perhaps he would suggest that, short of solving the new Goldilocks problem, it would be permissible to suppose the scale of miracle-working would be fairly small, as the human population was small. Perhaps he would try to finesse the problem that way. After all, William Rowe's 'not anything goes' idea enabled him to finesse the original Goldilocks problem.

But if van Inwagen did make that response, it would hardly do. For his Garden of Eden story seems to reflect God's expectation that the human race would continue to live in "the harmony of perfect love." If so, then presumably the scale of miracle-working would have grown proportionately with the human population, which is now well over three billion. Consequently, that maneuver to get around the new Goldilocks problem seems blocked. In addition, the rescue component of the hypothesis, which presumably would have been in God's mind from the start as part of contingency planning, would involve alternative miracle-working on a massive scale. For instance, think of all the freedom from aging and death that would come with the successful rescue of millions or even billions of people.

### A dilemma

Van Inwagen's Garden of Eden story is either a miracle story or not. That 'either/or' seems to issue in the following dilemma for his defense. If it is a miracle story, then, consistent with his demand of Rowe, Draper, and others, a new Goldilocks problem seems to come up. That is, specificity is needed regarding the cut-off point, below which miracles do not cause massive disruption. But if it is not a miracle story, then, consistent with his other demand of Rowe, Draper, and others, about the design specifications of a world with less evil than the actual world, van Inwagen must provide specificity about the laws of nature and so on that are operating in the Garden of Eden.

Now let us take up the 'rescue' portion of van Inwagen's conjecture, the situation following the fall from grace.

## Knowing about the rescue plan

A crucial point in this conjecture is that, to be rescued, human beings must come to know the error of their ways and to recognize that the only solution is atonement, plus love of God. For instance, the story goes, if they atone and love God, then, like their ancestors in the Garden of Eden, they will no longer be subject to death.

An obvious question comes up about the advertising of the rescue plan. Why isn't it adequately publicized? After all, it is a plain fact that many people never even know of it. For instance, think of all those who die young, with no inkling of this conjectured opportunity for atonement and freedom from death. Considering the current and past human populations of the earth, the number of people affected would seem to make the toll in the Holocaust small by comparison. Furthermore, as described, it is the only opportunity for human redemption. Consequently, wouldn't it be the right and the decent thing for the rescue planner, especially one who is omniscient, omnipotent, and perfectly good, to ensure there would be equal opportunity for all to be rescued? As things stand, however, the rescue plan seems to be 'tough love,' minus the love, for enormous numbers of innocent people.

I think van Inwagen's response might be that this merely takes us back once again to the original Goldilocks problem. For, if there is no 'just right' amount of evil in a God-made world, there may always be some amount of eliminable horror in the world. And perhaps the fates of those millions, if not billions, who never know of the rescue plan just fall into that category.

However, considering the numbers involved, to say that seems the equivalent of simply saying that anything goes. But, as we saw, that cannot be the theistic position.

## The plausibility of the rescue conjecture

A further question concerns people who do hear of the rescue idea but who, through no fault of their own, find it implausible and so ignore it. Take the supposed link between atonement and freedom from death. Even some people who describe themselves as religious find that implausible. After all, it is literal death that is meant. That is, unless the Garden of Eden story is seriously misleading, the freedom from death that comes up in it means that there are no funerals for dead people, no burials or cremations, in the Garden of Eden; for there are no dead people there. Considering that even many religious people do not believe in literal freedom from death, the question comes up: Why is the rescue plan not made known in terms showing literal freedom from death to be a plausible idea?

Another facet of the story that would strike many unbelievers, as well as many reflective believers, as implausible is the scale of the "horrific" consequences of the 'free will' rebellion in the Garden of Eden. Death, disease, natural disasters, and so on for several hundred thousand years and counting, as a fitting consequence for the abuse of free will by a small number of people, seems massively disproportionate. The disproportionality recalls that between the age of the universe and the time since the evolution of *Homo sapiens*, as well as that between the size of the universe and the size of the earth, in suggestions that human life is the point of the universe's existence.

But, in the previous chapter, didn't we see van Inwagen say that his conjecture did not have to meet a standard of plausibility? Yes. So how can we now be justified in bringing a point about implausibility against him? Hasn't he immunized himself against such questioning?

I hope a distinction will clear things up. When van Inwagen claims that his defense need not meet a standard of plausibility, and so ought not to be judged by one, he is talking about a criterion of admissibility for his story to get into the discussion in the first place. He is talking about winning a hearing for his hypothesis, alongside other hypotheses. But when we wonder why the rescue component in the story would strike many people today as implausible, we are talking about a key feature within the story. In raising the question, we grant that the story has already been admitted into the discussion. Granting that, the question asks about a character in the story, God, who is depicted as having a certain objective. And the question reflects the point that, within the story, we legitimately expect that character to behave in a plausible way, insofar as achieving his own objectives is concerned. If he does not, it is a defect in the story, which undermines the story, relative to rival stories with greater internal coherence, for instance the hypothesis of indifference.

Here is an analogy to clarify the distinction. Take the story of Goldilocks and the three bears. For the story's purposes, for it to be interesting to young children, say, or to be a morality tale for other people in addition to young children, do we have to think it is plausible that bears live in cottages, cook porridge, sleep in beds, speak in English, and so on?

No, of course not. In regard to all of those things, real-world plausibility can safely be suspended. It would be tiresome pedantry to object to the story on those grounds. Liken that to van Inwagen's point about his own story, namely, that it does not have to meet a standard of plausibility in order to be admitted into discussion of God and evil. Now to a different point about plausibility.

Within the story of Goldilocks and the three bears, within the world of the story, having granted all the points about living in a cottage, making porridge, and sleeping in beds, we can expect the bears and the little girl to act in character. That is, we expect plausibility in their respective behavior. For instance, we expect Baby Bear to think and behave one way and Papa Bear another, and so on. Likewise, within the world of van Inwagen's story, we expect plausibility of the characters and situations.

Now God, as a character in the Garden of Eden story, is depicted as having the objective of rescuing human beings, by providing them with opportunity to be saved from the "horrific" consequences of the fall from grace. The key to their salvation is their freely changing their lives. And the key to that is their believing various things, a crucial one of which is the link between atonement and freedom from literal death. But, for many people nowadays, it is not at all plausible to suppose human beings can avoid literal death, whether by atonement or otherwise. Nothing in their experience supports the idea. Indeed, virtually all of their relevant experience supports regarding it as just wishful thinking. Consequently, within van Inwagen's story, it is implausible that a rescue plan thought up by an omnipotent, omniscient, perfectly good God would not be more credible or realistic to those who are its intended beneficiaries and who, through no fault of their own, live in separation from God. And that is a defect in the story.

A variation on this brings up a question about justice in the Garden of Eden story. It is another question about credibility or plausibility within the story. In biblical language, think of it as a question about "the iniquity (that is, the sins) of the fathers." The question is an obvious one. How could it be right for a person's children or other descendants to be punished for his or her wrongdoing?

The God of the theistic religions is described as a God of justice and love, as well as of knowledge and power. But, according to van Inwagen's conjectured defense, this God permits the "horrific" consequences of the abuse of freedom by a small number of people in the distant past to be felt by all subsequent members of the human race. But what is their offense?

For all we know of justice and of the love that parents have for their children, is it really true for all we know that the innocent should suffer for the offense of the guilty? Is it fair for all we know that the youngest children in a family should be allowed to suffer for the bad behavior of the first-born?

How are we to understand the concept of a just and loving being who knowingly permits that, and whose rescue plan is either never known by many descendants of those original sinners or is never known by them as something that is plausible? At the least, the concept of such a just and loving being is deeply mysterious.

## True for all we know: three questions

Van Inwagen claims that his story of a Garden of Eden, a rescue plan, and the avoidance of massive disruption in pre-historic times is true for all we know. To evaluate this claim, and the defense that depends on it, we need to know what is meant by something's being true for all we know.

In the previous chapter, we saw that van Inwagen does not define the concept. However, we know that he means it to be a weaker standard than plausibility, but stronger than mere logical possibility. Guided by those points, let us now investigate the meaning of the term. Let us do so by posing three questions. And to save time, let us continue to concentrate on the Garden of Eden aspect of his hypothesis. Each of the three questions presents a way of understanding the idea that the Garden of Eden story is true for all we know.

### First interpretation of 'true for all we know'
Is van Inwagen's Garden of Eden story possibly true, supposing there is a God? The answer seems to be yes. There seems to be no contradiction in it. But mere possibility is not a sufficient answer to the challenges posed by either Rowe or Draper, and van Inwagen knows it. Against an argument aimed at establishing the improbability of something, a defense of that thing's possibility is not enough. You tell me it is improbable that someone would survive a 10,000-foot fall from an airplane. I respond that it is logically possible. Which of us has the better of that exchange over probabilities and improbabilities? You do, even though you do not (let us say) deny the truth of my response.

If 'true for all we know' comes to no more than this, it is not enough. But is that what it comes to? We have reason to suspect it is. In the previous chapter, I suggested that the core of the concept's meaning is the idea that we are not in a position to say for sure that something or other is false. To investigate what that amounts to, suppose I ask you if a person would survive a 10,000-foot fall. You say no. I respond by asking if you can say that for sure. You say yes. Then I ask if you can say it *for sure*. Now, in your imagination, say the words 'for sure' with stronger and stronger emphasis, while thinking of miracles or freakish happenings, and notice how that nudges the standard closer and closer to bare logical possibility. Hence the suspicion that van Inwagen's 'true for all we know' standard either may not be far from mere logical possibility or may not be able to draw a clear line between itself and mere logical possibility.

*Second interpretation of 'true for all we know'*
Is van Inwagen's story probably true, supposing there is a God? That is, supposing there is a God, is it more probable than not? Is its level of probability over 50 percent? To that, we cannot say. We don't have enough to go on. Van Inwagen seems to be right about that. Anyhow, as we saw, he denies that something's being true for all we know means that it is probably true. So we can dismiss this second interpretation of the term.

Given that van Inwagen wants (and needs) the standard to be more than just bare possibility, and given that we cannot say if the probability level of something's being true for all we know is above 50 percent, can we identify some probability range to which it belongs? That seems like an obvious question in the circumstances. And a good way to attempt to find out would be in comparison with its principal rivals. That is, it seems commonsensical to see if we can identify the probability level of the Garden of Eden story as being above, below, or approximately the same as that of the main opposition. For, given Rowe's finessing of the original Goldilocks problem, both Draper's and Rowe's respective versions of the indifference hypothesis remain viable challenges to, as well as viable alternatives to, the theistic hypothesis. Consequently, not to compare the three seems tantamount to avoiding the heart of the matter. So back we go to our pursuit of a comparative verdict.

*Third interpretation of 'true for all we know'*
Is van Inwagen's story more probable than, less probable than, or equi-probable to the indifference hypothesis? Notice that something important is missing from the question. It has no context for comparison of the two

things. By contrast, notice the context in the two previous questions. In each of those, context was supplied by the qualifying phrase, 'supposing there is a God.' Furthermore, that is the context van Inwagen himself emphasizes in presenting his defense hypothesis. Why is it omitted here? Clearly, that needs explanation.

The reason is that it has to be omitted. Otherwise, the third question will not be a fair question, reflecting a genuine inquiry, but only a sham. For, as we saw in the two previous chapters, the indifference hypothesis and the theistic hypothesis that God exists – the latter being an essential part of van Inwagen's conjecture – are mutually exclusive. So, if we frame the third question on the supposition that God exists, we are simply prejudging the indifference hypothesis false. Consequently, if we are going to attempt a genuine comparison between the indifference hypothesis and van Inwagen's hypothesis, as rival substantive hypotheses, we need the veil of ignorance or something much like it. We need a context with no prior commitment or even inclination to theism, to atheism, or to agnosticism. We need one that will give us a chance to see how things stand independent of those perspectives.

True, both by asking a comparative question and by changing the context, we are asking a different question from the one that van Inwagen himself wants to ask. Yet this third question is an obvious one to ask, in evaluation of his defense.

## The three hypotheses compared: Draper, Rowe, and van Inwagen

Let us compare the rival hypotheses in the four following areas. Doing so will summarize the foregoing evaluation of van Inwagen's second defense.

### Simplicity
Behind the veil of ignorance, van Inwagen's conjecture is far less simple and straightforward than the indifference hypothesis. For one thing, the justice and efficiency of the deity in his conjecture are difficult to square with the supposed all-around perfection of the theistic God. By contrast, Draper's and Rowe's versions of the indifference hypothesis are simple and straightforward, with the concept of God in them equally so. The core idea in the indifference hypothesis is that, absent God, the mix of good and bad occurrences in the world is not surprising, being in line with what we would expect from the blind and indifferent forces of nature. By contrast, on the theistic hypothesis, either the mix of good and bad

in the world is not in line with what we would expect and so it is surprising, or we are not entitled to any expectations or any opinions at all about that mix. But, either way, further questions come up and further explanation is needed. Either way, the theistic hypothesis at the heart of the Garden of Eden story is less simple than the indifference hypothesis.

_Miracle story or not?_
The Garden of Eden story is either a miracle story or not. If it is not, can we really agree that it is true, for all we know behind the veil of ignorance? After all, if it is not a miracle story, it seriously conflicts with what we know in various fields of science, for instance human biology. It could still possibly be true, of course, despite seriously conflicting with our current best scientific knowledge, but no more than that. So, if it is not a miracle story, and if we set aside the mere logical possibility that it is true, then it is not true for all we know behind the veil of ignorance.

Now suppose it is a miracle story, which seems truer to van Inwagen's intent anyway. But if it is a miracle story, then, behind the veil of ignorance, its being true for all we know seems to amount only to the mere possibility that it is true. Behind the veil of ignorance, that is the most that can be said for appeals to miracles.

Either way, then, behind the veil of ignorance, 'true for all we know' seems to boil down to the mere logical possibility of the Garden of Eden hypothesis.

By contrast, the indifference hypothesis conjectures neither miracles nor things deeply at odds with our best scientific knowledge. Its fundamental point is that, given what the sciences tell us of nature, the mix of good and evil, pleasure and pain, and so on is unsurprising.

_The new Goldilocks problem and design specifications_
If van Inwagen's Garden of Eden story is a miracle story, he faces a new Goldilocks problem. And, as we saw, he does so without the prospect of finessing it. By contrast, neither Rowe nor Draper faces the new Goldilocks problem. But if the Garden of Eden story is not a miracle story, van Inwagen needs to be specific about the laws of nature and other things in that conjectured period of the world's history. But if he must be specific about those design features, he is no better off in that regard than Rowe or Draper, in their conjectures about a world with less evil than the actual world. Taking both things together, then, his hypothesis ranks behind the indifference hypothesis here too.

*The original Goldilocks problem*
Neither Rowe nor Draper solves the original Goldilocks problem in the abstract. But we saw that theists must solve the same problem, and are no better off insofar as doing so is concerned. Things seem equal between the two sides in that regard. However, Rowe's point that not anything goes in a God-made world means that the theist cannot rest content with this parity. That is, the indifference hypothesis can finesse the Goldilocks problem, but it is not clear that the theistic defender can.

On the basis of the foregoing comparisons, then, van Inwagen's hypothesis ranks below both versions of the indifference hypothesis.

## A comparative verdict

Van Inwagen's hypothesis is incompatible with each of the two versions of the indifference hypothesis. If either is true, his is false, and vice versa. So, by ranking either of them above van Inwagen's, on the same scale of probability or plausibility, we rank the probability of van Inwagen's hypothesis as less than 50 percent.

Take Rowe's hypothesis, for instance. Behind the veil of ignorance, we rank it as more probable than van Inwagen's. Given their mutual exclusiveness, its level of probability reflects the level of improbability of van Inwagen's hypothesis. Consequently, the improbability of van Inwagen's hypothesis ranks higher than its probability. But that can only be so if the probability of van Inwagen's hypothesis is less than 50 percent. Probability of less than 50 percent means being less probable than not. That is, it means being improbable. So, ranking van Inwagen's hypothesis below Rowe's and Draper's, our verdict behind the veil of ignorance is that his hypothesis, his mixed technicality–substantive defense, is improbable.

True, behind the veil of ignorance, we cannot definitively rule it out. What he conjectures remains a possibility. And if the concept 'true for all we know' means only bare logical possibility, then van Inwagen's hypothesis is true for all we know.

It is also true, as we noted earlier, that perhaps an argument will be developed that will establish the probability of God's existence, even by the standard in effect behind the veil of ignorance. After all, it is the standard that the design argument we discussed in chapters 5 and 6 sets for itself. If such an argument were developed, that would curtail, and perhaps over-ride, this verdict.

For those reasons, then, this verdict is not unconditional. It is a verdict reflecting the perspective of ideal non-partisanship, and thus it disallows things that a committed theist would draw upon. And it is conditional upon the judgment that no argument has successfully established the probability of God's existence.

This verdict that van Inwagen's Garden of Eden hypothesis is improbable, behind the veil of ignorance, does not mean that either Rowe's or Draper's version of the indifference hypothesis is probable. Judging their hypotheses more probable than van Inwagen's does not mean that they are more probable than not. That remains an open question.

We will come back to these things in the final chapter.

## IV   Overall Verdict on Skeptical Defenses

A serious side-effect of both Wykstra's and van Inwagen's defenses is that they seem to make the concept of God virtually incomprehensible. In addition, Wykstra's defense seems to undercut the very concept of theistic morality. From our perspective behind the veil of ignorance, van Inwagen's substantive conjecture is improbable.

At the end of the previous chapter, we issued an interim verdict. It was that the skeptical defenses offered by Wykstra and van Inwagen blocked Rowe's and Draper's arguments. However, in light of further considerations, our verdict now is that they do not block or defeat Rowe's or Draper's arguments. Those arguments maintain that, judging from the facts of evil in the world, the existence of God is or seems improbable. So let us turn now to a different kind of theistic response to those arguments.

## V   On to Substantive Defenses

Suppose Swinburne's design argument succeeds. It would show that the existence of God is more probable than not. That would make an excellent, albeit indirect, defense against Rowe and Draper. To borrow terms from Peter van Inwagen, it would mean that the abundance of seemingly pointless evils was a "difficulty" for theism, but not a serious threat to falsify it.

But Swinburne's argument does not show the existence of God to be more probable than not, and no better arguments seem to be available. So that kind of indirect, substantive defense seems to be unavailable. Indirect substantive defenses of this sort are not theodicies. They are the exception, promised at the start of chapter 8, to my policy of equating substantive defenses with theodicies. Broadly understood, a theodicy is an attempt to explain, in a way that is compatible with theism, the fact that many terrible things happen in a supposedly God-made world.

Let us turn, then, to direct substantive defenses. The foregoing exception having been noted, what I mean by direct substantive defenses is what I said just above in definition of the term 'theodicy.' To repeat, then, direct substantive defenses are attempts to explain, in a way that is compatible with theism, the fact that many terrible things happen in a supposedly God-made world. Van Inwagen's second kind of skeptical defense, his 'mixed' defense, goes some of the way toward this, but let us now look to go further in that direction.

## Suggested Reading

Howard-Snyder, Daniel; Bergmann, Michael; and Rowe, William L. (2001) "An Exchange on the Problem of Evil," in William L. Rowe, ed., *God and the Problem of Evil*. Oxford: Blackwell. This excellent and accessible exchange is also available in Michael L. Peterson and Raymond J. VanArragon, eds, *Contemporary Debates in Philosophy of Religion* (Oxford: Blackwell, 2004).

Van Inwagen, Peter (2006) *The Problem of Evil*. Oxford: Oxford University Press.

# Part V

# Evil and Design (2)

# 10

# Greater-Good Defenses

The basic idea you will find running through this chapter and the next is that sometimes the ends justify the means.

## From technicality to substance

Unlike the defenses examined in the two previous chapters, those to be considered now accept that there is a case which theism needs to answer, and they take on the substantive task of trying to answer it. They do this by trying to explain the occurrence of terrible evils in a world supposedly made by God. The aim is to win on the substance of the issues discussed, not on a technicality involving either the admissibility or inadmissibility of evidence or our capacity justifiably to choose among rival hypotheses.

Recalling a point from chapter 8, substantive defenses of the sort we will be examining in this and the next chapter are sometimes called theodicies. A legal analogy would be when the defendant goes in the witness box to explain himself.

Substantive defenses are needed for three reasons. First, as I argued at the end of the previous chapter, the main skeptical defenses are not successful in keeping the facts of seemingly pointless evil from being serious counter-evidence to the idea that God exists. Second, the most influential of the skeptical defenses, Wykstra's noseeum defense, has serious implications for the theist's understanding of God as a perfectly good, omnipotent, and omniscient person. So, even if the defense succeeds, success is expensive. Third, we all have a strong desire to understand the world as much as possible. In line with that desire, reflective believers wish to understand why the world is imperfect in so many wasteful and destructive ways. Recall Pope Benedict XVI at Auschwitz asking: "Why, Lord, did you remain silent? How could you tolerate this?" His words show that the desire for understanding and explanation is evident at the top of the religious establishment, no less than lower down. And even if a skeptical defense were to succeed, that desire would remain unmet.

For some theists, substantive defenses are needed for a fourth reason. Those are theists, Richard Swinburne for instance, who try to infer the existence of God from various facts about the world. And, as we saw, skeptical defenses seem to pull against that enterprise.

## I  Hick and Swinburne

*Common cause on common ground, and two big disagreements*

As reported in the newspaper, the pope did not, on his visit to Auschwitz, attempt to answer his own questions. The two prominent theistic philosophers whose work we will now examine do. They are John Hick and Richard Swinburne, the most influential English philosophers of religion of the twentieth century. Each of them has put forth a substantive theory to explain the vast abundance of seemingly pointless evils. Their respective defenses share a good deal of common ground. In the following list, I set down the fundamental points on which the two defenses have significant agreement.

1  The need for explanation. In Hick's words, the defender of the theistic view must address "this baffling problem of excessive and undeserved suffering."[1] In similar vein, Swinburne says he is sympathetic to the puzzlement "why a God might bring about natural evil of the quantity and intensity which this world contains."[2]
2  The concept of a divine plan centered on human flourishing. If the world is indeed brought about by God, then presumably it reflects a plan. Both philosophers agree in speculating that humans' welfare,

---

[1]  John Hick, *Evil and the God of Love* (San Francisco: Harper & Row, 1978), 335.
[2]  Richard Swinburne, "Knowledge from Experience, and the Problem of Evil," in William J. Abraham and Steven W. Holtzer, eds, *The Rationality of Religious Belief* (Oxford: Clarendon Press, 1987), 165.

and especially our flourishing and self-realization, are an important part of that plan.

3   Libertarian free will and a free-will defense. Genuine self-realization presupposes free choice. Both Hick and Swinburne understand freedom of choice in the libertarian sense discussed in chapter 4. On the libertarian view, the expression 'caused free choice' is self-contradictory. On this concept of freedom, when I freely choose, I alone am the agent of my choice and I always have the viable option of choosing something else instead. A libertarian free-will defense is central in the account of evil developed by both philosophers. In Swinburne's words, it is "the central core."[3]

4   Justification by way of serving the greater good. Both defenses turn largely on the idea of justification of evil in terms of a greater good. Sometimes this involves the idea that evils are justified as the means necessary to achieving a greater good; sometimes it involves the idea that evils are justified as unavoidable byproducts of the means necessary to achieve a greater good. Broadly speaking, on greater-good defenses, evils due to free choice, moral evils, belong in the second category, while some natural evils, evils not due to free choice, belong in the first category.

5   Afterlife. The concept of life after death is an essential component of Hick's defense, and it plays a role in Swinburne's too. For Swinburne, though not for Hick, the concept is an addition to ideas that play a more central role in the greater-good defense.

Notwithstanding the considerable amount of common ground between their defenses, and apart from differences of emphasis in areas where they fundamentally agree, Hick and Swinburne differ on two important points. First, Swinburne's defense provides for afterlife compensation for unjustified evils, but Hick rejects this idea.[4] Second, Swinburne is the foremost contemporary advocate of the project to infer God as the original cause or source of the universe, but Hick thinks that project is stillborn.[5]

---

[3]   Swinburne, *Is There a God?*, 98.
[4]   Hick, *Evil and the God of Love*, 340–1.
[5]   Hick, *Evil and the God of Love*, 244.

*What a divine plan for human life might involve*

Both defenses reflect a theistic stance to begin with. As such, they are defenses of theism from the inside, as opposed to being externally based defenses. That being so, in order to examine these defenses fairly and comprehensively, we must grant their theistic perspective from the start. So, for the sake of argument, we do.

The theistic perspective reflects the idea of a divine plan for the universe. In a widely used term that Hick borrows from the poet John Keats (1795–1821), the main provision in that plan, as it applies to human life, is the idea that the world is intended to be a place of "soul-making." In close proximity, Swinburne speaks of the world as a place where human beings have opportunity to make "a free and responsible choice of destiny."

In the term "soul-making," think of the word 'soul' as meaning self or person. That is, the defense does not require any esoteric notion of a ghostly non-physical thing, though it does not dismiss that either, of course. The term 'soul,' in the expression "soul-making," is intended to reflect an essentially ordinary and uncontroversial concept of a person. So, substituting 'self' or 'person' for 'soul' will not weaken the greater-good defense in any way. Perhaps the contrary.

In chapter 6, discussing the fine-tuning hypothesis about conditions in the universe in the first seconds after the Big Bang, we worried about lapsing into the view that the entire universe exists for the sake of human life. But now, are we not agreeing, for the sake of argument, to that very thing?

The danger is mitigated by the fact that the concept of a divine plan in Hick's and Swinburne's defenses does not insist on human life as the point of the universe. Consequently, it will be sufficient to grant, for the sake of argument, the more modest idea of a divine plan that includes the flourishing of human life. Anyway, fairness requires granting the platform on which the defenses are constructed. So we can hardly go forward without permitting those defenses to make their case on the terms of their choice.

## II  Moral Evil and the Free-Will Defense

We discussed the free-will theory of evil, and the libertarian concept of freedom in particular, in chapter 4, so a sketch of the theory here should be enough to remind us of the essentials. A libertarian free choice by a human being is beyond even the infinite power of God to cause; libertarian free will is necessary for moral development; moral development is an important goal in the divine plan for the world; and a world with libertarian freedom is better overall than one without.

But freedom, being freedom, means that evils such as murder, torture, theft, dishonesty, cruelty, and so on, can result. However, according to the free-will theory, these outcomes are, on balance, justified from God's perspective. The responsibility and blame for them are said to be ours, the perpetrators', not God's. Accordingly, the free-will theory claims that moral evil can be justified in a God-made world.

Swinburne calls the free-will defense the central core of the greater-good explanation of evil. Consequently, the plausibility of the free-will defense is the key to the plausibility of that explanation overall. And the plausibility of the libertarian theory of free will is the key to the plausibility of the free-will defense. But in chapter 4 we saw that the libertarian theory of free will is controversial and by no means a sure thing.

In our context at the time, that didn't matter. For Alvin Plantinga's use of the theory required only the bare logical possibility of its being true. But now, incorporated into the greater-good explanation, what is required is the plausibility, not just the bare possibility, of the libertarian understanding of free will. To the extent it is not plausible, or to the extent that its compatibilist rival is more plausible, the defenses proposed by Swinburne and Hick stumble.

Nonetheless, in order to examine those defenses on their own terms, let us again grant the libertarian theory of free will for the sake of argument. But this time, unlike the last, doing so is a significant concession. For now, if time and space permitted, it would not be unreasonable to expect the greater-good defenders to make out a good case for the plausibility of the libertarian theory. And to the extent they do not, we would be justified in seeing that as a serious shortcoming in those greater-good explanations.

### Full freedom as a difficulty in understanding God

According to the free-will defense, once full-time libertarian freedom is granted, the giver of the freedom is absolved of all future responsibility for its use.

However, in our experience of granting freedom to others, we know this is not always true. Suppose I give freedom to my child in some particular situation, and she gets into trouble. Am I automatically free of responsibility? No. Whether I am or not depends on a variety of things. For instance, did I give too much, or too little, freedom on this occasion?

But perhaps the proper analogy to use in thinking about libertarian free will is adult freedom. For children's abuse of freedom may trace ultimately to their parents' poor judgment in giving them too much or too little, thus to the poor judgment of adults. So let us probe the free-will defense only in terms of the freedom of adults.

Two questions stand out. Why grant equal freedom to all adults? Why is there no intervention to stop serious abuses? The first of these questions reflects the commonsense core of J. L. Mackie's question about the free-will defense. It is: Even if we grant that libertarian freedom is subsequently beyond the power of omnipotence, couldn't God control who gets it in the first place?

According to the free-will defense, you have full libertarian freedom and so do I. But so do psychopaths, serial rapists, child abusers, and genocidal dictators. Does that seem prudent? After all, if we were in charge of granting freedom, surely we would not give it to those people. Recalling our discussion of Mackie's challenge to the free-will defense in chapter 4, think again of the function of parole boards. When we have responsibility to grant or to withhold freedom, we typically grant it selectively. On the free-will defense, however, the concept seems to be that of a blank check, full freedom granted equally to all.

This makes it hard to understand the kind of being that the theistic God is supposed to be. It makes it hard to admire the kind of being that, insofar as the apparently indiscriminate granting of freedom is concerned, the theistic God seems to be. This echoes a point from the previous chapter about an effect of skeptical defenses, namely, that they tend to make the concept of God incomprehensible to us. Let us now take up the lack of intervention, when freedom is seriously abused.

### Hitler's freedom and God

Hitler is not the only monster in history, of course, but he is so clearly in the top rank of the worst that he can serve both as an exemplar of evil in his own right and as a proxy for the likes of Pol Pot, Stalin, and

Chairman Mao, as well as for the many who pre-date the twentieth century. Furthermore, Hitler was not the only person responsible for the Holocaust, but he was more responsible than anybody else. Without his policies and orders, it would not have happened.

Now imagine yourself as a perfectly good being, omnipotent and omniscient. Would you remain on the sidelines while the Holocaust was going on? Wouldn't you intervene, directly or indirectly? Wouldn't you feel some responsibility to do so, since you were the one to give Hitler his freedom, as well as his temptation to do evil things, in the first place?

One obvious example of direct intervention would be to see to it that he didn't wake up one morning in 1935, or in late 1938, when it was clear to many people, and so, surely, to God, with or without foreknowledge, what was likely to happen. Or, if not then, in 1942. But surely by 1944, when, without him around, the war might have been concluded early. We may safely surmise that no one would have known his death was a homicide. For it would have been brought about by an omnipotent and omniscient being, and such a being, surely, would have been well up to the task of making Hitler's death seem to have been due to natural causes. Furthermore, contrary to Peter van Inwagen's hypothesis, no massive irregularity need occur. A peaceful (or not) death in his sleep would surely have been a good thing, from our human perspective, certainly from the perspective of the victims-to-be and their families.

True, causing Hitler to die in his sleep, to prevent him getting on with the 'final solution,' would have compromised his freedom. But why would that be a bad thing, compared with the good it would do? Surely David Lewis (1941–2001), one of the most influential philosophers of the second half of the twentieth century, is right in saying that, viewed on that balance scale, Hitler's freedom would be a "weightless consideration" for any moral person.[6]

## Libertarian freedom and you, blank checks and robots

Suppose you see your young sister or daughter being savagely attacked. Suppose you do nothing to help, not even calling the emergency services. Later, a friend asks you why. She asks if you held back out of fear, either of making the situation worse or for your own safety. Suppose you say

[6] David Lewis, "Evil for Freedom's Sake?" *Philosophical Papers* 22: 3 (1993), 155.

it was not fear, but the high value you place on freedom, the attacker's freedom in this case.

Your friend might or might not have understood a failure to act because of fear. But surely she would find it very hard to understand how respect for the attacker's freedom could be a good reason. Again, wouldn't, indeed shouldn't, that be a weightless consideration?

The point is that it is hard to understand the idea that the value of free choice is so high that it always, even automatically, trumps the value of preventing great suffering or loss of innocent life. True, that is possible. But is it plausible? Do you believe it? Are you sympathetic to non-intervention out of respect for the attacker's freedom?

It is very hard to understand or to value a being who would issue freedom as a blank check. And it would be even harder if human beings suffered from the kind of depravity we discussed in chapter 4, Plantinga's conjectured transworld depravity.

A mind that would grant freedom without restraint or exception, a mind that continues doing the same thing, without fine-tuning based on experience of abuses of freedom, looks far more like a robot mind than a human mind. In chapter 6, we saw that the vast regularity in the natural world might also be viewed as more consistent with a robotic source than with a source in a mind like ours.

Here is a second suggestion about the lack of calibration of freedom to fit the capacities of its recipients. Perhaps the one-size-fits-all quality of uncalibrated freedom is due to the fact that its source is indifferent. Paul Draper's suggestion seems to fit well with indiscriminate freedom. On his indifference hypothesis, no questions come up about the intelligibility of the source, such as those that come up if the source is supposed to be God. The same applies to the indifference implicit in William L. Rowe's naturalistic hypothesis.

### Freedom and limited temptation

We saw earlier that freedom alone is not enough for moral development. Temptation to do evil is required too. Without the appeal of things, good and bad, we do not need to resist temptation, and that resistance is part of developing strength of character. But, even granting that, the obvious question is: Why there is so much temptation?

In response, it may be proposed that a Goldilocks problem would come up. It is: Where exactly is the 'just right' level of temptation? But, drawing on our earlier discussion, it seems reasonable to think that this form of the Goldilocks problem can be finessed. For the level of temptation could be capped at a level lower than that exhibited by genocidal dictators, or by those people who prey on young children, and so on. Without being able to specify the 'just right' level, we can still be pretty confident that Hitler's level was too high. And so on for other major criminals. So, a Goldilocks objection to the idea of capping temptation seems implausible.

True, there would be less temptation for some people than at present. And so their success in resisting or overcoming it would be less heroic than their success at present. But two points counter-balance that.

First, think of the improved lives of the potential victims, saved because of reduced temptation in those who would have succumbed to greater temptation. Second, do we really think that a world where certain people have to fight very hard against their strong temptation to engage in sadism, or rape, or child abuse, say, is better than a world where people either have no such temptation at all or a far milder case of it? If we do, that is a very peculiar idea.

### Interim verdict on the free-will component in the greater-good defense

As we continue to grant the libertarian idea of free will for the sake of argument, the free-will defense must be deemed successful up to a point. Freedom of choice is a good thing, whether understood the libertarian way or the compatibilist way. Furthermore, some kind of free choice is necessary for morality and human flourishing, both of which are also good things. And moral evils do indeed issue from freedom of choice. So, broadly speaking, the free-will component in the greater-good explanations offered by Hick and Swinburne must be judged successful.

But the details matter too, and there success seems much less assured. Why is there so much freedom, why is it so indiscriminately given, when clearly some of its recipients are obviously and massively unfit? If we were the donors, we would give out freedom more prudently. And we would intervene in certain circumstances, even after granting freedom in the first place. In some circumstances, it would be our moral duty to intervene.

The upshot is that it is very hard to understand an all-good, all-knowing, all-powerful giver of freedom either granting freedom indiscriminately or never subsequently intervening. The free-will defense's hypothesis of unrestricted freedom as a grant of God's reminds us just how alien to our comprehension such a being would be.

As with freedom, so with depravity and temptation. We can see the need for some temptation on the free-will theory, but why so much? True, from the perspective of eternity and infinity, things may look very different from how they look to us. We are in no position to deny that outright, or to claim to know otherwise. But is that admitted possibility sufficient basis for a plausible and reasonable answer to Pope Benedict's questions?

In sum, the free-will defense works at a level of broad generality, but it looks very puzzling when we try to get into the details.

### III   Natural Disasters and other Terrible Things, and the Free-Will Defense

The 2004 Indonesian tsunami killed over 230,000 people and left many more injured, homeless, or destitute. The Pakistani earthquake the following summer killed over 73,000 and left almost 3,000,000 homeless. How can those occurrences be for a greater good? What could a good outcome, otherwise unachievable, or a worse or equal evil, otherwise unavoidable, be?

For both Hick and Swinburne, the key to answering these questions is to extend the free-will component from moral evils to evil occurrences issuing entirely from natural causes. Broadly speaking, there are three kinds of extensions of the free-will defense from moral to natural evils.

One, suggested as a possibility by Alvin Plantinga, develops the long-established theistic idea of a supremely evil being, Satan, as the moral agent responsible for diseases, disasters, and so on. On this idea, those things seem to us to result just from natural causes, but appearances are misleading. On this hypothesis, all those things are really due to Satan. In effect, on this hypothesis, all evils are moral evils.

A second, partly similar, idea is the theory of Manichaeanism, mentioned in chapter 7 as one of four hypotheses considered by David Hume. Essentially, it is the idea that the universe is a battleground for a perpetual struggle between two more-or-less equal, supernatural, forces, one good, the other evil. On this idea too, all evils are moral evils.

I propose to give no further consideration to either idea. Our topic here is the probability or improbability of God, given the facts of evil in the world. Absent a decision on that, it seems a needless complication to speculate about the probability or improbability of other kinds of supernatural beings. Accordingly, my use of the term 'moral evil' in this book restricts it to the wicked doings and omissions of human persons.

On the third model for extending the free-will defense from moral evils to natural evils, much pain, suffering, and so on, continue to be seen as issuing just from natural causes. They are not re-described as really moral evils in disguise.

### Freedom, temptation, character development

The idea of soul-making presupposes that the world is a place where genuine hurt and harm are live options. For character development involves coping with an environment in which things go wrong, where there are dangerous things and situations. So, assuming God desires character development to occur, the divine plan could reasonably be expected to provide an environment where danger and loss, pain and suffering, destruction and accidental death, are live possibilities for us. On this line of thought, diseases and natural disasters can reasonably be seen as contributing to an environment suitable for testing and building character.

The essential claim in this extension of the free-will defense is that natural evils are justified in a God-made world because they provide some of the necessary difficulties, challenges, and opportunities that character development and genuine self-making require. The point is emphasized by both Hick and Swinburne.

Along with freedom, temptation, genuine challenges and risks, the development of moral responsibility and self-realization requires knowledge. Broadly, the knowledge needed is of two kinds.

We need to know various moral principles, for instance the Golden Rule of treating others as you yourself would wish to be treated. In addition, we need practical knowledge. For instance, we need to know the good and the harmful consequences of various actions that we might consider doing. This second kind of knowledge is sometimes basic, and sometimes refined and sophisticated. For instance, we need to know that fire burns and destroys, that food nourishes, that children need love, affection, and encouragement. But we also need to know that suffering pain now, while in itself a bad thing, is sometimes worthwhile in the long run, and that this may be one of those times. We need to know that the world is a dangerous place, and that we ourselves are capable of doing great harm as well as some good.

How are we to acquire these kinds of knowledge? It seems that we could come to know moral principles through acquaintance with the wisdom or good sense of others, that is, by being told, or through reading. But it seems that we would need to experience harm and loss, pain and suffering, at first hand, to acquire the practical knowledge needed for moral development. Richard Swinburne, especially, emphasizes the latter point. For the sake of argument, let us suppose he is right.

His core point here is that we know something only when, among other conditions, we are justified in believing it true. And in the last analysis, the touchstone of justification is experience. So, in the last analysis, our justification for believing that certain actions hurt and do damage is our actual experience of such occurrences in reality. In making this point, Swinburne is drawing on the resources of an influential, perhaps the most influential, philosophical theory of knowledge. The essence of the theory is that knowledge is belief that is justifiably arrived at from things that establish the truth of the belief.

Swinburne's point, then, is that if we are going to know about the good and evil consequences of actions, the world has to be a place where genuine harm as well as genuine good occurs. For it is by our experience of both that we come to know we are able to cause good or evil consequences. On this view, the world has to contain natural evils. If it did not, then we could not acquire the necessary practical knowledge for moral development, and so would not be able to engage in genuine exercise of moral choice.

### Three questions

Granting the point for the sake of the argument, three troubling questions come up. First, why is there so much pain and suffering and waste of human life? Surely the actual amounts go far beyond any that would be justified in that way. Second, what about the moral development and soul-making of victims who die young? And third, why is there so much and so intense suffering by animals?

Although Hick does not emphasize the knowledge component in moral development as much as Swinburne, the three questions just asked apply equally to his attempt to justify natural evil as a necessary condition of soul-making.

*Why so much?*
Why are there so many forms of cancer? Why all the earthquakes and floods? Why all the suffering of children? True, granting the point that a world fit for soul-making would need to contain disease and danger and suffering, we cannot specify exactly how much is necessary for that purpose. We still have no solution in the abstract to the Goldilocks problem. But it seems obvious that there is far more disease and waste of life in the world than is necessary for human beings to know the full extent of our capacities for doing good and evil. That seems obvious to believer and unbeliever alike. For instance, think of all the pain and suffering and waste of life in pre-historic times, or today in the wild. In John Hick's words, quoted before, even granting the greater-good idea at the heart of the conjectured divine plan, the believer still faces "this baffling problem of excessive and undeserved suffering . . . [which is] . . . unjust and inexplicable, haphazard and cruelly excessive . . . with its alien, destructive meaninglessness."

Here too, then, as previously when we wondered about so much unchecked freedom of choice and so much temptation to do evil, the problem comes back to the enormous quantity of terrible occurrences in the natural world. The amounts seem far in excess of any we can imagine to be necessary for educational or soul-making purposes. Like Hick, Swinburne acknowledges the problem.[7]

*Why their suffering for our benefit?*
Imagine a mother letting her young child suffer horribly, without any sign of love, without any comfort, and then letting the child die an excruciating death, alone and frightened. Dostoevsky describes such a thing in his book *The Brothers Karamazov*. Then imagine that mother claiming to justify that suffering and that death, as well as her withholding of affection and comfort from her child, because it was an opportunity for another child to learn a valuable lesson. Wouldn't we think that was a monstrous reason? Wouldn't we think that mother was far more depraved than if she had outright shot her child dead?

Neither you nor I died in an earthquake or tsunami. But recently many hundreds of thousands of people did. And, also unlike us, vast numbers

---

[7]  Swinburne, "Knowledge from Experience," 166, 167.

of others suffered enormously from those disasters. Now, if we grant the extension of the free-will component in the greater-good defense, some of us among the living learned from the suffering and death of people less fortunate than us.

But how could that justify their suffering or death? Why should they suffer or die for our benefit? Do you think it would be OK to reverse the favor? Would your death be OK, if a person in Pakistan benefited from seeing a picture of it? How about your suffering horrible mutilation?

It is sometimes said in the theistic religions that God loves all human beings equally, as good mothers or fathers love their children. True, other things are also said in some of those religions, suggesting otherwise. For instance, in the Jewish scriptures, the Jews are described as God's chosen people, and Calvinists speak of some, but not all, people as the beloved of God. Nonetheless, let us ask a question on the basis of the idea that all persons are loved equally by God. It is: How can that idea be reconciled with the suggestion that pain, suffering, waste of life, and so on, endured by some people, are sometimes justified on grounds that other people thereby learn valuable lessons? And keep in mind that, in the sorts of cases in question, the victims do not volunteer to suffer so others may benefit.

A good parent would never sacrifice one child for another. And if, in some appalling circumstance, a good parent had to do that, the parent would curse the circumstance. Think, for instance, of the circumstance for which William Styron's novel *Sophie's Choice* is named. A good parent would never knowingly engineer such circumstances. Yet the core of the greater-good defense – a divine plan for a world facilitating soul-making – seems to be the blueprint for that very thing.

Albert Einstein (1879–1955) famously said that God does not play dice with the universe. True, it was in a wholly different context. He was expressing his disbelief in quantum theory. And he didn't intend his use of the word 'God' to suggest a belief in the theistic God. We know from other things he said and wrote that he did not believe in such a being. He was using the word as a figure of speech, to reflect his reluctance to accept as ultimate reality the randomness that, on the quantum theory, prevails at the level of sub-atomic particles.

But the distributions of suffering and death caused by diseases and natural disasters seem to be random. So, if we start out with the idea of the theistic God, then it does look like God plays dice with the universe. It looks like God plays dice with the lives of many people. Being a victim, or not, of a particular disease or disaster seems to be a matter of chance. Peter van Inwagen agrees.[8]

Insofar as the distribution of suffering and early death is concerned, the world does not resemble a moral and rational system so much as a lottery with an unfathomable randomizing feature. If you survive to a decent age in decent health, you can count yourself lucky. Lucky to have been born here instead of there, and so on. But if you die young, as a child victim of an earthquake, say, then you weren't lucky. And so on.

*What about the suffering of animals?*
Medicines and other products under development are sometimes tested on animals, before they can be certified fit for use by humans. Nowadays, in Great Britain, the United States, and other developed countries, the regulations governing such tests and experiments are tight. The regulations governing the cultivation and harvesting of animals for food are tight too. The purpose of those regulations is to minimize animal suffering and to avoid cruelty.

The regulations are in place not just because many animals are property, and governments often enact regulations to protect property. The main reason for the regulations issues from the recognition that animals are sentient beings, that many species have nervous systems not very different from our own, and so the pain they would suffer would be as bad as the pain we would suffer, if the tests or experiments were performed on us.

We know there is a vast amount of animal suffering in the natural world. With the greater-good defense, let us suppose some of that suffering is justified by serving a greater good. The main good the defense tells us about is our ability to learn from suffering, including animal suffering. The best analogy would seem to be our use of animals in tests and experiments.

But, as noted, when we use animals in that way, there are strict regulations to prevent extreme or excessive suffering. In nature, by contrast, there is nothing that lessens or mitigates animal suffering. So if the greater-good defenders have it right, and God permits a lot of animal suffering for our benefit, then it also seems that, unlike us, God is not taking precautions to lessen animal suffering. And, at the least, that

---

[8]    Van Inwagen, "The Problem of Evil," 212.

seems odd and surprising behavior from a perfectly good person, when persons who are only pretty good do take such precautions.

Apart from that, most animal suffering is unknown to us. Consequently we never learn from it. For instance, think of all the animal suffering before the emergence of *Homo sapiens* on this planet. Or think of all the suffering in the various jungles and savannahs in the world of which we have no experience. What greater good is served by that suffering?

It is hard to think of any. Consequently, as far as we can tell, much animal suffering is just pointless. But how can there be pointless suffering in a world made by God? If the suffering of animals is most reasonably interpreted as indeed pointless, then, absent some compensating good, it will be equally reasonable to conclude that probably there is no God, but only blind and indifferent nature.

Some people may be tempted to dismiss the point about the suffering of animals in the wild, on the ground that it is natural, that it is simply what happens in jungles and so on. It is the idea that nature just is "red in tooth and claw."

But now consider your own dog or cat, or a friend's, if you have none. Suppose it gets injured and is suffering terribly. Would you do nothing? And what would you think of an animal owner who did nothing? But your animal's suffering is no worse than the suffering of animals in the wild. After all, pain is pain.

Now, perhaps it is reasonable to think of the relationship between God and animals as something like your relationship with your animal, that is, a relationship in which you are the responsible and caring party. Your role includes a large providential aspect. On the theistic story, so does God's. So, just as you would wonder about the moral status of an animal owner who did nothing, when his animal was suffering terribly, so it is natural to wonder about the apparent inaction of God vis-à-vis animal suffering in the wild.

But perhaps, as Peter van Inwagen suggested, any interference by God in the regular, lawlike operations of nature would cause massive irregularity in the natural world. And perhaps the resulting state of things would be as bad overall as the state of things with vast animal suffering.

Let us recall that idea from chapters 8 and 9, and press it into the service of the greater-good defense. So conscripted, the point becomes this. A large part of the benefit of lawlike regularity in nature is that we learn from it, and organize our societies and lives accordingly. On this idea, we, the human race, are the principal beneficiaries. On the divine plan, perhaps we are the intended beneficiaries.

In the previous chapter, we saw various difficulties in this massive-disruption idea. Those points still stand, but let us not rehearse them here. However, there is a question from chapter 6 that now comes up again. It is whether it is reasonable to suppose that the entire cosmos is for us. The idea seems massively disproportionate, even granting the theistic idea of God as the original source of the universe. Linked with the issue of animal suffering, it seems to suggest that even the suffering of pre-historic animals was for our good in the long run.

Combined, the three questions just set out – Why so much? Why the suffering and waste of life of the innocent? Why so much animal suffering? – are the crux of the problem of natural evil. Their connecting thread is the fact that there are enormous amounts of suffering and death that seem to be neither justified nor compensated.

## Suggested Reading

Hick, John (1978) *Evil and the God of Love*, Part IV. New York: Harper & Row.
Swinburne, Richard (1999) *Is There a God?*, ch. 6. Oxford: Oxford University Press.

# 11

# Evaluating Greater-Good Defenses

As we have been seeing, the basic idea in greater-good defenses is that sometimes the ends justify the means. An important back-up concept is compensation, especially compensation for things that may be unjustified.

Justification and compensation are different. The basic idea in justification is that something or other is permissible, perhaps even good, although it may cause suffering or harm. Think, for instance, of a justified punishment, or of a surgery to save a person's life. In contrast, the basic idea in compensation is a balancing out of harm after the event. It is the idea of making recompense, of making up a loss to someone. Think, for instance, of compensation to a person injured at work, or to a victim of libel in a newspaper, or to the owner of a house that the town council zones for construction of a new road. The last of these illustrates compensation for possibly justified harm.

## I  Justified and Compensated Suffering and Death

### Justified suffering and the silence of God

In chapter 7, I listed some typical circumstances in which we can be justified in causing or permitting others to suffer. An obvious example is suffering that is an unavoidable aspect of achieving another's own good. But we saw as well that causing or permitting another to suffer can be justified when the victim does not benefit – as for instance in some punishments, some quarantines, and so on. Cases of the latter kind may be ones where compensation is appropriate.

When a good parent permits his or her child to suffer greatly in the course of receiving medical care, or to be very frustrated through being quarantined because of the measles, or worse, typically that parent is present with the child throughout, comforting and reassuring the child. As William L. Rowe points out, however, the available evidence strongly suggests that God, supposedly akin to a loving parent to all human beings, is not lovingly and reassuringly present to many who suffer, or who die seemingly pointless deaths.[1]

In addition to explaining suffering that seems pointless, then, the greater-good defender needs to account for the silence of God in the face of such terrible things. Recall one of the questions posed by Pope Benedict XVI at Auschwitz: "Why, Lord, did you remain silent?"

Let us switch now from justification for suffering to justification for death, the death of the innocent in particular.

## Justified death

Can permitting the avoidable death of an innocent person, say the death of a child, be justified? If so, then perhaps it is in the best interest of the child himself or herself. After all, that is most often how justification works in cases of justified suffering, and it seems reasonable to wonder if the same logic applies here too. Surely we would not think it morally justified or permissible to bring about, or to permit, the death of a young child in order to benefit another person or a group of other persons, except, perhaps, in extraordinarily extreme circumstances. And, even then, it is not obvious we would be justified.

In Dostoevsky's novel *The Brothers Karamazov*, one brother asks the other whether, to bring about peace on earth, he would be willing to permit a young child to be tortured to death, and gets the answer, no. You might answer differently. The point is that the different answer is not obviously correct. If you think a different answer is correct, ask yourself if your view would be the same if the child were your own and not a stranger's. On the theistic view, none of us is a stranger in the sight of God, so that basis for preferential treatment would not be available to God.

Sometimes we are justified in killing an animal for its own good, for instance to relieve it of terrible suffering. In certain cases, we would consider mercy killings of animals not just permissible but obligatory.

---

[1]   Rowe, "An Exchange on the Problem of Evil," 130–1.

In some of those cases, it is a failure to kill the animal that we would regard as cruel.

Does the same thing apply in some cases of terrible human suffering, when the victim is beyond saving? The question is not about the legality of such a killing, or the way it would be viewed from certain religious perspectives. After all, insofar as the latter are concerned, we are behind the veil of ignorance, and so we do not know how, as Jews, Christians, Muslims, atheists, or agnostics, we think of such a thing. The question is a moral question, a question about what, in an extreme circumstance, might be an act of decency and compassion.

Suppose a child victim of an earthquake is trapped in the rubble, horribly mutilated, and in terrible pain, and there is no hope of rescue or survival. Suppose no painkillers are available. Can you imagine, for humane reasons, killing the child in order to relieve him or her of suffering, as we would an animal?

The point here is not whether we answer yes or no. The point is that we are trying to imagine circumstances when the death of an innocent person is both justified and beneficial to the victim himself or herself. After all, the theist, on the greater-good defense, presumably thinks that some innocent deaths are justified and serve the best interest of the victim. We are probing to try to find such cases.

There is an obvious difference between the greater-good justification of death and the greater-good justification of suffering. Often, in the case of the justified suffering, we are anticipating a good future for the victim, as a consequence of the treatment or cure. But in the cases of justified death we are imagining – the child in the rubble, suffering terribly, beyond hope of rescue, or the injured animal in horrifying agony – there is no better future. The benefit is the ending of terrible suffering, not the provision of the means necessary for good experiences in the future. The justification for mercy killing is forward-looking only in a negative sense. The aim is the elimination of present suffering plus the prevention of future suffering.

Before looking at the greater-good defense's response to questions about justification, let us bring in the topic of compensation.

### Compensated suffering and death

Suppose your five-year-old child gets measles and now cannot be Cinderella in her kindergarten play. In addition to her suffering and discomfort from the measles, she is terribly disappointed. For she has been dreaming and planning for weeks to be Cinderella. She was looking forward so excitedly to riding in the carriage and to wearing the dress at the ball, not to mention the subsequent business with the shoes. Now she has to miss it all.

There is no question of justification here. She got measles at a bad time. She had bad luck, and nothing can be done to change that.

But you try as best you can to make it up to her. You take her to a show she would love to see, followed by pizza and ice cream. You try hard to balance out her disappointment, maybe even to outweigh it if you're lucky. And you try as well to use the episode to help shape the little girl's outlook for the better.

If you succeeded in making up for your child's disappointment it was because she had a future. But what about the suffering of the child trapped in the rubble after the earthquake, whose agony was ended by death? Or the terrible suffering of the fawn burned in the accidental forest fire?

Can death be compensated for the victim in similar fashion to suffering? Can an innocent person be compensated for his or her death? Can an animal be compensated for its death? These are strange questions. However, in the context of the greater-good defense of the theistic view of the world, Swinburne's for instance, they are important ones.

### First-party compensation, and what seems to be third-party compensation

The essence of compensation is recompense to a victim for his or her loss or harm or suffering. Let us call it first-party compensation.

True, there is the concept of compensation to the victim's family, say for the death of the victim. But when we look carefully at that, it seems to turn out to be compensation to the members of the victim's family for their own loss. For instance, the compensation is calculated on the basis of the family's loss of income from the victim, or their loss of the victim's affection, and so on. So the fundamental point in the concept of compensation remains recompense for loss to those who suffered the loss.

Consider compensation to a farmer for the death of his or her livestock. The purpose is to make up to the farmer the farmer's loss. But the life lost was the animal's, not the farmer's. What the farmer lost was the property value of the cow, including its value in milk to be produced, or in calves born, or in meat sold. It is not the loss of life, as such, that is being compensated, for that loss was the cow's. For instance, the loss to the cow of its own valuable future, measured in pleasant experiences, say, is not compensated when the farmer receives a check from the insurance company. Nor, presumably, does either party to that transaction suppose that it is.

The problem, now, insofar as first-party compensation is concerned, is obvious. Death cuts off the individual's future. So how is compensation to the victim for his or her own death even logically possible, to say nothing of practicable? There is a like problem with animal deaths. And, for both people and animals, there is the related problem of compensation for terminal suffering.

There seems to be a significant difference between the idea of a justified death of an innocent person or of an animal, on the one hand, and the idea of a compensated death of a person or animal, on the other. For, considering the nature of death, we have no acquaintance with first-party compensation for death. That is, we have no experience at all of the dead victim himself or herself being compensated for loss of life. And the same applies to terminal suffering.

The challenge for the greater-good defense turns on the expectation that, if the world is God-made, the occurrence of terrible things will be justified, compensated, or perhaps both. It seems a reasonable expectation, and a pivot in the essential difference between the theistic idea and the hypothesis of indifference. But, in the cases of unjustified death or terminal suffering, how can there be compensation?

# II   Afterlife

The theistic idea of a divine plan behind the world includes the idea of life after death.

### Being specific about a post-mortem world

In chapter 8, discussing skeptical defenses against the arguments of William Rowe and Paul Draper, we granted the legitimate demand for more specificity in those arguments. Peter van Inwagen, among others, requested details about the natural laws that would operate in a world with less evil but no less good than the actual world, as well as about the initial conditions in that world, and so on.

It was a fair point then, and it is no less so now. But now it is the theistic adherent to a greater-good defense who conjectures a possible world. Of what raw materials will this post-mortem world be composed, if not the sub-atomic particles making up the physical universe? What laws will that world run on? It seems fair to request as much specificity now as van Inwagen and others request of Rowe and Draper. Without some reasonable degree of specificity, how are we to counter the suspicion that the hereafter possibility is just empty, feel-good talk?

Without waiving that request, but out of consistency with granting the theistic idea of a divine plan, let us grant for the sake of argument the idea of an afterlife, pending specificity.

### More than a hereafter needed

Perhaps suffering by the innocent, for which we can find no justification, is justified posthumously. However, the very same question must be faced as when we search for a justification here in the world. That is, by what is the suffering justified? For instance, what, in a hereafter, justifies the suffering of a child victim of the 2005 Pakistani earthquake? If a good suggestion is not forthcoming, then we are entitled to treat that lack just as we do the failure to find a good justification here in this life. For the idea of a hereafter, in itself, contributes nothing to a solution of the problem. More time, in itself, is no answer to the question.

The situation is parallel to that of responding to the existential question – What is the meaning or purpose of life? – by appealing to a life after death. For extra time, in itself, contributes no meaning, thus no extra meaning, to my life. Likewise here, with the question about justification, extra time in itself contributes nothing.

### The pre-existing condition problem

The prospects for a good answer to the question about afterlife justification appear dim. To see why, take a typical case of justified suffering of the innocent, say a child suffering the effects of aggressive, invasive treatment of her brain cancer. The justification of the child's suffering is that her pain was an unavoidable byproduct of the best efforts of the doctors to cure her. The justification comes from the expected outcome of treating the child's pre-existing condition.

But what is the parallel pre-existing condition of the Pakistani child? If we stick to the analogy with the sick child's cancer, then, presumably, the Pakistani child's entrapment in a collapsed building would be viewed as the treatment. But of what is it supposed to be a treatment? Means–ends justification works only to the extent that we are able to give some account of both the ends and the means.

However, to suppose that the means–ends analogy with justified painful treatment of a pre-existing medical condition holds up in this case seems absurd. The idea of the earthquake, or just the collapse of that particular building, as treatment of some pre-existing condition, seems an obvious non-starter. The point is acknowledged by T. J. Mawson in a recent book.[2] Mawson, an Oxford philosopher and greater-good theorist, is sympathetic in particular to Richard Swinburne's version of the greater-good defense.

Absent a solution to this pre-existing condition problem, it seems that afterlife justification of seemingly pointless suffering will not work. If the greater-good defense is to be able to cover innocent suffering in a hereafter, then, it seems that it will have to be as compensation, not justification.

### *Afterlife compensation for innocent suffering*

The basic idea is that compensation would be a life after death, where the victim's quality of life makes up for the victim's suffering in this life. For instance, the trapped Pakistani child's suffering would be compensated in a way that satisfies the child herself. On this idea, justification would not be involved. Considering the pre-existing condition problem, it seems more promising than the idea of posthumous justification.

As before, we are entitled to ask for some details. In particular, what would it be reasonable to suppose the compensation might consist in? Perhaps the greater-good defender could plausibly answer that it is the

---

[2]   T. J. Mawson, *Belief in God* (Oxford: Oxford University Press, 2005), 208.

child's own personal experience of God. Clearly, on any version of theism, that would be a very great good. But some difficulties arise.

*Afterlife compensation and the laws of nature (1)*
Many human beings die too young to exercise moral choice, to choose their own destinies, or to progress in soul-making. In their conjectured afterlife, will they have those lost opportunities? Either they will or they won't. But serious problems arise either way.

If they will, then, presumably, the laws of nature, or something closely approximate to them, will be in effect in the afterlife too. For, on both Hick's and Swinburne's versions of the defense, character development and soul-making can come about only if we experience the pleasures and pains that result from natural processes.

But if the laws of nature are operative in the hereafter, then we should expect there to be horrendous unjustified suffering there too. And then there will need to be a solution for that. This is an especially acute problem for Hick's version of the greater-good theory, as Hick envisages soul-making to continue after death.[3]

But perhaps afterlife compensation will involve soul-making and the development of moral choice without learning from experience of natural forces, thus without the pleasures and pains that those forces cause. But then, the laws and forces of nature are not strictly necessary for moral choice and development. And that raises the question: Why could God not have arranged moral choice and development to be possible that way here on earth? It would have saved both us and other animals from unimaginably vast amounts of pain and suffering.

A further question emerges from a hypothesis we examined earlier. It is Peter van Inwagen's suggestion that, if God prevented or eliminated great evils, it might, for all we know, cause massive disruption in nature. The suggestion is that such disruption might result from divine interference with the laws of nature. But if soul-making is now imagined to be possible after death without either vast amounts of natural evil or massive disruption, then why not now in the actual world?

Two additional questions come up. First, if the laws of nature apply in this conjectured afterworld too, then we need some specificity about how that is supposed to work, if this afterworld is not made up of

---

[3]   Hick, *Evil and the God of Love*, 347.

sub-atomic particles. Second, if other laws are in effect instead, then a request for some specificity about them seems reasonable too.

### Afterlife compensation and the laws of nature (2)

As Hick's concept of soul-making, unlike Swinburne's, includes the idea of further personal development after death, this second difficulty does not apply to him.

Perhaps afterlife compensation bypasses moral choice and moral development for those victims who died too young to have experienced them. But if so, then won't those people be second-class citizens in the hereafter, compared to the people who did experience those things in this life?

If not, then a human life without moral choice, and without undergoing moral development, turns out to be no worse than a human life with those things. But if that is so, how can the moral development of the latter be of such great value that it supposedly justifies all the evils that result from the freedom of choice that, on the libertarian free-will defense, is a prerequisite for moral development? And how can moral development be of such great value that it justifies so much evil resulting from natural forces, namely, the natural evils supposedly necessary for us to learn about good and evil?

Either way, there seems to be a serious problem for the idea of afterlife compensation.

Let us apply another idea of Peter van Inwagen's to our request for specificity about laws of nature in an afterlife. Speaking of the concept of heaven, presumably the ideal of an afterlife, van Inwagen suggests it is not a place, but a condition.[4] If the afterlife is not in a place, but reflects a condition instead, then perhaps it might be suggested that laws of nature would not obtain there.

Letting that pass, an obvious question is: Of what is it to be a condition? If of a physical thing, then the prior question about laws of nature returns in full force. If a condition of a non-physical thing, then the question is about the meaning of that. Perhaps that question would take us back to points discussed in earlier chapters about the plausibility of postulating non-physical selves.

---

[4]   Peter van Inwagen, "The Magnitude, Duration, and Distribution of Evil: A Theodicy," in *God, Knowledge and Mystery*, 112.

## The problem of animal suffering

Then there is the suffering of animals. It is as legitimate to wonder about this as about the suffering of innocent human beings. After all, suffering is suffering, regardless of the species of the victim. Furthermore, on any reasonable reckoning, there would seem to be a far greater quantity of animal than human suffering. In addition, not all human suffering is worse than animal suffering. And if suffering is objectively a bad thing, then why would animal suffering matter less to God than the suffering of humans? Presumably, it wouldn't.

Thoroughness, as well as both moral and intellectual consistency, then, would seem to require the greater-good theory to provide for posthumous compensation to animals for their suffering too. And the aforementioned T. J. Mawson does.[5]

Hick is very skeptical about the concept of afterlife compensation for animals.[6] We cannot, then, extend Mawson's idea to him. Swinburne is not explicit on the point, but the drift of his thought seems to incline toward something like Mawson's position. He says:

> God does have [the] right [to allow humans (and animals) to suffer] so long as the package of life is overall a good one for each of us . . . if there are any lives which nevertheless are on balance bad, God would be under an obligation to provide life after death for the individuals concerned in which they could be compensated for the bad states of this life, so that in this life and the next their lives overall would be good.[7]

In context, his word "individuals" seems to cover animals of other species as well as humans.

How are we to think of this idea of posthumous animal compensation? If in physical terms, then, among other things, the problem discussed in (1) below comes up. If in non-physical terms, then in what sense is it that animals live on hereafter? For so much that seems intrinsic to animal nature seems inseparable from their physicality. Whether we are supposed to think of it in physical or non-physical terms, the problem discussed in (2) below comes up.

---

[5]  Mawson, *Belief in God*, 207–8, 211–12.
[6]  Hick, *Evil and the God of Love*, 316.
[7]  Richard Swinburne, *Providence and the Problem of Evil* (Oxford: Oxford University Press, 1998), 235, 236.

*The problem of animal compensation (1)*
Like us, animals need certain kinds of habitats to survive. But the habitat necessary for the survival of one species is often a habitat in which another species would quickly go extinct.

Then there is a difficulty with animals that share a habitat. For some animals survive by preying on others for food. Doing so is intrinsic to their nature. Tigers do not become predators through a career choice. It is nature, not nurture. Nurture may influence how good at it they will be, but not whether they are predators in the first place. Being killed and eaten for food is an important source of animal suffering.

So a serious difficulty facing the idea of animal afterlife compensation is that it seems to perpetuate the very problem, unjustified animal death and suffering, that it is supposed to be solving.


*The problem of animal compensation (2)*
But there is a bigger and more fundamental problem that comes from what seems to be a necessary condition of compensation in the first place. Compensation seems to require understanding by the victim that the present gain is to be set alongside the previous loss, so as to balance it out, or perhaps even to outweigh it. Without that understanding, what we would have is only past loss or pain followed by present gain or pleasure. If the concept of the gain as redress for the loss is not grasped, then all there would be is a sequence of bad experiences first, followed by good experiences second.

Perhaps, on the theistic idea of an afterlife for human beings, the problem is soluble in the case of infant victims or mentally retarded victims. Perhaps the theist could suppose in both cases that, in the afterlife, those people would be able to understand eventually. But there is nothing in zoology to justify the idea that the essential nature of animals could include such understanding. Consequently, it seems there could not be compensation to animals. John Hick, in declining to subscribe to the idea of hereafter compensation for animals, makes a similar point.

But if compensation to animals is not possible, then it seems that much suffering in the world would be neither justified nor compensated. But how can this be, if God exists? The greater-good defense needs a solution to this problem, otherwise the defense will fail. But the prospects seem dim. The same reasoning, the same problem, and the same dim prospects apply to afterlife compensation for unjustified animal death as for unjustified animal suffering.

The impossibility of compensating animals for either suffering or death raises a serious question about certain forms of the greater-good defense. However, in itself, that impossibility is not direct evidence against the existence of God. For, as we agreed in chapter 2, inability to do the logically impossible does not cancel omnipotence. But there is no comfort in that point for Mawson and other proponents of the form of greater-good defense now under discussion.

### *Far from common sense*

The thoughts we have been pursuing have taken us far from common sense. But the questions that started the pursuit are obvious and robustly commonsensical. On a greater-good defense, how can there be justification for the suffering of the innocent who die young? How can those early deaths be justified? And the same goes for the suffering and early death of animals. The questions are straightforward. But the greater-good theory's answers seem to get ever more baroque. They come more and more to look like thinly disguised versions of 'I don't know.'

## III  A Theistic Variation on the Hypothesis of Indifference

On Paul Draper's indifference hypothesis, it is not surprising that lots of terrible things happen, or that they seem to have no purpose whatever. John Hick suggests that the occurrence of terrible evils that seem utterly pointless, and seem to have no redeeming features whatsoever, may not be surprising to the theist either. The idea is an important addition to the greater-good defense.

### *"Epistemic distance"*

The *New York Times* reported Pope Benedict XVI at Auschwitz saying: "We cannot peer into God's mysterious plan." John Hick expresses a similar thought, and incorporates it into his formulation of the greater-good defense.[8]

The core idea is a skeptical one. But it is a more limited skepticism than we found in either Wykstra's or van Inwagen's skeptical defenses of theism. Its role is to supplement the greater-good defense, not to supplant it, or to make it unnecessary. Hick's point is to incorporate our incomprehension of why there is so much horror and misery in the world into his conception of the divine plan itself. The key to doing so is his suggestion that it would make good sense for God to remain at a fairly considerable "epistemic distance" from us.

*Episteme* is one of the Greek words for knowledge. Hence the name, epistemology, for the philosophical study of the nature and extent of knowledge. An epistemic distance, then, is essentially a knowledge gap. The knowledge gap that Hick is thinking of here is a deficiency in our understanding of God and of God's plan for the world. His suggestion is that this deficiency may be deliberate on God's part.

Why might God want to keep us in the dark about such important things? Hick's suggestion is that it may be for essentially the same reason that the world is a hard and dangerous place. That is, it may be part of the divine plan for us to have opportunity to develop moral responsibility and to become good persons. How?

Hick's idea is that the best way to answer that question may be by first asking, and answering, another. That other question is: Why would God want us to engage in, and succeed at, soul-making? The answer, presumably, is because of the goodness implicit in it, the goodness of being a good and decent person. It is the idea that God would want us to do good things, to avoid harming others, and so on, for their own sake, not for any external reason.

What might an external reason be? One might be fear of God's disapproval and punishment. Such reasons are more prudential than moral reasons. And it seems plausible that God would want us to be good persons for reasons other than prudential or self-regarding ones.

Now, suppose that it seemed pretty clear to us, on the evidence of our own experience, that there really is a God. Then, Hick conjectures, perhaps our reasons for good behavior might be more prudential than moral. If it seemed pretty clear to us that there is indeed a God, then it

---

[8]   Hick, *Evil and the God of Love*, 335–6.

might seem equally clear that there would, in the end, be a reckoning for our misconduct. And if that were so, then perhaps we would choose and do good in order to avoid punishment more than for its own sake. And, in that case, our moral and spiritual development might be less meaningful than they are in the actual world. For, in the actual world, it is far from obvious or certain that God exists. Swinburne expresses a similar point about the value of moral over prudential reasons for doing good, although he emphasizes this skeptical aspect of the greater-good defense less than Hick.[9]

In this part of his theory, Hick is acknowledging serious grounds for doubt about God's existence. For instance, he is acknowledging that the universe does indeed seem indifferent to pain and suffering. His aim in doing so is to make additional room for faith.

## IV   Verdict on the Greater-Good Defense

*Tackling the right question, but problems in the answers*

The greater-good defense operates on a plausible, commonsensical idea. It is that, in human affairs, when injury or harm issues from some plan or action, as opposed to just blind, brute nature, questions of justification and compensation come up.

If the basic theistic idea is true, then, in the last analysis, there is no blind, brute nature. Instead, the basic laws of nature reflect a divine plan. They reflect intention and purpose, thus responsibility. So the matter of justification and compensation for injury or harm resulting from them comes up. Clearly, then, the greater-good defense is tackling the right substantive question.

However, when we examine its answers, we find a problem that leads to a bigger problem. The problem is that we can find no justification for vast amounts of suffering and waste of life.

Turning, then, to the back-up idea of posthumous compensation for the victims, it is very unclear how the idea could work. Without rehearsing the difficulties previously discussed, let one suffice now as a reminder. It is the problem of afterlife compensation for animals. The core

---

[9]   Swinburne, "Knowledge from Experience," 157.

of the problem is that no such thing seems even logically possible, and so the idea is useless to greater-good defenses.

Turning next to Hick's theory of epistemic distance, it is hard to see how that theory helps with the substantive issues under discussion. To see why, grant Hick the point. Grant that epistemic distance is part of God's plan from the start. Perhaps we are meant not to understand, at least in this life, the justification or the compensation for various evils.

But if the world is indeed God-made, presumably those evils are in fact either justified or compensated. And yet, to stay with just one example, we have serious reason to think that compensation for unjustified animal suffering and death is impossible on logical grounds. If that is so, then it is impossible for God to provide, thus there is no compensation. Thus, more would be lacking than just our comprehension of compensation procedures.

What about justification? Could keeping us in the dark justify all the pain and suffering in the natural world? It seems a steep price. In addition, it seems to rely on the idea that we are the point of the natural world's being as it is.

## Fideism and the surprise principle again

If the theistic response is that the unanswered questions provide a good illustration of faith picking up where reason runs out, then we would seem to be, again, knocking on the fideist door. The previous occasion was in our investigation of the skeptical defenses, Wykstra's noseeum defense in particular.

How does the greater-good defense measure up against the idea that there is no God, thus that much suffering is just a brute fact of blind nature? The latter idea is simple and direct, and requires no elaborate metaphysical add-on of a densely populated afterlife.

To compare the two, let us bring back the surprise principle that we used in discussing probabilistic arguments and skeptical defenses against them. And we keep in mind that we are still behind the veil of ignorance, so we don't know our religious preference, if any.

On the indifference idea, it is unsurprising that vast amounts of seemingly unjustified and uncompensated suffering and death exist. It is what we would predict.

On the theistic idea, filtered through the greater-good defense, is it surprising or unsurprising that, over and above biologically useful pain, vast amounts of seemingly unjustified and uncompensated suffering exist? To be fair in answering, we must add in the further point of Hick's, and Swinburne's to a lesser extent, namely, the idea of an intended deficiency in our grasp of the divine plan for achieving the overall greater good. On that idea of epistemic distance, a difficult and often bewildering God-made world is unsurprising. It is unsurprising, if the world is one in which God intends good to be done for its own sake, and in which faith exists without assurances of a happy ending.

This idea that God might want us in the dark, to a large extent, is plausible in the abstract. But the details matter too. And the crucial detail is the vast abundance of suffering and waste of life. That remains surprising on the theistic hypothesis, even with the concept of epistemic distance added in. Furthermore, it is surprising on Swinburne's idea that natural evils need to exist so that we can learn practical lessons about good and evil. By contrast, on the rival hypothesis of indifference, it is unsurprising. In a comparative reckoning, then, using the surprise principle, the greater-good explanation fares worse than its rival, the indifference hypothesis.

Does the greater-good explanation come up so short than it can be dismissed? The answer to that is no. If there is a substantive theistic explanation at all, it seems plausible to think it would be along the lines of the greater-good explanation. But, to repeat, the details matter, and the greater-good defense leaves important questions unanswered and perhaps unanswerable. At best, then, it seems to be addressing the right substantive questions and, in its answers, it seems to be facing in the right direction.

## Verdict overall, and back to Draper

With basic details remaining so problematic, the greater-good defense is not a successful explanation on its merits.

In chapter 7, we saw Paul Draper qualify his conclusion about the improbability of God. His qualification was that a successful proof of God's existence or a convincing theistic explanation of seemingly pointless evils might be developed, or a crippling defect in his own argument might be discovered. But in chapters 5 and 6 we found that a prominent version of one of the most prominent arguments for the existence of God failed, and we have just found that the two most prominent versions of one of the most prominent theistic explanations fail. Furthermore, we saw in chapter 9 that both Draper's and Rowe's arguments are not blocked or demolished by the most prominent skeptical defenses. True, other, more successful, arguments for God's existence cannot be absolutely ruled out. And neither can more successful explanations or defenses. Nonetheless, in light of the failures of those we examined, we may upgrade the strength of Draper's, and likewise Rowe's, claims on the truth.

## Suggested Reading

Hick, John (1978) *Evil and the God of Love*, Part IV. New York: Harper & Row.
Mawson, T. J. (2005) *Belief in God*, ch. 12. Oxford: Oxford University Press.
Swinburne, Richard (1999) *Is There a God?*, ch. 6. Oxford: Oxford University Press.

# Part VI

# Taking Stock

# 12

# Taking Stock

## I  Two Questions

We have been examining the relationship between the fact that terrible things happen in the world and the belief that there is a God who made it. Do the two things square with one another, or does the fact undermine the belief? That is one question.

Some things tell against the existence of God, but other things support it. If we take both kinds of things together, are we justified on balance to conclude that God exists? That is another question.

Religious belief can be a touchy subject to discuss, especially in a way that aims to go beyond innocuous politeness. Obviously, then, it can be a touchy subject to investigate philosophically. But religious beliefs are widespread and influential, and so it is important to evaluate them carefully and critically. Investigating them philosophically is one part of doing that. To facilitate impartiality in our philosophical investigations here, we borrowed John Rawls's tactic of imagining ourselves behind a veil of ignorance. Tailoring this approach to our two questions, we imagined ourselves cut off, first, from knowledge of our own religious preference, and then from knowledge of the entire subjects of religion and philosophy. The pretense enabled us to put the concepts of God and design and the facts of evil in a crucible for unbiased investigation.

## II  Three Verdicts

*Does the world testify to a divine origin?*

We grouped together the fact that the universe, though vastly complex, is orderly and regular, the fact that, against very long odds, conditions at the Big Bang were right for life eventually to evolve, and the fact that many terrible things happen for no apparent good reason. This grouping gave us a composite picture of some deep features of the world which go to the core of the theistic view of it as a creation. On the basis of this group of facts, we investigated whether the world plausibly testifies to a divine source. Our verdict was no.

The verdict covers two points. First, without the fact of seemingly point-less evil in the mix, the facts of order, complexity, and suitability for life are not sufficient to warrant concluding that God is the original source of the universe. Second, with the abundance of seemingly pointless evils in the mix, the evidence is sufficient to block that conclusion. With that mix as a base, a perfect designer-creator cannot justifiably be inferred, no more than, to re-use a previous analogy, a perfect cook can be inferred from a mix of excellent, mediocre, and terrible meals.

The verdict does not mean there is no such being. It does not mean that the existence of God is improbable, or that belief in God is unjustified or unreasonable. As we saw, and as our common sense tells us, failure to support a point by argument does not mean that the point is false or probably false, or that believing it true is unreasonable. Those additional things require separate reasons of their own. Again, recall Al Capone.

But while belief that God exists is not automatically undercut as a byproduct of a failure to establish it as the conclusion of an argument, perhaps it is undercut directly by the fact that terrible things happen. We took up this issue in two ways. First, does that fact rule out even the possibility that God exists? And second, does it show the existence of God to be improbable?

### Do God and evil square with one another? (1)

We saw J. L. Mackie's argument to prove that God and evil are logically inconsistent with one another fail. Moreover, we saw it proved by Alvin Plantinga that the existence of God remains a logical possibility, even though evil exists. The answer to the first of the 'squaring' questions, then, is that God and evil do square with one another, in the sense of being logically consistent.

But we saw in chapter 3 that logical consistency means only the absence of a strict contradiction. In itself, the absence of a contradiction is no reason to suppose that the non-contradictory thing in question is true or probably true. For instance, recall from the earlier discussion that there is no contradiction in the idea of a person's surviving a 10,000-foot fall from an airplane every hour for twenty years. In David Lewis's memorable phrase, a logical possibility is "the sort of possibility only a philosopher could cherish."[1]

## *Do God and evil square with one another? (2)*

Do the two things square with one another in an evidential, as well as a logical, sense? Or does the existence of enormous amounts of awful things give us adequate evidence to judge it improbable that God exists?

We examined two arguments for the idea that it does provide adequate evidence for that judgment, one direct, developed by William L. Rowe, the other indirect, developed by Paul Draper. We examined two kinds of defenses against them, technicality defenses and substantive defenses, respectively.

The technicality defenses we examined are skeptical defenses. One of these, the noseeum defense, comes from Steven J. Wykstra, while Peter van Inwagen provides two, the second of which mixes skepticism with a substantive conjecture. The upshot of our examination of Wykstra is that his defense seems to make the concept of God incomprehensible. Furthermore, in a closely related point, his defense raises a serious doubt about the theistic view of morality, understood as a system of values that dovetails with the will of God. For, as we saw in chapter 9, noseeum skepticism seems to give us good reason to doubt that human goodness matches any conclusions we can draw about the nature of divine goodness. For those reasons, that defense seems seriously to compromise the very position it aims to defend.

Van Inwagen's first skeptical defense, centering on the Goldilocks problem, shows us Rowe and Draper unable to specify the line separating too much from not too much evil in a God-made world. However, as Rowe points out, and as van Inwagen agrees, the theistic position cannot be that anything goes. Accordingly, failure to solve the Goldilocks problem does not block or defeat evil-based arguments for the improbability of God. Furthermore, to be justified in the view that a God-made

---

[1] David Lewis, "Divine Evil," in Louise M. Antony, ed., *Philosophers without Gods* (Oxford: Oxford University Press, 2007), 231.

world is not a world in which anything goes, the theist, no less than his or her opponent on this issue, needs a solution to the Goldilocks problem.

Behind the veil of ignorance, we judged van Inwagen's other defense, his mix of skepticism and a substantive explanation, to be less probable than either Rowe's or Draper's versions of the indifference hypothesis. Based on that, we went on to judge van Inwagen's 'mixed' hypothesis improbable.

The straightforward substantive defenses that we considered, two converging forms of a greater-good defense, seem to make the concept of God incomprehensible, as well as leaving large classes of evils either unjustified or uncompensated. Consequently, we judged those defenses to be unsuccessful. In their wake, the vast abundance of seemingly pointless evil in a supposedly God-made world remains unexplained.

Our verdict overall is that the enormous amounts of seemingly pointless evils give us sufficient evidence to think that, probably, there is no God.

Certain qualifications apply to this verdict. One is that a successful argument may yet be developed for the idea that the universe had a divine origin. If so, our verdict would be outweighed and set aside. However, we should note as well that, over and above Rowe's and Draper's arguments, additional arguments may succeed in showing there is no God. A second qualification applying to our verdict is that, although the skeptical defenses offered by Wykstra and van Inwagen do not block or defeat Rowe's or Draper's arguments, other forms of technicality defense may be developed that do. And a third qualification is that, while the substantive defenses offered by Hick and Swinburne do not explain the abundance of seemingly pointless evils in a supposedly God-made world, other substantive defenses may be developed that do. In the meantime, in the absence of those better arguments, our verdict stands.

### Back to headhunting

Briefly, as we take stock of our verdicts, let us bring back the headhunting pretense from chapter 1. We imagined ourselves hired for two assignments. One was to vet the credentials of a candidate for the job already selected, while the other was to start from scratch and come up with the best candidate.

Is there something about the candidate selected that would disqualify him or her? Our first assignment was to answer that question.

We did not find a definitive disqualification. We found nothing that would make it absolutely impossible or unthinkable to hire the candidate. But we found enough probable reason to report that, judged on a less minimalistic standard, the candidate is unqualified. Translated back into the context of our first philosophical investigation, this mirrors our two verdicts in that investigation. First, we found that the existence of seemingly pointless evil does not make the existence of God logically impossible. It does not make the existence of God unthinkable. But, second, we judged the facts of evil in the world to be strong enough evidence to make it improbable that there is a God.

Starting from scratch, who is the best candidate for the job? Our second headhunting assignment was to answer that question.

In the end, we make no positive recommendation to the board, although we rule out recommending one candidate for sure. Translating this back into the context of our second philosophical investigation, we came up with no hypothesis that we could judge the best explanation of the origin and nature of the universe. But our inquiry did not come up completely blank. For we did make enough progress to discover that an open investigation would not come up with the theistic idea of a perfect supernatural creator. An open investigation would not support that idea as a conclusion.

## III   Out from behind the Veil of Ignorance

Those verdicts were reached behind our veil of ignorance. As such, they reflect religiously neutral philosophical investigation. The veil of ignorance facilitated inquiries drawing only on information available equally to believer and unbeliever alike. The point of view in our inquiries was third-person throughout, with nothing reflective of my life-experience or situation that is not equally reflective of yours. The influential American philosopher Thomas Nagel (b. 1937) provides a useful, as well as catchy, term for this type of perspective. He calls it "the view from nowhere." Viewed from nowhere in particular, then, the evidence we examined warrants those verdicts.

The participants in Rawls's thought experiment go back to their full experience and knowledge after the experiment is over. And so do we. Accordingly, with our individual religious preferences and so on known to us once again, let us take the measure of our two investigations and our three verdicts. In doing so, I will concentrate on the believer. The reason is that, for him or her, the difference between how things look behind, and out from behind, the veil of ignorance is greater than for the unbeliever.

## The possibility of God

For some religious believers, the verdict reached in the Mackie–Plantinga debate will be enough, giving them all they expect or ask of reason. It will be enough for some believers if the core content of their faith, the idea of a supernatural, personal creator, is not absolutely impossible. That being so, some believers will be content to let faith and religious experience cover things over and above that minimum. This view overlaps with the moderate fideism, or 'faith only' stance, briefly described in chapter 2.

## God as unwarranted conclusion: a setback for evidentialism

Some believers, including some of the type just mentioned, will be untroubled, perhaps even heartened, by a failure to establish through reasoning alone that God exists. In their view, the failure makes room for faith. Among philosophers, the most famous and influential to maintain that failure to prove the existence of God clears the way for faith is the German philosopher Immanuel Kant (1724–1804).

But many believers take a less austere view, and see their faith as a source of important information. They see it as providing important moral truths, as well as access to the prime exemplar of moral goodness. And some see religion as providing the fundamental truth about the natural world too. That truth, in their view, is that the world is essentially a divine creation, imbued with overall meaning and purpose.

However, our restored knowledge provides no new evidence to support an inference from the natural world to God as its creator.

Of the four understandings of the relationship between religious faith and reason described in chapter 2, it is the evidentialist view that is set back by this verdict. The other conceptions of that relationship have nothing at stake in either the attempt to reason from natural facts to a supernatural cause, or in its failure.

In the first place, they are not participants in the attempt. Indeed, among fideists, there would be opposition to it. Then, second, to repeat a point underlined before, failure to justify a conclusion that God exists does not mean that belief in God is false or unreasonable.

## Support, but not evidence, from experience

If belief in God is not warranted as a conclusion, is it supported in some other way? For some believers, faith is supported by personal experience. And now that, out from behind the veil of ignorance, religiously relevant experience is restored to the believer, some will appeal to certain parts or aspects of their experience in support of their faith.

Some believers report the sense of being in the presence of a divine being, or the sense of being in the presence of signs of a divine being, or a feeling that the world is intrinsically meaningful and purposive. Some believers cite those experiences to support and sustain their faith. The famous American philosopher William James (1842–1910), quotes the following report of a person feeling himself to be in the presence of a divine being: "God was present, though invisible; he fell under no one of my senses, yet my consciousness perceived him . . . God surrounds me like the physical atmosphere."[2] This appeal to religious experience is not a claim to possess evidence of God's existence. The point is not that God's existence is being inferred from those experiences. Instead, the claim is that such feelings are of direct or indirect encounters with a divine being.

For instance, when you call your friend on the telephone, and she answers, you do not infer that she is there. Typically, no such figuring out occurs in situations like that. Instead, you act on the supposition that your friend is right there. James's point is that the experience he is reporting belongs in the same class of experiences as that. So classified, he claims as much justification for accepting the one at face value as for accepting the other. True, when you recognize your friend on the phone, there is a cause–effect process at work. But cause–effect is not the same as evidence–conclusion.

Included among experiences that believers may regard as indirect, in contradistinction to direct, encounters with God are ones in which the world is felt to be a certain way. For instance, believers may report experiencing the world as intrinsically purposive, or they may report feeling

[2] William James, *The Varieties of Religious Experience* (New York: Modern Library, 1902), 71.

completely dependent on something apart from things in the world. Another form, which may be direct or indirect, is when people report feeling called to a mission or vocation in their lives. Here, the contrast would be with the person who reports (merely) choosing a certain path in life.

### Martin Heidegger

Martin Heidegger, the influential German philosopher mentioned in chapter 6, offers a general description of the phenomenon in question. He describes how, sometimes, our basic outlook on life reflects a state of mind more fundamental than any beliefs acquired through reason or reflection. Examples of such dispositional states of mind are optimism, hopefulness, foreboding, anxiety, and so on. In Heidegger's account, our experiences of particular situations are sometimes colored by, and so reflect, these states of mind. This account has no essential religious orientation or coloration, but religious outlooks seem to be good examples of the general point. Heidegger himself is difficult to classify in standard religious terms, but it seems safe enough to say that his position is not the theistic one.

A religious outlook or state of mind is one such basic stance toward the world. And now, out from behind the veil of ignorance, believers are free to draw upon such an outlook and its associated experiences.

But seeing the world a certain way is no guarantee of seeing things as they really are. The possibilities of error or illusion are as real here as with any experience or intuition. Nonetheless, the believer, out from behind the veil of ignorance and assured that the occurrence of evil in the world does not rule out the logical possibility of God, may reasonably draw upon his or her experience-based conviction about God, in responding to evidence that the existence of God is unlikely. However, unbelievers may just as reasonably and legitimately draw upon their experience to respond to evidence supporting the existence of God. But those experiences too are open to error and illusion. In both cases, the fundamental point is that the supporting experiences cited are not evidence.

Suppose you experience a certain place as menacing and spooky. Suppose being there makes you edgy and ill at ease. Suppose you tell a friend, who then goes there with you. Suppose that, once there, she sees nothing amiss, nor does she experience any particular feeling about the place. But suppose that you yourself, alongside her, feel the same as always there. It seems haunted to you, a troubled place.

Suppose your friend tries to nudge you out of feeling as you do by questioning you. Is it the shadows, or the silence, or maybe an association with a memory of something that frightened you as a child? Suppose your answer to each question is no.

The resulting situation would be a kind of stalemate. Your skeptical, or perhaps neutral, friend can't find anything convincing to you to explain away your feeling. But, similarly, you can't point to anything in the place to persuade her. Nonetheless, your own perception remains the same. And so does hers.

From a neutral, objective point of view, there is nothing to support your feeling. Suppose you accept that. After all, there was nothing you could point to as the crucial fact. But, on the other hand, there was nothing in the detached, neutral perspective that was dissuasive to you either. Perhaps the religious person's sense of the world as a providential place is analogous to the experience of a place as haunted, for both are ways of experiencing whole situations.

In principle, something could happen that would make you see the possibly haunted place differently. Likewise, something could happen that would cause a believer no longer to see the world as reflecting a divine presence. After all, as we saw in chapter 2, even on the experientialist view of the relationship between faith and reason, a defense is needed against evil-based arguments that there is no God.

The point is supported by the distinguished theistic philosopher Philip Quinn (1940–2004). He emphasizes that an intellectually sophisticated believer will recognize that experiences which he or she sees as encounters with a divine being may, like any experience, not reflect reality. Furthermore, the intellectually sophisticated theist will acknowledge that those experiences do not automatically over-ride serious reasons to think there is no God. The vast abundance of seemingly pointless suffering and waste of life is among the best of those reasons. The following parable by the English philosopher Basil Mitchell (b. 1917) illustrates the overall point.

### Mitchell's parable

Mitchell's is a tale of a resistance fighter, in a time of war, meeting an enigmatic stranger who deeply impresses him. The stranger tells the fighter that he, the stranger, is the overall leader of the resistance. And he urges the fighter to have faith in him, no matter what happens.

They never speak again. Sometimes the fighter sees the stranger helping the resistance. Other times, however, the stranger is seen, in the uniform of the police, handing over patriots to the occupation forces. Sometimes, through channels, the fighter asks the stranger for help, and receives it. Other times, he asks for help but receives nothing. On those occasions, he thinks, "The stranger knows best."

If he is reflective, the fighter will recognize that aspects of the stranger's ambiguous behavior count against his faith and trust in him. The question is: By how much? Perhaps the initial encounter with the stranger is sufficient to sustain and to justify the fighter's continued faith. Or perhaps not. It seems reasonable to suppose that would vary from one individual to another. Either way, a reflective person will surely be troubled by those facts that seem strongly to suggest the stranger is not what he said.

There is a parallel between Mitchell's parable and our investigations. The veil of ignorance supposition is equivalent to supposing that there is no initial, impressive encounter with the stranger. Absent any such encounter, all there is to go on is that, sometimes, the stranger is seen helping the resistance, but, other times, he is seen, in enemy uniform, working with the enemy. On the strength of those facts alone, are we entitled to judge that the stranger is the leader of the resistance? Clearly not. The facts do not testify to that at all.

Do the facts square with his being the leader of the resistance? Yes, in the sense of logical possibility. But, notwithstanding that, those facts give us serious reason to think he is not. Are they sufficient evidence to make it improbable that he is the leader of the resistance? That will depend on the balance of positive and negative evidence. But surely, not anything goes.

### Religious experience and skeptical defenses

Out from behind the veil of ignorance, a believer's outlook may include a sense of a divine presence in the world. That sense may be likened to the encounter with the stranger in Mitchell's parable.

Now, unlike earlier, failure to understand why God might tolerate evil, or even to understand the concept of God, in light of so much seemingly pointless suffering, may no longer be good reason to think belief in God is unreasonable or probably false.

Why not? On the skeptical defense, the reason is that now, convinced of having either direct or indirect experience of God, the believer may claim to have no expectation of understanding the ways of God. Indeed, the believer may even reasonably claim to expect to not understand.

Now, out from behind the veil of ignorance, the noseeum and other forms of skeptical defense may provide a theoretical base for the reasonableness of expecting to not understand. In this way, the skeptical defense may augment the (non-evidential) support that the believer's expectation of not understanding the ways of God receives from his or her own experience, or from the theistic community and tradition.

Furthermore, in contrast to the earlier situation behind the veil of ignorance, now the believer does not need the skeptical defense to meet a standard of persuasiveness sufficient for a person whose outlook is neutral. For instance, think of Peter van Inwagen's criterion of something's being true for all we know. Think of it two ways. First, think of it from the perspective of a believer out from behind the veil of ignorance. Then, second, think of it in the more austere and restrictive setting in force behind the veil. It is a standard that is far easier for the believer to meet in the former than in the latter context.

## Mystery and the surprise principle

The *New York Times* quoted Pope Benedict XVI at Auschwitz saying: "We cannot peer into God's mysterious plan. We see it only piecemeal."

This appeal to mystery seems to reflect a combination of two things. They are, first, surprise that a world made by God would contain such appalling horrors as the Holocaust, but also, second, the believer's lack of surprise that he or she does not understand the reason or justification for such horrors. The latter is the believer's expectation to not understand the reason. It is the essential point reflected in Hick's suggestion that an "epistemic distance" might be part of the supposed divine plan from the start. And perhaps we catch a hint of it as well in van Inwagen's 'true for all we know' standard. In effect, the concept of mystery suggests both the applicability and the non-applicability of the surprise principle.

Is the believer justified in classifying the enormous abundance of terrible things as, from a religious perspective, mysterious, without thereby embracing obscurantism? Behind the veil of ignorance, no. There, the theist is not justified. There, believer and unbeliever alike follow the evidence wherever, on balance, it points. There, appeals to mystery have no force of evidence. But, out from behind that veil, the believer reflects on the facts of terrible evil in a context that may include experience,

convincing to him or her, that God is present. In that context, committed to trust and hope that there is a divine plan, with provision
somehow for justification and compensation, perhaps it can be reasonable for the believer to see evil as a mystery, without seeing it as
sufficient negative evidence to warrant unbelief. Out from behind the veil
of ignorance, the believer may, perhaps, see the existence of seemingly
pointless suffering as a difficulty, even a serious difficulty, for faith, but
not as evidence to over-ride it. As previously mentioned, the distinction
between difficulty and negative evidence is Peter van Inwagen's.

Yet the thrust of our discussion of the two perspectives – that behind
and that out from behind the veil of ignorance, respectively – also means
that the believer can acknowledge both the reasonableness of the unbeliever's unbelief and the persuasive power of Rowe's or Draper's arguments.

A cartoon from the *New Yorker* magazine illustrates the two-sided
point. The scene is outside a church, with the minister shaking hands with
a man after a church service. The man says: "Oh, I know He works in
mysterious ways, but if I worked that mysteriously I'd get fired."

## Détente

Out from behind the veil of ignorance, the believer does not possess
or provide any more information than before, insofar as justification or
compensation for seemingly pointless evil is concerned. But, out from
behind the veil of ignorance, the significance of the failure to explain
may be different. Now, in some cases, if faith is secured by experience, a
believer may reasonably claim that seemingly pointless evils are somehow justified, without being able to say how. This does not mean that all
believers will be in a position to claim this. It is not a one-size-fits-all claim.

The issue of compensation is more problematic than that of
justification. The reason, as we saw in the previous chapter, is that compensation may be logically impossible in some cases. And if that is so,
then no amount of religious experience can make it reasonable to believe
in afterlife compensation for all evils.

Judged on the basis of impartial investigation of evidence equally available to all, and in particular the existence of vast amounts of seemingly
pointless evil, a naturalistic view fares better than a supernaturalistic,
theistic one. That is how things look behind the veil of ignorance.

But some believers may be justified in not committing to such an
impartial perspective. True, that seems odd, at first acquaintance. For

what could justify over-riding impartiality? In many contexts, nothing. But, in regard to religious belief, it may sometimes be the case that the believer is sincere in reporting experience that, to him or her, is either direct or indirect experience of divinity itself. So long as the believer does not suppose this counts as evidence, it can ground the believer's religious outlook, and perhaps enable it to withstand even strong evidence pointing the other way.

For analogies, think of the continued conviction that the place is haunted, while acknowledging no evidence persuasive to another person, or think of the resistance fighter continuing to believe in the stranger, despite serious evidence to the contrary.

The effect seems to be a détente between the two perspectives, belief and unbelief in God respectively. Approached neutrally and impartially, our verdicts in the two investigations that we conducted seem to stand up. But some believers may be justified in seeing things differently.

William L. Rowe acknowledges the détente just described, and at one point in his career characterized his own position as "friendly atheism." The friendly atheist maintains that atheism wins on the merits of the arguments, but accepts that religious belief may be a reasonable position nonetheless, even for people aware of the weight of evidence against it. Later on however, almost twenty years after the "friendly atheism" characterization, Rowe maintained that, given the facts of seemingly pointless evil, a rational belief in God would require strong supporting evidence.[3] From the foregoing discussion, and, in particular, from the provision in it of space for the fideistic outlook, I think you will see that my own view tilts more to Rowe's earlier than to his later assessment.

### "A world more full of weeping than [we] can understand"

Let us end as we began, with Yeats's line. I think both Rowe and Draper would agree with the thought in it. Their respective arguments may plausibly be viewed as moving out from that thought to the conclusion that probably there is no God. Mackie, too, would agree with the thought. But he would draw a stronger conclusion than either Draper or Rowe.

---

[3] For the contrast between the two claims of Rowe's, see his classic paper from 1979 in M. M. Adams and R. M. Adams, eds, *The Problem of Evil* (Oxford: Oxford University Press, 1990), 135–7, and his "The Evidential Argument from Evil," 282

He would conclude that the existence of God is out of the question, given the world's being as we find it. But what about Mackie's second thoughts? In light of those, let us say the earlier Mackie would conclude that the existence of God is out of the question.

I think Wykstra and van Inwagen would also agree with the thought in Yeats's line. But they would move out from it to the conclusion that we are in no position to judge, either way, on the probability of God. I think Plantinga would also agree with Yeats's thought. But he would disagree with the conclusions drawn by Mackie, Rowe, and Draper, respectively.

I think that Hick would agree with the sentiment in the line, and Swinburne too, but to a lesser extent. Neither of them, however, would go as far as Wykstra or van Inwagen. For their view, held in different strengths, is that perhaps we can understand, up to a point, how this world full of weeping could be brought about by God.

If you have read your way to this point, as opposed to just looking in here at the end, and if I have been as clear as I hoped I would be, then you know already that my own view lines up with those of Rowe and Draper, although I am sympathetic to much in the skepticisms of Wykstra and van Inwagen. And if you read your way to this point, I hope you found interesting things along the way to help you in coming to your own view on the topics of this book.

# Index